Semiotics of Rape

Semiotics of Rape

SEXUAL SUBJECTIVITY AND VIOLATION IN RURAL INDIA

Rupal Oza

zubaan

zubaan

ZUBAAN
128 B Shahpur Jat, 1st floor
NEW DELHI 110 049
Email: contact@zubaanbooks.com
Website: www.zubaanbooks.com

First published by Duke University Press 2023
This edition published by Zubaan Publishers Pvt. Ltd 2024
For sale in South Asia only

10 9 8 7 6 5 4 3 2 1

ISBN 978 81 947605 5 9 (paperback)

Zubaan is an independent feminist publishing house based in New Delhi with a strong academic and general list. It was set up as an imprint of India's first feminist publishing house, Kali for Women, and carries forward Kali's tradition of publishing world-quality books to high editorial and production standards. *Zubaan* means tongue, voice, language, speech in Hindustani. Zubaan publishes in the areas of the humanities, social sciences, fiction, general non-fiction, as well as books for children and young adults under its Young Zubaan imprint.

Typeset in Minion Pro by Westchester Publishing Services
Printed and bound at Raj Press, Inderpuri, New Delhi, 110 012

For Jayshree Oza

CONTENTS

AUTHOR'S NOTE

Throughout this book, names and places have been changed, with the exception of Bhagana. Stories about Bhagana are widely known, and I quote from them and from Satish Kumar, who has been the spokesperson for the continued protests. All given names that appear alone, including those of people I spoke with in Bhagana, are pseudonyms. Field notes and most interviews, likewise, have been anonymized.

PREFACE

I completed a draft of this manuscript between 2020 and 2021, in the wake of eighteen months of tumultuous events that began in Delhi in December 2019, and during a still-devastating global pandemic. It felt both dissonant and urgent to be writing about violence during this time.

In 2019, I had returned to Delhi just as the draconian National Registry of Citizens (NRC) and the Citizenship Amendment Act (CAA) went into effect. CAA creates a pathway to citizenship for those the government deems "illegal," but only if they belong specifically to Hindu, Sikh, Buddhist, Jain, Parsi, and Christian communities from three Muslim-majority countries—Pakistan, Bangladesh, and Afghanistan—and if they entered India before 2014. The act notably excludes Muslims from these protections, and it also excludes people fleeing violence and persecution from non-Muslim majority countries, such as neighboring Rohingya Muslims fleeing from predominantly Buddhist Myanmar. The related NRC aims to make a list of all the "legal" citizens of India, and where it has been implemented, it has forced residents to try to prove that they have been in the country since at least 1971. Those who fail to prove their citizenship, in many cases only because their names have been misspelled in official documents or because they left their papers behind when they fled their homes decades ago, have been threatened with imprisonment in newly built detention camps. The government has spoken about the NRC as critical to rooting out "infiltrators," a term many Muslim Indians understand as a derogatory code aimed at them by the right-wing forces in power. It is widely understood that while the NRC is carving out paths to statelessness for disfavored groups, the CAA is creating paths to citizenship for preferred groups, and that both aim to bolster a dangerous and mendacious anti-Muslim politics that casts Muslims in India as foreigners and Muslims abroad as barbaric. Of course, any serious student of Indian history will know that Muslims in India, today approximating well over 200 million people, have always been an integral part of the social and national fabric.

The Hindu right-wing–led Bharatiya Janata Party (BJP) made the NRC part of its election mandate in 2019, and in November BJP's home minister Amit Shah declared that the NRC would be applied all over the country. But both the NRC and CAA have been met with opposition. Protests against the CAA and NRC started in Delhi in December 2019, and soon spread across the country. As the scale of the protests grew, several state governments defied the central government and claimed that they would not implement these laws in their states.

In Delhi, the protests against CAA and NRC were centered around the neighborhood of Shaheen Bagh, where a group of Muslim women began a peaceful protest. These protests gained widespread support and were boosted by public disgust with the brutal violence police and factions of the BJP unleashed against students demonstrating in Jamia Millia Islamia and Jawaharlal Nehru University (JNU), two of the country's premier institutions of higher education. In both Delhi-based institutions, students had been actively participating in protests against the new CAA and NRC laws when, in early January 2020, a group of masked men and women armed with metal rods broke into JNU's campus and attacked students and teachers. Shouting slogans against "anti-nationals," these masked attackers belonged to Akhil Bharatiya Vidyarthi Parishad (ABVP), the student wing of the BJP. Various accounts by students, teachers, and journalists concurred that the Delhi police stood by while they were being attacked (*Caravan* 2020). Images of students being dragged with their heads bleeding led to trenchant public critique of the Hindu right and the Delhi police, and pointed to their joint complicity with the ethnonationalist, communal politics of the BJP.

When I went to Shaheen Bagh in January 2020, I saw posters of Ambedkar, Savitribai Phule, and Bhagat Singh adorning the tent erected by the community of protestors there.[1] One side of the tent was covered with the preamble of the Constitution in large font. Calls for *aazadi* (freedom) and slogans against the CAA and NRC resounded among those gathered, while poetry and songs of solidarity quickly spread through social media, bringing more people together. In an era of rising right-wing, authoritarian governments across the world, including the overwhelming electoral victory by the BJP in 2019, these protests across the country felt like the first glimmers of a shift presaging a different set of possibilities. After an era of right-wing consolidation and a sharp rise in communal tensions and sectarian politics, these protests against the CAA and NRC brought together diverse coalitions and groups of people across multiple divides. Dalit, Bahujan (subaltern), Advasi (Indigenous), and Muslim solidarity was powerfully on display and articulated in protest and song.

India's caste divisions, which include strict rules of segregation regulating against "pollution" from lower castes, were upended as people from across communities and castes ate together and shared songs, stories, and slogans articulating aspirations for a more free and just society. Spreading quickly across social media platforms, these images of solidarity spurred others to join. On a cold winter day in the middle of January, a group of farmers from Punjab—the state neighboring Haryana, where the rest of this book is based—began to unload large cooking utensils under an overpass and set up a *langar*—a community kitchen. They had come to Delhi to express solidarity with demonstrators in Shaheen Bagh, and they began to feed people. Bearing signs and posters that read "Bhai sey bhai ladney na payee phir se 47 banney na paaye" (May brothers never fight again, may 1947 never be repeated again), the images and stories of Punjabi and Muslim men and women coming together in solidarity moved and inspired millions. They also constituted a forceful response to the hateful divisiveness of the BJP.

Then, just as the protests and acts of solidarity were gaining momentum, a global pandemic forced everyone to sequester. In March 2020, when India instituted a nationwide lockdown, thousands of migrant workers, suddenly without jobs or ways to get back to their villages, were seen walking for hundreds of miles. The breathtaking lack of support for the poor laid bare the violence of the state toward the people who had built and run the cities and towns, and who were now abandoned and treated as disposable. Soon, students from JNU and other groups began to mobilize support for these migrant workers. I was back in New York to begin a new semester of teaching, joining others in the diaspora as we watched and witnessed in horror, and scrambled to find ways to support from afar.

As social distancing became the norm to deal with the COVID-19 virus, it exposed the evisceration of social infrastructures that has since the 1970s left the poor everywhere vulnerable to premature death (Gilmore 2007). In New York—a city ravaged by the early days of the virus, which left thousands dead—the most affected were people in the communities where I lived: mostly immigrants and people of color who are part of the brutal contingent economy. When my neighborhood shut down, the ambient sounds and smells of daily life—conversations in multiple languages, students walking to school, music blasting from cars, street vendors—were replaced by the unremitting sirens of ambulances. The public hospital in the neighborhood, one of the few still left in the city, overwhelmed by patients standing in a serpentine line to get into its emergency room. In those brutal early days, we learned that nurses and doctors at the public hospital did not have enough personal protective equipment to stay safe as they cared for the hundreds of sick and dying patients coming through the doors. Yet again, it took neighbors and a community to raise money to fund items urgently needed by public healthcare workers, exposing the utter failure of health infrastructure in the city and country at large.

In India, conditions were deteriorating fast. Following the shutdown there, the injunction to socially distance was untenable and ludicrous. Most people in India, except for a relative minority with caste and class privileges, live in small, crowded homes and communities. Moreover, efforts to deal with the pandemic using distance and segregation fortified dominant-caste customs of purity and pollution. As a result, the vulnerabilities that Dalits, Bahujan, Advasi, and other marginalized communities routinely experienced became more exacerbated during the pandemic. Charu Gupta, K. Satyanarayana, and S. Shankar (2020) write about dominant-caste Hindi literature from the early twentieth century, which is replete with commands to guard against pollution from Dalit men and women. This literature was deeply concerned with "intimate sexual liaisons and illicit collusions between savarna [dominant-caste] women and Dalit men." The regulation of touch, and the injunction to not touch in response to the virus, "mirrors . . . distinct social histories of preservation and upholding of caste hierarchies" (Gupta, Satyanarayana, and Shankar 2020).

Dalit literature has documented in painful detail the manner in which dominant castes have required the excessive performance of distance from those they consider subordinate, so that even their shadow will not pollute them (Bama 2012). These practices of separation are manifest in architecture such as an arch or doorway that leads to a powerful family's cluster of homes like the ones on the cover of this book. Villages, towns, and cities across the country have long practiced their own versions of social distancing by segregating Muslims through active discrimination in housing (Jamil 2017). In villages I visited, Dalit *bastis* (neighborhoods) were usually located on the outskirts, physically separated from the rest of the village. With the pandemic, these physically demarcated spatial arrangements found renewed sanction, and their apartness was reinforced by anxieties about maintaining social segregation.

Given the historic, structural discrimination against Dalit, Bahujan, Adivasi, and Muslim communities, there is no doubt that we will see a gravely disproportionate death toll in these communities once the impact of the virus is better discerned. The death in these communities is commensurate with that in Black neighborhoods in the United States, which have also historically faced severe discrimination, and which have been disproportionately devastated by the virus. A *Washington Post* report about the impact of the virus demonstrates that majority-Black counties suffered "three times the rate of infection and almost six times the rate of death" endured by white counties (Thebault, Tran, and Williams 2020).

In those early months of the pandemic, the starkness of institutionalized, structural racism upended liberal understandings of race as simply a matter of personal prejudice. While the pace of pandemic devastation slackened a bit in the summer of 2020, it was followed by the brutal killings of Ahmad Arbury, Breonna Taylor, George Floyd, and Jacob Blake by white police officers and vigilantes. In the days that followed, city after city across the United States erupted in protest and anger, leading to a summer of racial reckoning led by the Black Lives Matter movement. The juxtaposition of the pandemic, which exposed the inequities that made Black, brown, and immigrant people particularly vulnerable to the virus, against a series of brutal murders that exposed structural racism, shifted the terms of public discourse in the country. These murders further exposed white supremacy and police brutality, and again demonstrated their capacity to destroy lives within a juridical and political system that shields both from prosecution or meaningful accountability and redress.

In India, where the pandemic was unexpectedly muted during the last four months of 2020, the hope was that life would return to normal—ease for those who could enjoy it and to the status quo of normalized despair for those who could not—as the vaccines rolled out. However, by March 2021 a calamitous surge in the virus left hundreds of thousands dead. In the interim, another crisis would engulf the country. While falsely claiming victory over the virus, the BJP used this time to push through three agricultural acts, which are often referred to as the 2020 Farm Bills, and which directly undermined farmers and their livelihoods. These acts were the Farmers' Produce Trade and Commerce (Promotion and Facilitation) Act, the Farmers (Empowerment and Protection) Agreement on Price Assurance and Farm Services Act, and the Essential Commodities (Amendment) Act. These acts would fundamentally change the way "agricultural produce is stocked, marketed and sold" (Tur 2020). From the moment they were introduced as ordinances to when they were pushed through into law governing the whole country, farmers from Punjab and Haryana, later on joined by farmers from Uttar Pradesh—all states that depend heavily on agriculture—began protesting. They argued that these bills would introduce a corporatization of agriculture and would further immiserate them by eliminating the government-supported minimum prices they received for their produce. They expressed that even the minimum prices that they received from state granaries were woefully inadequate, given the rising cost of fertilizer, pesticides, and other expenses. The notoriously high numbers of farmer suicides in India, attributed primarily to steep debts borne by agricultural workers, should illuminate the seriousness and harm of government policy that further attenuates the capacity of farmers to sustain themselves and their families.

All of the farmers I met and spoke with in Haryana were in significant debt and struggling to make a living. As I show in the chapters ahead, their efforts to make a living and the inability of farming to support their livelihoods pervaded the stories I heard. As the state turned a deaf ear to the grievances of farmers, they began arriving in Delhi in droves to protest the farm laws. The BJP government directed the Delhi police to close the border and deploy water cannons against the arriving caravans of farmers. As news of this mistreatment of farmers spread, support for them grew and reached a peak in November 2020, when, according to one report, over 250 million people joined them in protest against the farm laws (Pahwa 2020). A year later, Narendra Modi—in an unexpected capitulation—repealed all three farm laws. Many view this as BJP's effort to appease farmers who are key to their electoral prospects in the upcoming assembly elections in Punjab and Uttar Pradesh (*Scroll.in* 2021).

The strategy of appealing of different segments of the population was also deployed by the BJP earlier in 2021, when another set of assembly elections loomed. BJP began to organize large rallies, particularly in states where they hoped to defeat political parties opposed to their right-wing mandate.

Aligned with this goal, BJP officials granted permission to the organizers of the Kumbh Mela, a Hindu religious gathering of thousands on the banks of the River Ganga, despite the persistence of the global coronavirus pandemic. These large gatherings, driven by BJP's political ambitions, contributed to a devastating surge of the virus in India, crumbling the weak infrastructure already vulnerable from years of divestment in public welfare. Hospitals ran out of oxygen even as state and local governments denied any shortages. Once again, it was community mutual aid that lessened the suffering caused by state neglect and organized abandonment. In this case, Sikh *gurudwaras* (temples) began to organize oxygen *langars*, offering free food and oxygen to those who came for help (Anand 2021). Their efforts helped alleviate hardships, but the death toll remained astronomical. Crematoriums ran around the clock, but many still had trouble laying their deceased loved ones to rest. Conditions were so dire that even more privileged people, with money and with the political connections to call in favors, were unable to receive adequate care or protection for themselves or their loved ones. Poor people from Dalit, Bahujan, Adivasi, and Muslim castes and communities had it worst, and they have been forced to secretly bury or cremate the bodies of their loved ones in the middle of the night, while fearing getting caught and being beaten by police for breaking curfew. For me, back in New York, the news felt unrelenting as we heard about friends, family, comrades, and activists succumbing to the disease. Grief took on a new shade and meaning.

Writing about rape in the wake of all of these events, I was left with questions, dilemmas, and discomforts in trying to make sense of a world eviscerated in so many ways. Drafting the final pages of a book on rape during a global pandemic made me acutely aware of the pervasiveness of violence at different scales—from the most intimate to the global. Profound structural inequities laid bare how caste, race, gender, and class shielded some from the devastation to which the majority were exposed. Local and national governments and institutions mandated with the responsibility to care for people were at best unable and in many instances unwilling to recognize and ameliorate harm endured by people whose lives they considered less valuable. This politics of unequal recognition made clear, once again, that from the perspective of the powerful some forms of harm are more deserving of redress and restitution, at the expense of others.

I want to conclude this brief preface by juxtaposing the response and recognition by the courts and the police of two rape cases that illustrate this difference between the recognition of harm to some and the lack of recognition or erasure of harm to others. The first case involves the gang rape by dominant-caste men of a young Dalit girl in Hathras in September 2020. The second rape case involves Tarun Tejpal, a prominent investigative journalist who was accused of raping his colleague in 2013. In the first instance, the brutal assault on the young girl in Hathras was overlooked, denied, and rendered invisible, and her rights were repeatedly denied by the police and local government. She had to die before she was finally recognized as a victim deserving of justice. Meanwhile, the Bombay High court in Goa acquitted Tejpal of all charges in May 2021. In her judgment, the sessions judge even blamed the woman who filed the rape case against Tejpal for not demonstrating what the judge considered to be sufficiently visible signs of distress after her assault, and for expressing solidarity with the young Dalit girl who had been gang-raped in Hathras (Asthana 2021). The young Dalit woman was denied recognition as a victim and thereby denied rights and restitution; meanwhile Tejpal, a dominant-caste and class man, was rendered blameless and freed from any responsibility for the harm he caused.

The politics of recognition reveals that some people, that some lives, that some subjectivities are worth more than those who are most vulnerable. I will have more to say about the politics of recognition toward the end of this book. I raise it here to anticipate how the recognition of a person's value and credibility in a rape case, and the recognition of the harm they have suffered, is tethered to a matrix of power and to the formation of the subjectivities of raped women, which is what I explore in the pages that follow.

ACKNOWLEDGMENTS

Researching and writing this book resulted in amassing an inordinate amount of gratitude to many friends, colleagues, interlocutors, guides, and family that make fiction of the solitary credit of authorship.

My first set of deep gratitude goes to the families of victims of assault I met in Haryana. The parents, siblings, and in particular to the women themselves: I am humbled by the generosity with which they shared their stories, offered their understanding of what occurred, and gave critical insights about the social landscapes they were navigating.

To Manisha Mashaal and Rajini Mashaal, fierce activists and amazing organizers, my profound gratitude. I have learned so much from both, their sharp perceptions of deep-rooted caste politics in Haryana offered an unparalleled understanding of rape. I am so grateful also for the generosity with which they shared their home. The memory of the days and nights spent together and the friendship we forged will remain with me all my life.

Rajat Kalsan was a generous and wonderful guide to the courts and cases in Haryana. Along with activists and others, our initial stay in Haryana was facilitated by him. I am so grateful for the wisdom, pathways, and sharp analysis of caste politics. His fierce and *bekauf* (unafraid) activism has made him a powerful force for justice in Haryana. Balvant Singh Bondiya offered generous friendship and was also a key guide to the cases and courts in Haryana. His long-standing activism on behalf of Dalit rights has made him exceptional for the vastness of his knowledge and respect he has garnered. I am also grateful to Lal Bahadur Khowal, who is well versed with rape cases and the manner in which they are navigated. His insights on compromise cases and the way the special sessions courts work was key to understanding how rape cases wind themselves through the court systems. I owe a debt of gratitude to the Tawar family for their hospitality. On many occasions they generously hosted us when we faced challenges in finding a place to stay.

To the many other people I met in Haryana through the course of this research, I am so very thankful for their incredible kindness. I refrain from naming them or even identifying the places where they reside in an effort to protect them. I remain circumspect about revealing details that could inadvertently divulge the identity of cases I researched. They are village panchayat members, *sarpanches*, and village elders who were so generous and hospitable. To the young women I met in the villages who spoke about their love for sport, their hope for themselves, who demonstrated their deep friendships with each other, their attempts to hold out on marriage, their deep appreciation for the sacrifices their families make, their conflicts and struggles, their understanding of violence and the rapidly changing world around them: words inadequately express my deep appreciation and gratitude for all that I learned in their company.

Travel through rural Haryana took us to a wide variety of places as I followed the cases I was investigating. During these trips I was occasionally accompanied by activists or lawyers working on some of these cases. Wherever we went, we were offered food and refreshment—always. In district offices, police stations, homes of village *sarpanches* and elders, hospital administrators, and lawyer's chambers, all of whom I met extended tremendous courtesy to me and to those I was with. In all these instances, even though I was familiar with the common cultural practice of offering refreshments to visitors, I was also aware that my class and caste position often played a role in opening doors and extending courtesies that are not always extended to those without the privileges I inhabit.

Women's rights groups in many of the districts I visited were particularly important. Some of the ones I visited were affiliated with All India Democratic Women's Association (AIDWA), which is associated with the Communist party of India (Marxist). Guidance by Jagmati Sanghwan and

Inderjeet Singh was instrumental in developing an appreciation of how the agrarian crisis saturated violence everywhere. They shared their time with incredible generosity, offering names and contacts of people I could speak with in different districts. Their reach and decades of organizing on the ground meant that they had deep familiarity with farmer distress and gender-based violence all over Haryana. I also met with members of Mahila Samakhyas in different districts. At these gatherings too, those I met opened their homes to us whenever we visited.

I first met Prem Chaudhry after I had read her books and articles. She was already a towering figure for her meticulous analysis of Haryana. Over the years as my research progressed, I would meet and talk with her about who I met, the dilemmas I faced, and the many concerns I had. She always found time for me to hear about my work. Her guidance and insights were key as I struggled with understanding what I was encountering in rural Haryana.

The bulk of my research transpired between 2015 and 2016. In the fall of 2015, I was at the Center for the Study of Law and Governance (CSLG) at Jawaharlal Nehru University (JNU) as a visiting fellow. I am deeply grateful for the warmth and welcome I received from Amit Prakash while I was there. In the nine months of the fellowship, I had the profound privilege of getting to know and befriending the many amazing faculty at CSLG. I was such a pleasure to get to know Chirashree Dasgupta, P. Puneet, Pratiksha Baxi, Ghazala Jamil, and Nupur Chowdhury. At JNU, I was also at the Jawaharlal Nehru Institute of Advanced Studies (JNIAS). My deep gratitude to G. J. V. Prasad for giving me the opportunity and the pleasure to meet with so many other fellows and present my work. While at JNIAS it was particularly wonderful to meet Gordon McOut, to whom I remain in debt for his advice and help. My time in JNU overlapped with the wonderful scholar and artist Mangai, whom I was fortunate to meet and befriended. I recall with great fondness the dinner we had together at JNU and then again when I visited her in Chennai. I look forward to the time when we may be together again. Just as I was finishing my time at JNU, Shirin Rai joined CSLG. The brief times together were memorable and such fun. My gratitude to Shirin for reading parts of the research that emerged from my work in Haryana and for taking the time to write letters of support.

My stay at JNU coincided with the incredible student uprising and lectures on nationalism. Beginning with backlash against students for an event they had organized in February 2016, the student wing of the Hindu right labeled these students as anti-national. The conflict inspired some of the most trenchant critiques of nationalism and who constitutes being part of the nation. In these uprisings the communal politics of the BJP and others were laid bare. The violence of authoritarian regimes was evidenced in their attempts to charge students under sedition laws for their critique of the Hindu right. There was increased distress and anger over the arrest of students some of whom remain in jail to this day. The campus in those months was vibrant with conversations and lectures. The fiery and inspiring responses by Kanhaiya Kumar, the then president of the student union, articulated trenchant critique of the BJP and the prime minister, propelling him to national fame.

Janaki Nair among many others helped organize these open lectures attended by hundreds of students and supporters filling the steps leading to the administrator's offices at JNU. The solidarity of faculty and students and staff was inspiring as those days revealed a different possibility in poetry, word, and song. My days at JNU were indelibly marked by these student uprisings that I had the privilege to witness.

I am also grateful to Janaki Nair for her friendship and the countless dinners she hosted during my days at JNU. Her and Devyani's warm home was a welcome refuge. My special thanks also to Pratiksha Baxi, whose friendship sustained me as I conducted difficult research in rural Haryana. Her reminders to take care of myself while doing research were acts of such generosity and kindness. Pratiksha introduced me to Malavika Parthasarthy, who was just finishing her training as a lawyer and helped me understand some of the legal language and terms. Working with her was delightful. To Ghazala Jamil, who also extended herself, I am so grateful for the warmth of her friendship. I remember still with great fondness the evening we spent at her home.

In JNU at the Center for Women's Studies it was such a pleasure to meet several friends and colleagues. I am so grateful to Navaneetha Mokkil, G. Arunima, Lata Singh, and Papori Bora for the warmth they extended. In January 2019, I was invited by the Center for Women's Studies to present on part of my research. I am so grateful to Navaneetha Mokkil and Lata Singh for organizing the talk and for members of the audience who engaged with it.

While in Delhi, Professor Ravinder Kaur from the Department of Humanities and Social Sciences at the Indian Institute of Technology offered generous advice and encouragement on the project. Professor Kaur also introduced me to Dr. Neerja Ahlawat from the Department of Sociology at Maharshi Dayanand University. My deep gratitude to both for their support and assistance during my research. It was through Professor Ahlawat that I met Suman Malik, whose knowledge of Haryana rural life and familiarity with the language and idiom taught me so much. I am so grateful for her help, guidance, and friendship.

I owe a debt of gratitude to Mary John for her friendship and deep generosity with which she offered suggestions, patiently heard my concerns, and enthusiastically encouraged by research. My time in Delhi and Haryana would have been vastly different and much less rich had it not been for the time that Mary took to guide and help me as I wrestled with so many dilemmas and worries. She was in so many ways a mentor par excellence. I am so grateful for her friendship.

Just as I was initiating my research, Women against Sexual Violence and State Repression (WSS) released their report on Bhagana, specifically linking the relationship between caste atrocities, land, and sexual violence. I am grateful to Mary for introducing me to activists in WSS, some of whom were old friends and comrades. At one of their meetings, I briefly met Rajni Tilak before her untimely demise. Her work on bringing attention to issues of sexual violence against Dalit women has been groundbreaking. It is also through Mary that I got to know the wonderful, Ajita Rao. Mary and Ajita were instrumental in organizing a panel at the Law and Social sciences Research Network (LASSNET) conference in December 2016, where I presented the early reflections on my research in Haryana.

At the Center for Women's Development Studies, I am also grateful for N. Neetha for her help as I tried to make sense of census and other data. My deep gratitude also to Uma Chakravarti for meeting with me in the early days of my research and for her advice. In Chennai, meeting V. Geetha was particularly wonderful. I am so very grateful for her generous read and engagement with my essay on consent. The evening with her remains a fond precious memory.

Since the Mirchpur atrocity in 2010, Human Rights Law Network (HRLN) had been deeply involved with organizing in Haryana with a network of activists and attorneys. As I was initiating my research, they put me in touch with key activists and attorneys in Haryana. My deep gratitude to Colin Gonsalves and Sneha Mukherjee for their help and friendship. I assisted Sneha and other lawyers at HRLN with some of the complex issues with the cases we were encountering in Haryana and went with them to villages as we researched cases. I am so grateful that our work together led to reinitiating HRLN's projects in Haryana after the May 2017 meeting in Jind. HRLN's support of young Dalit women advocates is remarkable and led to their support of Manisha Mashaal's important organizing work in Haryana.

In January 2015 I also met Asha Kowtal, who is the General Secretary of the All India Dalit Mahila Adhikar Manch, just as I was exploring research work in Haryana. I am grateful for the advice and caution that she offered during our meeting. While I had already made contact with Manisha Mashaal, my meeting with Asha helped me further comprehend and appreciate the significance and simultaneous precariousness of Dalit organizing in Haryana. Asha also introduced me to the scholar and artist Thenmozhi Soundarajan. In spring that year, along with my friend and colleague Smita Narula, we collaborated with Thenmozhi to organize a few speaking engagements at Hunter College for Manisha and other Dalit activists and scholars.

I am fortunate to have exceptionally supportive colleagues in the department of Women and Gender Studies (WGS) at Hunter College, CUNY. After spending nine years as director of the then program in WGS, when it became a department we were fortunate to hire Catherine Raissiguier as the chair. She was instrumental in my being able to take two years off: the first as a visiting scholar at JNU, and the second for my sabbatical. The two consecutive years afforded me time and space to do my research. I am so very grateful for the time off and for my colleagues who protected my time away. I know that having such support is not usual, and am especially thankful. Thanks to Jennifer Gaboury, who through all these years of struggle and organizing at Hunter has been a wonderful comrade and friend. My deep gratitude to Lisa Steadwell for her help and friendship. I was so fortunate to have Ros Petchesky as a colleague and wonderful friend at Hunter. I am so grateful for her support and encouragement. In the past few years, we added to our ranks and are lucky that Chris Mitchell, Kelly Nims and Deb Tolman joined the department and I am grateful to count them as colleagues and friends. The excellent adjunct faculty Boon Lin Ngeo, Carmelina Cartei, Daniel Polyak, Katherine DeLorenzo, and Portia Seddon have been the most generous of colleagues.

I am fortunate to have had wonderful colleagues and friends read and engaged with various parts of the book. My deep gratitude to Catherine Raissiguier, Dina Mahnaz Siddiqi, Jinee Lokaneeta, Linda Martín Alcoff, Mary John, Pratiksha Baxi, Srimati Basu, Sonali Perera, and V. Geetha. I want to especially thank the two anonymous reviewers for their generous reading and engagement with the manuscript. Their thoughtful suggestions for revisions pushed me to think through my theoretical and empirical work, and is just the kind of response one could hope for. I remain in their debt.

To Ken Wissoker, I am so delighted that the book is with you and Duke. Thank you so very much for your advice and support shepherding the book through.

I worked with two editors. Micha Rahder was able to copyedit the manuscript within a very short deadline. I am so grateful for her help. To Leili Kashani, a wonderful development editor who read and worked with the prose and was able to capture so accurately my intent and purpose: thank you, dear friend, for all your help.

I am fortunate to have wonderful friends in the United States and India who through the challenges of life have kept me grounded and helped ease my heart and mind. Their political commitments to justice are an inspiration and hope against growing authoritarian regimes. They are Ali Mir, Amita Swadhin, Anjali Kamat, Balmurli Natarajan, Biju Mathew, Jinee Lokaneeta, Prachi Patankar, Prerana Reddy, Ronak Kapadia, Ragini Shah, Saadia Toor, Sangay Mishra, Sangeeta Kamat, Svati Shah, Sreevidya Kalaramadan, Tejasvi Nagaraja, and Tony Alessandrini. To the wonderful friends from the South Asian feminist reading and writing group—Anu Sharma, Dina Siddiqui, Jinee Lokaneeta, Madiha Tahir, Ritty Lukose, Saadia Toor, Sanghamitra Padhya, Sareeta Amrute, Sonali Perera, Tejaswini Ganti, Vasuki Nesiah—my gratitude for reading parts of the manuscript and offering sharp incisive comments. The profound challenges that the pandemic wrought on our lives would have been so much worse had it not been for a vibrant community of friends in Jackson Heights. My thanks to Anjali Kamat, Arun Venugopal, Chris Stone, Gonzalo Casals, Kavita Misra, Leili Kashani, Manijeh Moradian, Meera Nair, Manu Bhagvan, Sandra Gresl, Sahar Romani, Sohl Lee, Sweta Vohra, Ryan Gerety, and Sree Bhagvan. To friends new and old in India, it is always such a joy to see them during my trips back. They are Anusha Khan, Balvant Singh Bondiya, Feisal Alkazi, Keval Arora, Jatinder Marwaha, Manisha Mashaal, Mary John, Mukul Kishor, Navneetha Mokil, Neena Singh, Neha Dixit, Pankaj Rishi Kumar, Preeti Singh, Pratiksha Baxi, Rajat Kalsan, Rohan Shivkumar, Shriti Malhotra, Shalini Singh, Shuddha Sengupta, Vidya Das, and Vijay Krishna Acharya. Special thanks Anjali Kamat, Ali Mir, Kavita Ramdas, Ragini Shah, Saadia Toor, Sanjay D'Souza, and Zuli Ahmad for their wonderful friendship. Their presence in my life has made it rich, comforting, and warm.

My family has been a source of joy and their support for me is unwavering. My gratitude to cousins in Bangalore, Mumbai, Pune, London, and Germany. To aunts and uncles, I recall with great fondness the times we shared through the different events and occasions. I am glad that I had the opportunity to have those memories before so many of them passed away. I deeply feel the loss of that generation of my family and with them the stories and narratives that filled our gatherings with laughter and delight.

My nieces are tremendous sources of happiness. It has been a special pleasure to see them grow; to Priya Venkat, Meghna Purkayastha, Kajori Purkayastha, Anya Oza, and Yamini Oza: I love you all so very much. To my brother Nilay, my gratitude and love for his unwavering support and for always welcoming us to his home. To my sister-in-law, Sarah, thank you for all the love and support. To Bhuvana and Dipanker, Kalpana and Ramesh: their homes have been places of love, laughter, and very good food. Thank you for your love, generosity, and support.

To Ash, whose partnership in my life has given me immeasurable love, laughter, and happiness. With tremendous patience and generosity, he has accepted my long absences as I researched this book, always supportive and encouraging of my work. He has been my most steadfast of champions. Thank you—always—for being my *humsafar*.

My tremendous gratitude also to Badam Singh, who tirelessly accompanied me on my various trips to Haryana, befriending the many people I met. He remains in touch with many of them and keeps me abreast of their news. His open generosity and enthusiasm for our journeys into rural Haryana made the long the trips comfortable and delightful.

My mother-in-law, Sharada Rao, did not see the book in print. But she has always championed my work and been a strong fierce supporter. Her support and wisdom I miss every day. My father-in-law, Professor S. R. V. Rao, is one of the most resilient and accommodating people I ever met. The graciousness with which he accepts life's vicissitudes are a source of inspiration. I am always delighted to spend time with him. I was fortunate to spend the year doing this research in the company of my father, Ashok Oza. He was always incredibly proud of my achievements and supported my choices without reservation. I deeply regret that did not get to see this book published. I keenly miss his presence every day. Finally, to my mother, Jayshree Oza, who has been my staunchest supporter. Her steadfast belief in justice for all has guided her incredible work on education in India. She is also gracious in her love for everyone and embodies enormous capacity for kindness. It is to her and all that she continues to teach me that I dedicate this book.

This research which was supported by funding from the American Institute of Indian Studies senior short-term fellowship (2016) and the

PSC-CUNY Enhanced award (68851–00 46). I am also grateful to the CUNY Mid-Career Faculty Fellowship program for giving me the opportunity to work on parts of the book. An earlier version of chapter 1, "Consent," appeared in the Autumn 2020 issue of *Signs: Journal of Women in Culture and Society* as an essay titled "Sexual Subjectivity in Rape Narratives: Consent, Credibility and Coercion in Rural Haryana." I have had the good fortune to share parts of the book in various forums with scholars who engaged with it. To Lila Abu-Lughod, my gratitude for inviting me to the 2018 Religion and the Global Framing of Gender Violence Workshop at Columbia University where I shared an early version of the chapter on consent. During the 2020–2021 academic year I was fortunate to be a fellow at the Center for Place, Culture, and Politics at the CUNY Graduate Center. My gratitude to Ruthie Gilmore for encouraging me to apply and to Peter Hitchcock and Sonia Vas Borges, as well as all the other participants who read and offered wonderful feedback on the chapter on land.

Introduction

I first met Sanjay on a hot summer afternoon in 2016. His T-shirt was rolled up to his biceps, and a crude tattoo was barely visible from under his left sleeve. Sanjay was a shy young Dalit[1] man around twenty years old who in August 2015 was accused of kidnapping and raping Kavita, a Jat girl he knew from his school. He was out on bail when we met.[2] A few weeks later, Sanjay was acquitted of both crimes by the special sessions judge. There is a long legal history in India of leniency toward men in rape cases (Satish 2017). This case, however, was not an instance of that kind of corruption. Sanjay's case was different: he and Kavita were in a two-year relationship and had decided to run away together to get married. However, Kavita was just shy of turning eighteen and was therefore not legally recognized as an adult. When her family discovered her affair they contacted the police, who apprehended the young couple while they were hiding in Mumbai and brought them back to the village.

Sanjay and Kavita's story is not unusual. Affairs made public, or those considered illicit for breaching boundaries of caste or class, are often disciplined through a series of violent measures. Dominant castes and classes, and the people and institutions invested in safeguarding their power, often deploy the charge of rape in these cases to mobilize the power of the state—specifically its police and courts—into restoring and guarding these boundaries. The accusation is part of a structure of revenge and retribution by dominant castes against the subordinate caste or class for going above their station. Sanjay and Kavita's families, their lawyers, the judge, and the police were all aware that this was not a story of kidnapping and rape, and yet they all played a role in the drama of filing a case and participating in the subsequent trial that unfolded. In this story of revenge, the state, in the form of the police and courts, colluded in restoring boundaries of caste and class. But Sanjay and Kavita's story is also about how the drama of revenge was interrupted by the judge who acquitted Sanjay. It is a story about young love and defiance, and about how these forces grate against existing social mores. It is a story emblematic of changing social landscapes.

Semiotics of Rape: Sexual Subjectivity and Violation in Rural India is about rape in rural Haryana, a small northwestern state in India. In my three years of researching the subject, I read about hundreds of rapes in multiple reports documented by feminist groups and human rights organizations and followed eight cases in depth through a series of interviews and conversations with the accused, the women, their families and community members, and the authorities involved. Of course, I could not speak to women who died or were killed during or after their rape, but in each of the eight cases a different assortment of people with some relation to it were willing to speak with me about the rapes.

Rather than speculate about why rape occurs or attempt to explain its persistence, this book focuses on what a rape charge does. I look at a rape case as a site where anxieties and battles over changing gender politics, rural crisis, complex sexual subjectivity, and caste politics are articulated. Rape is a particular kind of violation that is often treated as a social dispute rather than as a crime (Baxi 2014).[3] In other words, a rape charge is not only about bodily violation; it is also a mechanism and language through which other crises and tensions are navigated and revealed. Sanjay's case, for instance, exposes growing resentment by Jats about what they perceive as Dalit mobility set against their own decline. The dominant perception among Jats is that "Dalits take their jobs and then their girls" (Chowdhry 2009a). Several times in the course of this research I heard the lament that economic mobility had enabled Dalits to acquire fashionable attire. The lament, spoken with a degree of resentment, exposed dominant-caste concerns over losing political, economic, and cultural prominence.[4] Intercaste relationships, especially between dominant-caste women and Dalit men, as in Sanjay's case, generate upper-caste apprehensions about losing control over domestic sexual economy. Rape cases then become the venue where lawyers, judges, police officers, and village elders adjudicate what they all consider to be a pernicious fraying of the social fabric in an effort to stem it.

Consider for instance my conversation with the attorney Kavita's family had hired. Mr. Sihag has a chamber (lawyer's office) in the court complex. As we sit facing his large table, our conversation begins more generally about rape in the village. He bemoans that there is no longer any difference between the village and the city. In a clever turn of phrase, he says, "Gaon mein fasal kharaab hai, par sheher mein nasal kharaab hai" (In the village crops are bad, but in the city lineage/progeny are bad). In the context of our conversation, his allegorical alliteration suggests that the loss of family values is no longer limited to people in the city. "Kharaab" is a particular phrase used in the vernacular to mean bad and immoral, and rape is often referred to as "kharaab kaam." Speaking specifically about Sanjay's case, Mr. Sihag said prior to the courts reaching a judgment in the case, that the special session's judge for rape cases was very good and that the girl was not innocent of having eloped with the boy. Even though he was Kavita's attorney, Mr. Sihag acknowledged that this was not a case of rape and that Sanjay had been falsely accused. Mr. Sihag knew that the case was being prosecuted even though Sanjay had clearly not committed a crime, and that it was being litigated for reasons that went well beyond any questions about Sanjay's guilt or innocence.

As this case demonstrates, rape trials exceed the specificities of particular cases and are the terrain through which punishment for caste violation, loss of power, and changing gender politics are all expressed. The mobilization of state power in this case, as expressed by the police who apprehended the young couple and the courts that charged Sanjay with rape, reveals the state's investment in preserving and consolidating caste hierarchies by prohibiting intercaste relationships and alliances. Yet when the courts acquit the accused, as they did with Sanjay, this collusion and effort to consolidate caste hierarchies is rendered incomplete. I am interested in how caste structures are simultaneously consolidated, challenged, produced, devolved, reformulated, and realigned in the wake of a charge of rape.

I suggest that love affairs and sexual violations substantially impact both individual and community status and honor, can reshape the reputation of an entire village, animate conflicts over caste and land, and generate new sexual choices and intense battles over them.[5] Rape cases both bother and sediment patriarchal structures and relationships, and are a lens through which the architecture of subordination is both consolidated and defied. Messy conflicts emerge in the aftermath of rape, exposing dilemmas, struggles, alliances, and compromises, all of which appear in unexpected ways. In the wake of a rape charge, feminists and human rights advocates in particular often face unexpected and difficult questions and challenges.

The complex and multifaceted landscape of rape cases enfolds a very wide range of constituencies—including police officers, feminists, and human rights activists—each of which, in very different ways, marshals these cases to advance particular scripts. Police officers, for instance, draw on stories such as Sanjay and Kavita's to advance their deceptive claim that most rape cases are false and are only filed to manage reputational damage from an illicit affair. Human rights groups and feminist activists, on the other hand, focus on documenting how women and their supporters are discouraged from filing rape cases and how they are often coerced against filing a report, especially if that report aims to accuse those in power.

Reports by different Dalit, feminist, and human rights groups tracking rape cases in India have a record of offering compelling evidence of police and court malfeasance, sometimes clashing with members of a victim's or survivor's own community. This clash happens when these reports champion a rape survivor's story, while members of her community choose to instead echo police efforts to undermine her credibility and claim that her rape allegations are false. In other instances, the woman's kin fight bravely to defend her, while at the same time still blaming her for the shame her rape has brought upon her family, community, and village. And finally, for the young woman, who is the focus of a rape case, it forces an uncomfortable reckoning with the village and her family.

As I slowly parsed through the multiple narratives in the rape cases I read about and those that I followed more closely, I did not focus on determining which of the contesting claims were most credible. Instead, I examined how the different narratives functioned as a series of "scripts" produced to secure particular outcomes. I theorize scripts guided by an astute observation made by Manisha Mashaal, a feminist Dalit activist who explained that rape cases usually feature three different stories: one crafted by the courts and attorneys, the other by a woman's family, and the third by the woman herself.

In my research, I found that even though the scripts about rape cases were different and at times contradictory, they were all nevertheless exceptionally unified in the common subject of their scrutiny. As the subject of investigation, the woman alleging rape was central to the scripts that her rape would generate, and the outcome of rape cases rested on how her subjectivity was crafted. I understand subjectivity in two ways: first as the production of an identity that is recognized by the courts, such as a raped victim demonstrating a distressed mien. I go on to suggest that such identities are produced by structures such as the law, the state, and the patriarchal family. The raped woman's identity crafted in these structures attenuates her autonomy to craft a different sovereign narrative about her subjectivity. The second manner in which I understand subjectivity is by following how women navigate their rape cases and, through them, express their autonomy.

For instance, among police officers, a raped woman's subjectivity was crafted as morally compromised: a woman who voluntarily engaged in an unsanctioned affair. Members of the woman's community at times repeated this narrative, stigmatizing her for disgracing the reputation of her family. In contrast, among activists and attorneys on her side, the raped woman's subjectivity was crafted by highlighting her vulnerability, where justice for the victim/survivor often depends on a narrative of innocence to afford protection and restitution of her rights from the courts and law. Excluded from these different scripts is the subjectivity of the victim/ survivor herself, and it is her story and her own sense of reality that I am most concerned with uncovering in this book.

Semiotics of Rape is about how rape cases become the venue where women's sexual subjectivities and the sexual violations they have endured are debated. My inquiry into what rape cases do elicits three questions around which this book is anchored: What is the sexual subjectivity of the raped woman in Haryana? How is this sexual subjectivity forged through and against multiple scripts at different scales? What does sexual justice mean, and how does it intersect, in uneasy and sometimes conflicting ways, with social and political justice? In asking these questions, I parse out the different forms of subjectivity that are generated under conditions of violence. In my effort to grasp the relationship between subjectivity and violence, I turn to Saidiya V. Hartman's (1997) work, which theorizes the agency and will of people under conditions of slavery. I do not draw on Hartman to construct a false parallel between enslaved people and raped women. Instead, I draw on Hartman's capacity to deftly capture the subjectivity of those who are subjugated without reducing them to the dehumanizing scenes of their abjection. By paying attention to the subject formation of women who have been raped, and by refusing to see their subjectivities as defined entirely by the violent act of rape, I aim to apprehend how raped women can reclaim autonomy and sovereignty over their subjectivity.

I deliberately use the term "sexual subjectivity" rather than "sexual agency." They are not the same. Sexual agency is evident in cases like Kavita's, in which women are compelled to file rape cases after their illicit affairs are discovered, pressured by the need to mitigate the effects of reputational harm, as well as in cases that are colloquially referred to as "breach of promise to marry" cases, in which women file rape charges against lovers who lure them with the commitment to enter into a matrimonial alliance only to later abandon them. These cases are not rape cases—they do not involve violation of bodily integrity—but they do demonstrate sexual agency by the women who enter these relationships. While these cases are certainly evidence of deception by men, some of whom are of dominant caste and class who lure women into relationships with them, they also demonstrate particular kinds of sexual agency in that these women enter into these alliances even when they cannot be certain of the outcome of the relationship. However, by focusing on sexual subjectivity, my efforts pivot in a different direction. I pay attention to how women navigate their cases, what they have to say about the choices they make, and how they—at times—defy the abjection to which they are subject. By focusing on subjectivity, I examine what is possible to reclaim.

I'll elaborate by briefly discussing a case I deal with later in chapter 2. This case entails the alleged gang rape of a young Dalit woman I call Komal by two Jat and two Other Backward Classes (OBC) men.[6] It ended in a compromise, or an out-of-court settlement, after dragging on for four years. Cases like this, involving gang rape, and more critically, violence against lower-caste individuals, are often marked by threats and coercion against victims and survivors, who are generally forced to settle out of court. Dalit attorneys and activists who had organized around Komal's case feared that the compromise happened because Komal's family was coerced by dominant-caste men into settling. However, Komal insisted that the compromise was a just outcome. Her demeanor after the case ended demonstrated relief and a steadfast belief that the settlement was a fitting end. An inquiry into subjectivity in Komal's case allows me to ask: What did the compromise allow her to recuperate? While the outcome of her case is contrary to more conventional notions of justice that seek a guilty verdict and accountability through incarceration, and while the outcome was disappointing for activists who wanted to see whoever raped and beat Komal be convicted for the crimes against her, what can we understand about Komal's own insistence that the outcome was a good one? What can we learn by taking her claim seriously, and not dismissing it as merely misguided or a simple product of fear and exhaustion?

In explicating the difference between sexual agency and sexual subjectivity, I also seek to dislodge the idea that subjectivity in rape cases is only tied to the sexual encounter. In so doing, I ask: What can we discern about the sexual subjectivity of the raped women that escapes the flat and stultifying characterization of her as solely a broken, powerless victim or as a sullied, disgraced woman? (Or, I might add, that refuses caricaturizing her as a strong, heroic survivor?) Through my research, I found that raped women refused to remain confined by the sexual scripts about them. They crafted a subjectivity that continually ventured outside these narratives, frustrating attempts to congeal a single, flattening story about them. In some of the cases I followed, the subjectivity of raped women was evident in the articulation of their will or, as in Komal's case, in their insistence on an outcome contrary to more conventional notions of what justice looks like. The stories I followed revealed more complex subjectivities than what a victim/ survivor framing allows for. I was able to discern them by looking closely at how subjectivity enables a more expansive understanding of subjection. I argue that the sequestering that the shame of rape anticipates bringing to women tainted by it is never quite complete. In other words, I am looking at the production of agency in abjection, and it is to an understanding of subjectivity in abjection that I now briefly turn.

SUBJECTIVITY AND ABJECTION

According to feminist historian Dubra Mitra, from the mid-nineteenth until the mid-twentieth century, the prostitute was a foundational concept in the study of social life in India (2020). Mitra writes, "everyone was invested in an explanatory reasoning that could narrate the failures of female sexuality as a symptom of uneven social development" (18). I suggest that if the prostitute served to "delineate deviance" at the turn of the century, then the raped woman in the contemporary moment functions as symptomatic of social degeneration. In multiple conversations, including the one with Mr. Sihag I referred to earlier, many of my interlocutors pointed to the growing number of rape cases as evidence of growing perversion. Since they understood rape cases as a mechanism through which women and their families often dealt with illicit affairs, these interlocutors also pointed to women's sexual agency as a source of moral degeneracy. Identifying deviant bodies, such as the prostitute and the raped woman, offers a way to mark that which is profane, corrupt, and stigmatized. Literary theorist Richard Pedot, drawing on Julia Kristeva, says that this maneuver of identifying that which is abject is about "what society must exclude to persist" (2013, 2). The raped woman in this formulation is the abject figure that must be excluded or sequestered to maintain societal order.

The raped woman is considered abject because she is a source of stigma, held responsible for her own violation, and consequently a specter against which all other women must be perpetually vigilant. Dubra Mitra (2020) writes, "Dictates of shame and stigma not only were enacted in everyday forms of social control of women's sexuality but were also key in making disciplinary forms of social knowledge" (1). Consider for instance my conversation with young women in the village of Malud, for whom the "haunting presence" of deviant female sexuality was a persistent concern.[7] The five women gathered were keenly aware of the threat posed by the stigma of rape. They knew that if tainted their families would face social ruin, and they spoke with some frustration about how women were considered the *izzat* (honor) of their families, while also facing social scorn for being raped and molested. While some changes over the last few years had resulted in more autonomy in their lives, and they were now able to study longer, this new autonomy had also brought increased vigilance from their families. The daily dose of news about rape and violence against women generated a sense of perpetual peril against which young women had to actively inoculate themselves. They spoke about how women's attire, their use of cellular phones, their presence in public, and who they spoke with were all arbitrary measures of potential deviancy against which young women's reputations were gauged. Through our wide-ranging conversation, the specter of the raped woman emerged as a disciplining device that produced and shaped subjectivities.

Dominant social forces at once reject the raped woman, subject her to social abandonment, and at the same time perpetually recuperate her haunting presence to underscore the threat she represents and to keep people, and women in particular, in line. In a recently edited collection on abjection, Maggie Hennefeld and Nicholas Sammond (2020) write that "the abject exists in necessary opposition to the productive fantasy of the individual or social body as an agential or sovereign being" (12). For the women in Malud, the figure of the raped woman produced increased vigilance by their families so that they would not be tainted by its deviancy. In contending with the "productive" capacity of abjection, I intend to delineate the subjectivity of the raped woman. Understanding how the raped woman functions as an abject figure allows us to understand and name how she generates shame and stigma, while simultaneously instigating perverse fascination.

Abjection has been the source of considerable academic interest. A concept first developed by Julia Kristeva (1982) in her study of self through psychoanalysis, the abject is that which generates revulsion. For Kristeva, abjection is central to subject formation. The abject is a source of fear and fascination and something that must be rejected for the subject to exist. But Kristeva elaborates that the abject was not discarded and excluded; abjection "does not radically cut off the subject from what threatens it—on the contrary, abjection acknowledges it to be in perpetual danger" (9). It is this co-constitution between subject and abject that serves to generate subjectivity. Theorizing abjection in relation to minoritized populations in Britain, Imogen Tyler (2013) develops the concept of social abjection. In it, she is concerned with "the process through which minoritized populations are imagined and configured as revolting and become subject to control, stigma, and censure, and the practices through which individuals and groups resist, reconfigure and revolt against their abject subjectification" (4).

I turn to the concept of abjection to make intelligible the subjective potential that is not fully ensnared by the subordination of the raped woman. I draw on Saidiya V. Hartman (1997), who articulates how may we discern the agency of the enslaved, who is in an "indefinite and paradoxical relation to the normative category 'person'" (56). In the exhausting determinants of slavery, Hartman is looking for the "infinitesimal ways in which agency is exercised" (56). So while the abjected person is rejected as revolting, this person is nevertheless "not without the possibilities of a perverse form of agency" (Hennefeld and Sammond 2020, 18). And it is in these perverse forms of agency that I identify the subjectivity of the raped woman. It is this agency of abjection that Hartman captures when she argues that "the abjection of the captive body exceeds that which can be conveyed by the designation of or difference between 'slave' woman and 'free' woman" (83). The abjection of the raped women, similarly, exceeds that which can be confined by the shame and stigma to which they are subjected.

In narrating Komal's story and the stories of several of the other raped women, I make their subjectivity legible precisely to underscore the agency they exercise. The raped women I met and spoke with had complex responses to the stigma and rejection they faced. They were deeply aware of how they were shunned as sources of shame in their families, and yet they articulated their own positions, which at times diverged from those of their families as well as from those who were seeking justice on their behalf. Komal's story in some ways exemplifies this complex subjectivity but was not an exception among the cases I followed.

While I am concerned with how raped women construct their subjectivity, I draw on abjection not to showcase their passive resistance, but to expose the limits of their abjection and to understand the disbelief, rage, and social isolation that they are forced to endure. In articulating their suspicion of raped women, the police and attorneys, the neighbors, and the women's own kin generate a script in which the subjectivity of the raped woman is cast as deviant. But their rape script itself was productive of the investments it revealed.

SEXUAL SUBJECTIVITY AND THE FORMATION OF A RAPE SCRIPT

Explored in some detail by Sharon Marcus (1992), the term "rape script" suggests that the "violence of rape is enabled by narratives, complexes and institutions which derive their strength not from outright, immutable, unbeatable force but rather from their power to structure our lives as imposing cultural scripts" (389). Marcus here is pushing back against masculinist understandings of rape that constructs it as something that "is tantamount to death" and can only be "feared or legally repaired, not fought" (387). Marcus suggests instead that rape be understood as a language and a narrative, which can be changed, therefore allowing us to "resist the physical passivity it directs us to adopt" (392).

While Marcus understands the rape script as a discursive formation that ossifies to generate passivity, I use the term differently. In this book, I theorize the rape script as a language crafted to be audible to particular audiences in order to generate desired outcomes among them. It is a deliberately produced narrative that is honed to be recognized by its target audience. When a compromise on a rape case is reached—meaning when a plaintiff drops charges and reaches an out-of-court settlement—each side generates a script to narrate the story of the rape and to explain how an outcome was reached. Each side labors to create a script that casts its side in the best possible light. In the chapters that follow, I track when a script is formed, to whom is it audible, and what it does. I pay attention to the times it works and to when it falls apart. Kavita and Sanjay's case is an example of the latter, a case in which the rape script crafted to punish a Dalit man fell apart when the judge recognized it as a story fashioned to get revenge and refused to play along.[8]

I diverge from Marcus's understanding of script by theorizing it as the formation of a deliberate narrative. I differentiate between script and narrative by identifying scripts as a sedimentation of narratives that congeal into an audible form. By referring to a script as audible, I mean that it has been shaped into something readily recognizable among its intended audience, among whom it will resonate because it has already been rehearsed multiple times. So for instance, those in positions of power such as the police or dominant castes rehearse particular claims about Dalits (as untrustworthy, dirty, and criminal) and rape cases (as predominantly based on false allegations by unvirtuous women). The challenge then for those in subordinate positions is to make their own claims audible in a mainstream soundscape that denies the possibility of their existence as they see it themselves. What Miranda Fricker (2008) theorizes as illegibility, I understand as inaudibility. For Fricker (2008), an aggrieved person whose complaints have been rendered inaudible suffers an injustice that amounts to what she calls hermeneutical injustice, something which "occurs at a prior state, when someone is trying to make sense of a social experience but is handicapped in this by a certain sort of gap in collective understanding—a hermeneutical lacuna whose existence is owing to the relative powerlessness of a social group to which the subject belongs" (69). So against powerful existing scripts and the institutions that support them, those who are marginalized have to craft their own scripts in order to make themselves audible.

Civil rights and feminist groups have for years attempted to fight back against the "deflated degree of credibility" accorded to women and people from subordinate castes by documenting the unceasing violation of women's bodies. Through this work, they have been able to identify repeating patterns of structural injustice. Their documents, fact-finding reports, testimonies, anecdotes, prose, and fiction are all part of what I consider thick layers of narratives that have congealed into an audible, recognizable script. These layers of narratives are particularly significant because they have forged a language through which sexual violations can be identified and named, and around which claims for justice can be made.

When people from subordinate castes are violated, they are forced to face a rape script shaped with an additional layer of caste violence. The violation of Dalit women functions as the means by which dominant castes humiliate and maintain access to Dalit bodies. By access to bodies I refer not only to sexual access, but also to the dominant castes' capacity to extract labor from Dalit bodies and to secure their compliance with modes of behavior and deference that are in line with dominant-caste ideological hegemony. It's an exertion of terror and power that helps dominant castes ensure, for example, that Dalits perform their subjugated status by maintaining physical distance so as not to "pollute" their caste superiors, lowering their eyes in their presence, and by acquiescing to the injunction to live only in the segregated, dilapidated outskirts of villages and towns. There is a long history of dominant-caste men abusing Dalit women's bodies as retribution, punishment, and as a means of expressing and consolidating their power (Kannabiran and Kannabiran 2003; Rao 2011). There is now also a rich and growing archive of stories, prose, poetry, and testimonies—created by Dalits and their allies—that together generate a vocabulary and scaffolding through which atrocities against Dalits can be named, identified, and challenged.

To understand how particular scripts are crafted, it is critical to uncover and examine the history and political landscape of a place (Teltumbde 2019). Charu Gupta (2016), for instance, examines how in precolonial India, in the United Provinces, "the image of the Dalit woman's body as the site of evil and pollution gave way to a vision of her suffering and victimized body" (55). For Gupta, this shift in thinking about Dalit women provided upper-caste reformers with "a stamp of historical legitimation" (56). Attending to these place-based histories, as Shailaja Paik (2018) has shown, is also key to understanding that "Dalit women's agency belonged to them as well as to the culturally specific and historically contingent arrangement of power in which they were located" (4). In Haryana, two significant political moments led to greater Dalit awareness and political organizing, which also helped congeal a particular script about sexual violation.

The first of these political moments occurred in April 2010 in Mirchpur village. After a skirmish between a young Dalit boy and some Jat youth, Jat men looted, ransacked, and burned eighteen homes in the Dalit-caste Valmiki community as retribution for what they perceived as an insult by Dalits. During the rampage, a disabled seventeen-year-old Dalit girl, Suman, and her seventy-year-old father, Tarachand, were burned alive. Even though elders of the Dalit community had asked for forgiveness from the Jats in the village, the Jats responded with brutal vengeance. The police were informed, but they did not intervene to stop this violence against Dalit families.

Unlike many other instances of dominant-caste violence against Dalits, the Mirchpur incident, and more specifically the political mobilization that followed it, compelled the police to file a complaint against 103 Jats from the village. After advocates for the Dalit community in Mirchpur successfully argued that trial courts in Haryana would never hold the Jat men accountable for their crimes, because local Jat judges would never indict members of their own caste *biradri* (community), the case was moved to Delhi (Human Rights Law Network 2011). In a landmark judgment, fifteen

Jats were convicted for their crimes in Mirchpur, while eighty-two people were acquitted (*The Hindu* 2011). When the case recently came up for appeal, the Delhi High Court rejected it and sentenced the fifteen defendants to life imprisonment, calling the attack premeditated (Singh 2018).

The second significant political moment for Dalits in Haryana followed the brutal rape and subsequent death of a young woman in Delhi in December 2012. Her rape and death were followed by a national outpouring of grief and outrage, and political mobilizations in her support took place across the country. Nirbhaya became a household name.[9] Meanwhile, a range of activists and feminists noted and increasingly voiced a troubling, sharp contrast: namely, that equally brutal incidents of rape and violence against Dalits, Muslims, and Adivasis had consistently failed to garner attention or generate commensurate outpourings of grief (Dutta and Sircar 2013, 299). Feminists and Dalit scholars have of course long pointed out that whether or not an instance of extreme violence against a woman receives attention and results in public outrage is intimately tied to her caste and social position, and that such support and outrage is almost entirely absent when the violated woman is Dalit (Anandhi and Kapadia 2019; Ciotti 2019, 79). The massive reaction to Nirbhaya's rape and death generated renewed attention to the comparable silence about violence against Dalit women. This development, along with the fact of rising crimes against Dalits, mobilized civil and human rights groups to document cases of rape in Haryana and to support the women filing charges. These groups focused on Haryana, because reports indicated it has the third highest rate of crimes against women after Assam and Delhi (National Crime Records Bureau 2018, 195).[10]

Consequently, over the next few years, several reports emerged detailing the challenges Dalit women face while attempting to file rape charges in Haryana. In response to a particularly complex case involving the gang rape of a Dalit girl and a land dispute in Bhagana (a village in Haryana), a joint report was produced by two groups concerned with civil rights and violence: the Association for Democratic Rights (AFDR) and the People's Union for Democratic Rights (PUDR). Women Against Sexual Violence and State Repression (2014) also generated a detailed independent report on the relationship between sexual violence, caste-based atrocities, and land disputes in Bhagana. Simultaneously, Human Rights Watch (2017) documented the systematic efforts by members of the police and judiciary to stop Dalit women from pressing charges alleging rape. In addition to these civil and human rights groups, Dalit rights groups like the All India Dalit Mahila Adhikar Manch (AIDMAM 2018) also generated reports on atrocities against

Dalit women. Feminist activists such as Rajni Tilak, who was part of the National Confederation of Dalit and Adivasi Organizations and Rashtriya Dalit Mahila Andolan, was central in drawing attention to the specificities of violence against Dalit women and the forms of oppression they face.

In the wake of anti-Dalit violence in Mirchpur and the rising number of rape cases in Haryana, organizing efforts by human and civil rights groups, particularly Dalit activists and lawyers, drew much-needed attention to caste and gender violence in the country. Their efforts were part of a larger intellectual and political shift led by increasingly assertive Dalit activists and intellectuals (Anandhi and Kapadia 2019). This shifting terrain was the context for the emergence of a rape script that recognized the sexual violence inflicted on Dalit women and that insisted that Dalit women deserve protection and restitution. This rape script helped mobilize resources. Notably, it pushed back against the bias built into police stations and courts against women who allege rape, thereby challenging institutions that have historically prevented women from accessing justice.

But efforts to craft this important script necessarily truncated the contradictions and paradoxes of particular cases, and more significantly, flattened the agency and subjectivity of Dalit women (Ciotti 2014). At the scale of political mobilization, the script of rape and compromise—in which a raped woman is forced to drop her case in exchange for financial compensation—followed a template, albeit one derived from multiple stories of disenfranchisement and hundreds of cases where justice was denied. This script made a compelling case for paying attention to violence against Dalit women and to how dominant-caste threats can force subordinate castes to acquiesce, drop rape charges, and settle out of court.

However, at more intimate scales, such as that of the victim herself and her home, this script about rape and compromise changes and refracts. A closer look at this rape script makes apparent that a particular woman's story is often more complex than what the script can accommodate. This is not to say that the script is inaccurate; instead, I suggest that it is incomplete. Through my research, I saw various advocates for women's rights navigate between different "scripts" to try and "fit" a particular story of rape or compromise into one that would allow them to make a particular claim. In most of the cases I researched, a gap between a scripted narrative and the untidy details of the case persisted, despite efforts to align the two. In this gap, paradoxes emerged that compel difficult questions about what justice looks like at different scales. What are we to do when the story of rape differs among different publics, or when the desired outcome of a rape case, and the very definition of justice, diverges across scales? I suggest that thinking at the intersections of different scales may help us navigate diverging ideas about what constitutes justice in a rape case.

SCALE AND JURISDICTION IN RAPE NARRATIVES

To understand how rape animates different publics in rural Haryana, I draw on rich discussions of scale within geography. Since the 1980s, geographers have engaged in a long and varied discussion on scale as a way to understand social and political phenomena. Scale in human geography is about the relationship between particular jurisdictional boundaries, such as the national and global. While the field of human geography has extensively theorized how scales are made, contested, and transformed in relation to capitalist production, feminist geographers have pointed to a lack of attention to social reproduction in these theories (Katz 2001; Marston 2000). Drawing attention to how intimate scales such as the home and body are deeply imbricated in capital relations, feminist geographers have suggested that the "global and the intimate constitute one another" (Mountz and Hyndman 2006). The most common understanding of scale is as a nested hierarchy of smaller to larger scales, even if many geographers have come to contest and enrich this framing (Brenner 2001; Cox 1998; Howitt 1998; Marston, Jones, and Woodward 2005; Smith 1984).

I draw on this work by geographers to consider the publics and conflicts that rape in Haryana animates by thinking through the relationships between bureaucratic and intimate scales. I understand bureaucratic scales as village boundaries, wards, and districts that have an administrative function. Jurisdiction by these units is established through mundane governmental practices. The bureaucratic scales of districts and wards are codified through everyday mechanisms of administration and taxation, which reproduce their boundaries as ontological givens. Negotiations by village council officials with district offices over resources, compensation for crop failure, or a water dispute generate bureaucratic processes that render the scale and hierarchy of village and district as established, undisputed, and solidified. These scales are recognized because members of the state bureaucracy occupy positions such as district magistrate or district collector, making concrete the district as an administrative unit. Similarly, villages have specific boundaries and elected representatives who are assigned to negotiate with district officials on behalf of the village.

Intimate scales, in my understanding, are the space of the *basti* (neighborhood), home, and the body. S. Anandhi and Meera Velayudhan (2010) ask that feminist geographers be attentive to how neighborhoods are sharply divided and how boundaries of caste and religion are violently enforced (40). Contests over who has sovereignty and jurisdiction over these intimate scales are animated in the wake of rape cases. In these contests, previously invisible boundaries of caste and gender are enforced. In rural Haryana, men retain control and jurisdiction over both the home and the women in their household. Domestic sexuality is under the purview of the patriarch and needs to be protected, and in the case of young women, bartered with in marriage (Das 1996).

In cases of intercaste violence, the relationship between intimate and bureaucratic scales is made especially relevant. It is the gendered Dalit body that is subject to brutal violence in response to the perceived or actual upward mobility of Dalit lives. In her theorizing of the massacre of a Dalit family in Khairlanji in 2006,[11] Anupama Rao (2011) argues that "the brutal ritual desecration of the gendered Dalit body is a technology of violence that resurrects *archaic* forms of sexual violence and punishment in direct proportion to the politicization of Dalits, and the state's efforts to outlaw practices of caste violation." She continues to say that this technology of violence is "a counter response on the 'creative' semiotic ground of violation and violence that relocates struggles over Dalit identity to streets, homes, and to spaces otherwise invisible to the state's modern, nonarchaic glance" (612). In chapter 4, I show how despite laws against brutalizing people based on their caste status, caste violence remains illegible in rape cases. This invisibility of violence at an intimate scale on the Dalit body, which exists despite laws that prohibit it at the bureaucratic scale, is precisely what Rao points out.

I am interested in understanding how the rape charge is navigated between bureaucratic and intimate scales. Who has jurisdiction and control in these different scales? What is rendered visible and audible at intimate scales that is otherwise made invisible by the courts and the law? What scripts are generated? How are jurisdiction and sovereignty over intimate spaces challenged and consolidated in the wake of a rape charge? These questions guide my understanding of the contests over jurisdiction and sovereignty in two specific ways.

First, I am interested in who is invested in establishing jurisdiction over the intimate scales of the body, home, and *basti*. Exposing those who are invested in having jurisdiction over these intimate scales helps uncover who has a role to play in the construction of a rape script. By focusing on the intersection of intimate and bureaucratic scales, I suggest that at each scale the narrative of rape shifts and changes, animating various publics, each invested in different outcomes. The bureaucratic scales maintain patriarchy, so what does it mean when those invested in intimate scales collude with the police and the courts to establish jurisdiction over the home? What forms of control and caste politics are solidified?

Second, I consider how efforts by village elders and the male head of the household to maintain jurisdiction over the home may entail, for the woman who files a rape case, losing sovereignty over other intimate spaces, such as her body. In chapter 1, I explore the story of a young woman in a consensual relationship who is forced to file a rape charge against her lover. In an effort to establish jurisdiction over the neighborhood and the home, Dalit village elders and the young woman's father compelled her to file a rape case. For the young woman, her affair was a demonstration of her jurisdiction over her sexuality. Her village community and family did not sanction such a display of sovereignty, and their efforts to wrest back control required that she acquiesce jurisdiction over her body and sexuality.[12]

Rape is a violation of sovereignty at the intimate scale of the body and sexuality. It makes visible and disrupts contests of jurisdiction over these scales. In the context of patriarchal control over women's bodies and the home, rape is a violation of not only a woman's bodily integrity, but also of male jurisdiction over the household and over sexual access to the women who reside in it. Rape animates all of these scales, and responses to a violation entail efforts to restore jurisdictional boundaries and hierarchies. In the chapters that follow, I employ this framework of scale to think through what a rape charge does at different scales. How might these incongruencies help form a more robust understanding of political negotiations in the wake of a rape charge, and consequently push us toward more nuanced constructions of justice?

THE QUESTION OF JUSTICE

In January 2019, I was working with Dalit lawyers and activists from Haryana, along with a Delhi-based human rights organization, to draft a petition addressing compromise cases for the Supreme Court. Courts in India have long known that there is an unofficial "culture of compromise," where the two parties involved in a case come to an out-of-court settlement, and the plaintiff agrees to drop charges. These compromise settlements are not only against the law in criminal cases, but in instances of sexual violation, they are often produced through intimidation and coercion. Activists and lawyers in Haryana have for years been documenting cases of rape and various atrocities against Dalits that end in compromise. They argue that Dalits are often threatened with more violence and social boycott if they do not drop charges or if they do not agree to compromise on their cases. Social boycotts can have a very serious impact on the lives of those they target, and can include, for example, denying a person access to work and a livelihood. The petition we were crafting together sought to convince the Court to recognize the coercion and violence in compromise cases, and to take steps to mitigate them.

Because compromise in criminal cases is illegal, court records do not document whether a case was compromised. A tell-tale sign is when they note that the witness for the prosecution turned suddenly hostile toward their own lawyer, abruptly changing their story and claiming that no rape took place or that they cannot identify who the perpetrator was. However, not all cases in which the witness turns hostile are compromise cases, so the numbers of compromise cases are difficult to estimate. Anecdotal evidence by activists and lawyers suggests that up to 70 percent of rape cases end in compromise. Dalit activists I worked with affirmed that when a case involves Dalit victims and perpetrators from dominant castes, it almost always ends in compromise. I heard over and over again about how dominant castes used social boycotts, threats of violence, routine humiliation, and coercion as tactics to suppress Dalit claims for rights and justice. This narrative about compromised cases and the urgency to have something done about them was compelling.

However, as we began to document cases where compromise had occurred, the activists began to explain that in many instances, the families no longer wanted to talk about their case and had moved on. As we talked further and unearthed details about specific cases, the story about compromise became much more complex and at times contradictory. Some of the cases fit the "script" about how compromise is usually inextricable from coercion and threats. But in other cases, the story differed or was more ambiguous. In some instances, compromise occurred with the express intent of the victim, such as in the case of Komal, which I briefly mentioned earlier. We were forced to confront stories that lacked a clear narrative of coercion, and which were perplexing. The gaps and inconsistencies of these stories brought into sharp focus what Shailaja Paik (2018) and other feminists have argued, that "Dalit women's fragmented, flawed, complex, and contradictory lives cannot be confined to linear readings" (3). Throughout a day-long meeting, the political intent of the petition we were drafting, and its necessity, grated against some of the incongruities in the cases we discussed, creating dissonance. There was a gap between, on the one hand, a political strategy needed to address real systemic coercion by dominant castes, and on the other, the messy inconsistencies of the cases, which did not neatly fit the script of coercion.

The differences we encountered between the neat script of coercion and the more ambiguous, messy cases underscore how justice (encompassing fairness, the repair of harm, and/or respect for a victim or her wishes) is sometimes but not always aligned with conventional forms of social and legal justice, which entail making every effort to punish perpetrators as a means of securing accountability for their crimes. What, in light of these divergences, does sexual justice mean? My research following rape cases and interviews with attorneys and activists converged with what other legal scholars have argued: that the law and courts do not offer justice—in the sense of a meaningful repair of harm—to rape victims or to society.

While the activists and lawyers I worked with were clear on how juridical structures were failing to provide justice by consistently failing to hold violators accountable for their crimes, they spent less time examining what the divergent strategies, "failures," compromises, and resistance told us about how we might think about justice in the first place. It is one thing to agree that the court system and law, saturated by those in power, are not concerned with safeguarding the lives and rights of the subjugated, and that they frequently fail to provide any modicum of justice. It is quite another to then look carefully at the quiet refusals, silent resistance, and deliberate disengagement by victims/plaintiffs as efforts to craft an alternative to the types of justice on offer through legal institutions. In the third question of justice around which this book is anchored, I look closely at some of these strategies as a way to consider what sexual justice might look like. Such an inquiry would ask, for instance: How are we to understand Komal's exoneration of the four men accused of raping her? Might we consider her refusal as a way to think about sexual justice that allows her to reclaim a degree of control and autonomy over the narrative of her assault?

If subjectivity in rape cases emerges through the recognition of the victim/survivor as a person in need of restitution, then that subject is constituted through those structures. For instance, victims/survivors have to appear and be made audible as distressed and vulnerable to be "recognized" as victims or survivors of rape. In such a formulation, "the subject recognizes itself in opposition to that which is different" (Thomas 2019). Such a theory of recognition imperils the subject such that "if subjectivity is the result of hostile conflict, then recognition must inevitably exist as a relation of domination" (215). But what if compromise in cases such as Komal's allows for disengagement with conventional justice and its limitations? Could such withdrawal reveal what Kamari Maxine Clarke (2019) says, that "contemporary . . . legalisms are part of the larger tyranny of violence that does not stop with the individualization of criminal responsibility and trial performance" (15)? While Clarke is here writing about the International Criminal Court, her critique nevertheless echoes what feminist legal scholars have long claimed: that the courts advance a form of violence rather than stem it. What forms of subjectivities may be possible with disengagement from systems of law that imperil more autonomous possibilities? This central question animates the chapters in this book.

ARC OF THE BOOK

The chapters follow how the story of rape in rural Haryana was told to me. I begin in chapter 1 with the story of *marzi* (consent). I heard over and over that the majority of rape cases were false because they stemmed from relationships that were illicit but consensual, or that rape charges were filed as retaliation against a lover in a failed affair. In this chapter, I track how *marzi* is perverted to mean "corruption" rather than "permission" and "agency." The case I follow is of a young Dalit woman I call Vineeta who was in an impermissible relationship with Pradeep, a Jat man.[13] When a rape case was filed in response to this illicit affair, it seemed to corroborate police claims about how rape cases stem from false allegations. But I argue that both the rape case and the use of consent to discredit it are about disciplining unruly sexuality. Changes in women's sexual subjectivity in rural Haryana are a source of tremendous concern and anxiety. *Marzi,* then, is not about recognizing or respecting sexual subjectivity; instead, it is a narrative of perversion deployed to bring straying women back into the libidinal folds of domestic patriarchy.

In this chapter, I draw on Saidiya V. Hartman's (1997) deft analysis of "will" in *Scenes of Subjection* to understand how we might think through subject formation under conditions of coercion. I use this work to consider how women's sexual subjectivity is illegible and unacceptable even when she gives consent. Hartman is drawing on historical narratives of enslaved women who were raped. Toni Irving (2007) writes that the import of these histories is manifest in the contemporary mistreatment of Black women who are assaulted. She says, "How the law currently deals with rape reinscribes the historical notion that for black women sex is never against their will" (69).

I draw on the violation of Black women's bodies as a way to theorize the harm done to Dalits, following scholars who are calling for exploring such parallels. Shailaja Paik (2014), for instance, suggests a "'margin to margin framework' for the production of knowledge and the practice of political solidarity" (75). The issue of consent/nonconsent for particular kinds of women, those who were enslaved, Black women, and Dalit women is outside of dominant frameworks of discernment, rendering invisible the autonomy of personhood accorded to these women. *Marzi*, I argue, raises the specter of women taking control of their sexual choices, a possibility which patriarchal society considers intolerable. I draw on Vineeta's case to demonstrate how she crafts her sexual subjectivity through deliberate choices, a rejection of shame, and claims of autonomy. Despite her efforts at autonomy, Vineeta's rape case ended in compromise, and was about compensating her father for the loss of her value in marriage. Since these extra-legal out-of-court settlements were so frequently evoked by village elders, the woman's kin, and even attorneys as a way to deal with rape cases, chapter 2 deals with compromise in rape cases.

Chapter 2 picks-up where Vineeta's case ended, with an out-of-court settlement called a *shamjauta* (a compromise). If the first most frequent story I heard about rape cases was that they were in fact consensual, the second most frequent story I heard about rape cases was that most end in compromise. Here I draw on the second argument I make, about how sexual subjectivity is forged in and through multiple scales, animating different publics invested in its outcome. In rape cases, once a First Information Report (FIR) is lodged and the accused is located,[14] the accused perpetrator is usually taken into custody unless bail is granted. It is at this stage that the family of the accused initiates measures to pressure the victim's family into a *shamjauta*. While common, compromise in criminal cases is illegal in India. In the courts, judges and attorneys are deeply aware of compromised cases and participate in them through the drama of false testimony.[15] By "false testimony," I don't mean a fabricated accusation of rape, on which a prosecution's case is sometimes based. I'm instead referring to the testimony that withdraws the allegation of rape under conditions that everyone knows involves coercion, but participates in as if it doesn't. Some judges, recognizing the frequency of rape cases ending in compromise, even ask victims during the trial if they were coerced into dropping charges. Such questions reveal how contradictions and divergences from the rape script are animated at different scales to anticipate particular outcomes.

I draw on three compromise cases to illustrate, in different ways, the gaps between the script of rape and the actual intimate details of each case. These gaps force us to consider what justice means in these cases. At each scale, the illegal out-of-court settlement animated different concerns and forms of relief. But what did justice entail in these cases? Conflicting alliances and contradictory outcomes are part of the story of compromise, in which what is just is not simple or easily discernable. In this chapter, I draw on Audra Simpson's (2014) theorizing of refusal as a way to consider compromise not as a failure, but as generative of autonomy and deliberate disengagement. Through these cases, I ask what refusal allows. Of course, it's one thing if a woman refuses to press charges against a man because he didn't actually rape her or because she doesn't draw satisfaction/repair from punishing/imprisoning him. It's another if she refuses to press charges because she has been threatened with violence if she does.

Dalit scholars, activists, and lawyers, as well as extensive documentation in fact-finding reports, prose, and fiction, illustrate how dominant castes have the resources to convince or coerce Dalits and those of subordinate castes into compromise. In cases such as Vineeta's, for instance, the possibility of a compromise exists because Pradeep's family has land and can compensate her family for dropping charges. In Bhagana, the tale of rape emerges in the wake of a conflict over land, and the land-owning, dominant-caste defendants can explicitly or indirectly force the Dalit plaintiffs to drop their charges, because the latter rely on working on the land owned by the dominant caste. Because social relationships between different social and caste groups are navigated through who has access to and control over property, issues of violation, secrecy, and power are metastasized through these thick relationships.

Chapter 3 follows this story of land and the political-economic conditions that stem from it. In this chapter, I show how social relationships in rural Haryana are navigated through differential caste and community access to land (Chakravarti 2018). For instance, Dalits and people from subordinate castes are often compelled to settle rape cases out of court because of the precarity of their political and economic conditions. They cannot afford to refuse the demands of the powerful without paying a very steep price; their refusal to acquiesce would result in social boycott and a backlash that would threaten their very existence.

This chapter shifts the scale of analysis to situate the trajectory of neoliberalism in Haryana. The paradox between a high rate of gross domestic product (GDP) generated by the service, manufacturing, and real estate sectors and a declining rural economy marks the crisis in Haryana. This shift of scale and lens is important because it reveals the political-economic construction of Jats as a powerful caste who hold dominion over rural

Haryana. Understanding this caste's decline in power over the last two decades helps situate their violence and anger toward those of Dalit and subordinate caste who, in the same period of Jat decline, experienced a modicum of upward mobility. Jats perceive that these subordinate castes and classes advanced at their expense. So when Jats are accused of rape by Dalits it fuels their anger, and they can use their political clout to suppress such accusations precisely because they control the land.

If the prevailing narrative is that most rape cases are false and end in compromise, then when, and under what circumstances, are rape cases believed? Chapter 4 concentrates on cases in which death follows a rape case, and determines that death is what makes the allegation of rape more credible. I examine why spectacular death in rape cases, whether of the rape victim or of a member of her family, elicits gravitas in cases that, before the death, were not taken seriously or were viewed with suspicion. I suggest death credits the violation with veracity. I do not mean to suggest that rape allegations are only believed when they are followed by death, or that there must be a death for there to be a conviction for rape. My aim here is to examine how cases of rape that are followed by death compel acknowledgment by a state whose primary mode of response to rape has otherwise been disbelief. In so doing, I return once again to Saidiya V. Hartman's (1997) work to think through what death in rape cases makes possible. I use Hartman's analysis of how only some types of harm inflicted on an enslaved person are visible to the law as a theoretical scaffolding to understand how death generates recognition of the harm caused by the act of rape.

Juxtaposed against death that follows rape, I examine how women who survive are often referred to through a zombie metaphor of *zinda laash*, the living dead. What purpose does it serve to think about raped women as the living dead? In this chapter, I argue that the term *zinda laash* reveals the disquiet that rape survivors generate. So while death after rape makes the case believable, life in the aftermath of rape is offensive. Following two cases in which death followed rape, I examine the perverse validity granted to rape in the wake of death. I also draw on Ruth Wilson Gilmore's (2007) oft-quoted definition of racism as "the state-sanctioned and/or extralegal production and exploitation of group-differentiated vulnerability to premature death" (247) and apply it to understand premature death among Dalits. Drawing on Gilmore, I see that what Akhil Gupta (2012) calls the "structural violence" of the state renders some people more vulnerable to death than others.

I conclude this book by reflecting on a series of questions that emerge through the rape cases I follow and document: Which institutions, social groups, and caste politics are drawn into the conflict, and what investments do their positions divulge? How do we understand consent in the context of larger structures of coercive practices and caste violence? Does *marzi* matter? Why is women's sexual subjectivity only acceptable under secrecy? What do changing neoliberal politics in rural Haryana generate for women's mobility and subjectivity? These queries expose the architecture of the social life of rape and consequently propel a reflection on what justice may mean in rape cases. I suggest that sexual subjectivity turns our attention to a consideration of how harm is recognized and by whom, who gets to be considered a victim, and what a victim's refusal to seek justice through the courts might do to our understanding of justice. I dwell on three terms: refusal, recognition, and justice. In parsing out each of these terms, I am looking to see how the cases I draw on offer different notions of justice beyond the carceral.

THE CASES

Let me briefly address the rape cases I followed. As I explain further in the section on method, finding cases of rape was extremely challenging. In my effort to be sensitive and careful, but also because I wanted to closely investigate the cases and how they were navigated in the village, I followed eight cases in depth. There are three issues I would like to explain about the nature of the cases I followed. First, the eight cases are not illustrative of a statistical sample or majority, rather they are instances that illuminate the social life of rape. Second, the cases I follow seem to echo claims made by the police, attorneys, and bureaucrats. I intentionally chose to examine cases that seem to mirror the claims of these authorities in order to understand and expose the discursive maneuvers they employ to make, for instance, women's agency corrupt. I also sought to understand how compromise is at times facilitated by malfeasance and is at other times evidence of it. Finally, unlike the previous chapters on consent and compromise, both of which feature cases that ended in out-of-court settlements, the chapter on death deals with rape cases that better fit what convention dictates they should look like. The two cases I followed here were the only cases that led to a conviction. While the argument I make in this chapter is that death brings more credibility to rape cases, I want to be clear that not all cases in which death occurs are believed. I specifically looked at rape cases that were granted a degree of credulity in the wake of death to expose how the law and courts treat such cases differently than others. While the stories of all the cases inform all the chapters, some cases are more central to the arc of certain chapters than others.

I foreground the nature of the rape claims I followed rather than detail the brutal violations in case-after-case for two reasons. First, there already exists extensive documentation in reports by civil and human rights groups that details the trauma of rape and narrates the great difficulty of getting rape to be taken seriously and addressed. Such reports and documentation have effectively discredited claims by police and others that rape allegations are in the main false allegations. Scholarship on rape in South Asia and elsewhere has also offered sophisticated ways to consider how the law and state help those in power evade punishment or accountability for their crimes. This scholarship has also reiterated the violence women experience. The strategy I employ instead looks closely at police claims in order to understand how they are constructed and in order to unmask the biases baked into their logic and structures. Second, in a field already saturated with documenting violence against women, I wanted to veer away from also reciting this violence, and instead sought to excavate a different set of concerns, look at the unexpected places where agency is expressed, and consider the unconventional ways that stories of rape unfold.

WHY RURAL HARYANA?

Rape occurs everywhere; it does not occur uniquely in Haryana. But Haryana is crafted in the popular imagination as a place that is exceptionally violent toward women. Even though it does not have the highest rate of crimes against women, Haryana is perceived as particularly unsafe. Other states like Gujarat and cities like Mumbai distinguish themselves from Haryana and Delhi as being "safe" for women. Pratiksha Baxi (2014), in her eloquent ethnography of trial court in Ahmedabad, writes about how rape in Gujarat was viewed as mostly nonexistent except for a "few aberrant cases" (xliv). The commonplace view is that unlike "north India" (meaning, unlike states such as Haryana and Delhi), Gujarat was safe for women. This, of course, conveniently forgets the spectacular violence against women that occurred in Gujarat during the pogrom against Muslims in 2002 (Sarkar 2002).

Haryana has the highest rate of gang rape in the country outside of the northeastern states of Assam, Meghalaya, and Mizoram (National Crime Records Bureau 2018, 196). But before the perception of Haryana's hypermisogyny was based on crimes against women, the state was infamous because of its strong preference for sons and for its practice of deliberate sex selection in childbearing. Even though prenatal sex determination is illegal, Haryana, along with some other states, continues to use clandestine sex-selection technologies. This preference for male progeny has led to the most imbalanced sex ratio in the country: 834 girls to 1,000 boys (John 2018). Such a skewed sex ratio, Haryana's conservative sociocultural fabric, and high crime statistics together serve to forge a place that is hostile to women and girls. Crimes against women and Haryana's poor response and failure to curb it frequently make newspaper headlines. Consider these three headlines in the *Hindustan Times*: "21-Year-Old Woman Gang Raped for Four Days in Panchkula" (2018a); "Crime Against Women on Rise in Haryana, Rape Cases Up By 47 Percent" (2018b); and "Patriarchy, Popular Culture, Unemployment: Why Haryana Is India's Rape Capital" (Dhingra 2018)." Rising rates of violence against women in Haryana have been so notable that the Indian Supreme Court sent a notice to the state's government, asking about its efforts to curb crime (*Indian Express* 2014).

In the context of these stories, Haryana emerged in the popular imaginary as a place of excessive violence. The frame of "excess" is mine, and I use it to convey how the unrelenting news about violence in Haryana generated a sense of helplessness, which in turn demanded an immediate response by already overextended civil rights and activist groups. I discuss the construction of Haryana as a place of excess in a discursive sense, drawing on sources including the popular media just noted, as well as multiple conversations with bureaucrats, lawyers, and activists. Through these mediums, Haryana emerged as somewhat indifferent to crimes against women and recalcitrant to change. I heard several bureaucrats and activists say with frustration, "Yahaan kuch nahi ho sakta" (Nothing is possible here). In this study, I attempt to dislodge this ontological frame, which fuses place and people with violence. My intent is not to negate horrific violation, but rather to open to critical scrutiny how rape generates ferment among different publics with investments in particular outcomes.

I was spurred to begin this study by a story that made national headlines and spilled onto the streets of Delhi. In March 2014, four Dalit girls were gang-raped by five Jat men in the village of Bhagana, in Haryana. The girls were all under the age of eighteen and were kidnapped and found several hundred miles away at Bathinda railway station in the neighboring state of Punjab. This horrifying event drew numerous news stories and spurred human rights and feminist groups to generate fact-finding reports, like the joint report by the People's Union for Democratic Rights and the Association for Democratic Rights (2012). As the case garnered more publicity, a macabre tale unfolded in which it became clear that this was not only a case of gang rape, but also a dispute over common land to which Jat villagers were denying poor Dalits access.

Bhagana became emblematic of crimes against Dalits and revealed the particular vulnerability of Dalit women to dominant-caste men's violence. The history of a rural agricultural society where Jats owned most of the land left Dalits to serve in various modes of indentured labor. The consequences of this were that Dalit women who worked on these lands were often subject to violation by Jat men.[16] This history of systemic abuse by Jats was well known, generating a space of credibility which made it possible for the story of Bhagana to resonate. The case became a stark instantiation of Dalit vulnerability and generated outrage over the violence, resulting in public demonstrations in Delhi and overwhelming support for the victims. Bhagana offered a rare and unique opportunity to right—in this instance at least—a systemic wrong.

Through the course of this work, however, the story of rape became much more intricate than what I had initially understood. When I began my research in 2016, two years after the Bhagana case, many warned that I should avoid the Bhagana story because it had become "very complicated" and there were "multiple, different reports." Some suggested that there were rumors that one of the girls was possibly in a relationship with one of the accused. Others flatly denied this. Some said that the girls' families had been happy to compromise for money, while others claimed that they were coerced and threatened into compromise by the dominant caste in the village. Through my research, I came to understand how particular versions of the incident facilitated particular constructions of reality. The facts of the story and its implications were narrated differently from one group of people to another. I came to understand that rather than help determine the "truth," the multiple versions of the story revealed more about the concerns, conflicts, and power relations that rape animates. They foregrounded Michael Bakhtin's (1982) theory that "language is not a neutral medium that passes freely and easily into the private property of the speaker's intentions; it is populated—overpopulated—with the intentions of others" (294). While I did not begin my research with Bhagana, I ended with it, speaking to those who continue to sit outside the district offices and courts in protest seven years later: the mothers of the young women, activists, and attorneys with differing positions.

Over three years of research, I looked at rape in rural Haryana because it was a site of spectacular systemic violence. Unfolding in the context of a profound rural crisis, Haryana offered an opportunity to understand what the violation of women and girls means. The rising incidents of rape and Haryana's distinction as having one of the highest rates of gang rape in the country contributed to the emerging popular imagination of the state as anachronistic, intractable, and hypermisogynistic. This research pushes back against such deterministic frames to open the question of what rape in Haryana does. It is undeniable that brutal incidents of rape do occur and solicit rigorous responses, protests, and, at times, swift justice. But leaving aside the complexity of what rape does acquiesces to flat geographies, which fit places to human traits. My effort here is to provide a robust account of incidents of violation that help us understand how village reputation, family honor, caste politics, coercion, and consent are key aspects of the story of rape in rural Haryana.

METHOD: THE POLITICS OF WRITING ABOUT RAPE AND CASTE

I began my research on rape in rural Haryana in the wake of the huge publicity that followed the December 2012 Delhi rape and the 2014 rape in Bhagana. The complex imbrication between caste, sexual violation, and land disputes loomed large in these stories and offered an exceptional opportunity to better understand the relationship between gender, violence, and neoliberalism, which has been the trajectory of my previous work. I began by speaking with civil and human rights groups and Dalit activists in Haryana and Delhi about the cases they had followed and supported. Some of these cases were part of reports and other organizing efforts against rape in Haryana. I initiated my research by following up on the cases that were already part of prior fact-finding and organizing efforts. But I was soon confronted with the serious challenges and dilemmas around research on rape, including the politics of speaking with women who had been violated, the risk of retraumatizing them, and the adverse visibility that my meeting with them might cause. In particular, I was concerned about the ethical and political implications of conducting interviews, as a dominant-caste and dominant-class woman, with women who did not share my privileges.

Dalit and other feminists have pointed to the neglect of Dalit and other subordinate-caste women in the history of the feminist movement in India (Anandhi and Kapadia 2019; Paik 2018; Rege 1996; Tamalapakula n.d.). Since the 1990s there has been much more visibility of Dalit women writing their own history (Pawar and Moon 2008); an articulation of a Dalit feminist standpoint (Rege 1998); and an autonomous Dalit women's identity and need to "talk differently" (Guru 1995). A rich body of vernacular fiction and nonfiction work by Dalit women demonstrates the long lineage of their intellectual tradition (Anandhi and Kapadia 2019; Sarangi 2018; Tomar 2013;). Some of this rich work has recently been translated into English from Marathi (Dangle 2009) and Tamil (Bama 2012), and much of it cautions against members of dominant castes writing for and about Dalit women without being attentive to how doing so appropriates space. It also cautions against writing with a savior fetish, against writing that assumes a familiar "project of recovery" and rescue that elite women and women with an unexamined imperial lens have a history of producing (Akbar and Oza 2012; Paik 2018).

Attending to these cautions articulated by Dalit feminists meant treading particularly carefully as a researcher of rape. Dalit women had already been overdetermined as victims in literature and academic work, and there was a call to engage more fully with Dalit women's subjectivities as "transgressive agents" (Paik 2018). When I began this work, my focus was on the relationship between caste, rape, and land. My investigation of eight rape cases was my entry point to understanding dominant-caste discourses about false claims, compromise, consent, and death that were generated within dominant-caste structures such as the village council, the police station, the courts, and the district offices. Each of the rape cases I followed is therefore not representative in any statistical sense, but is an incident that guides my navigation into the social worlds in which these issues emerged and were adjudicated.

The biggest challenge, however, was finding cases of violation that I could investigate, and it was here that issues of caste were acute. While I began with wanting to understand what rape in rural Haryana mobilizes, I did not realize that access to people willing to speak with me would be so profoundly circumscribed. To exercise the utmost care, particularly against retraumatizing victims, I followed eight cases that had either been part of prior reports (in which the victim had already met with human rights groups, activists, and lawyers), or that were more recent cases recommended by the lawyers and activists with whom I collaborated. In each instance, the victim's lawyer, an activist, or both accompanied me as I explained my project and asked if she would be willing to speak with me. If granted permission, I would return for additional conversations that were open-ended rather than directly related to the rape.

Because my access to victims was limited by these connections to activists and lawyers, it in some ways determined who I spoke with. My relationships with lawyers and activists in Haryana were through civil and human rights organizations in Delhi; these activists and lawyers were part of Dalit groups fighting against atrocities in Haryana in the wake of the Mirchpur case. Since the cases they dealt with primarily concerned Dalit victims, most of the cases I followed featured either Dalit or OBC victims and families. Despite my efforts to get access to rape cases that involved dominant-caste victims, this proved to be difficult. I spoke with dominant-caste lawyers in the districts and asked if they had cases in which the families would be willing to speak with me. In all three districts where I conducted research, lawyers explained that cases involving dominant castes were usually suppressed immediately. I asked several lawyers who dealt with rape if they had cases involving dominant castes, and while they did, the lawyers explained that the families were reluctant to speak with anyone from the outside for fear that doing so would compromise their reputation. In the case of Sanjay and Kavita (who is dominant caste), with whose story I began this chapter, I asked Kavita's lawyer if her family would be willing to speak with me. While he shared her father's number with me, he also discouraged me from speaking with him. According to him, the family had gone through enough with the case; Kavita was now married, and the family would not want anyone to discuss the case with them again. Given the lawyer's opposition, I did not follow up with Kavita's family.

In other districts, I also met with several lawyers who reiterated that cases involving dominant castes were usually resolved in the village or between the parties involved. Given the increase in the number of rape cases in the past few years, it was obvious that cases were being reported and filed, but getting access to them remained extremely difficult. The only time I gained access to a case of rape or molestation among the dominant castes was when a case occurred in one of the villages I had previously visited. We became aware of the case while in conversation with the station house officer of a *mahila thanna* (women's police station).[17] The case involved the molestation of a young girl by an older man. Both families belonged to the dominant-caste Pandit family, albeit from different classes.

One of the main reasons it was so difficult to access dominant-caste cases was that there were no dominant-caste organizations that supported victims of rape. There was no parallel to the Dalit groups, lawyers, and organizations that advocated on behalf of Dalit victims. The organizations that supported the interests of the dominant castes were the *panchayats* (village councils) and *Khap panchayats* (caste councils), which are invested in issues of lineage and disputes. The caste councils have garnered a reputation for meting out brutal punishment against those who breach caste and subcaste boundaries and alliances. They are deeply imbricated in patriarchal structures and in efforts to maintain control over domestic sexuality. Since rape cases challenge those domains by opening them to scrutiny, caste councils work hard to make sure that such violations are not spoken about publicly. The resulting impenetrability demonstrated caste and patriarchal power, which meant curtailed support for victims of violation among dominant castes. In contrast, cases involving Dalit families had the support of Dalit activists and organizations, which emerged in the decade since the Mirchpur atrocity. These Dalit and human rights organizations, as well as women's groups in Haryana and Delhi, were involved with these cases and helped the families navigate the court system. Since victims had met with and spoken to multiple organizations, and in some cases, media outlets about their stories, some of them were open to my request to speak with them as well.

These circumstances meant that I could only follow subordinate-caste cases in my research, and this reality led some activists to question my politics as a dominant-caste woman writing about the rape of Dalit women. While I tried to meet with rape victims from different caste backgrounds, my lack of access to dominant-caste victims and the fact that only select Dalit and OBC families felt comfortable speaking with me led me to eight cases, all of which involved exclusively Dalit or OBC families. Caste politics and power dynamics were deeply apparent in this dilemma, because it was Dalit families and victims whose narratives were "open" or "available," while people in dominant castes could inoculate themselves against such scrutiny. While limited by these complex power dynamics, the cases that I examine offer a lens through which to understand the larger phenomenon of rape and the way that rural crisis, caste conflict, and poverty all intersect with sexual violation.

I followed the selected eight cases closely over the past three years, speaking with the young women who were assaulted and their kin. These interviews were conducted over several days, sometimes with activists present and at other times on my own. The conversations began not with the assault, but more broadly, allowing a tentative relationship to be forged. While the rape victims I interviewed were all either Dalit or OBC, I also interviewed dominant-caste members of the villages, including younger and older men and women. My attempts to understand how rape is navigated in the bureaucracy and by the police entailed conversations and interviews with police officers, attorneys, and bureaucrats, many of whom also belonged to dominant castes. Collectively, these interviews and observations illuminated dominant-caste biases, distress over farming and diminishing authority, and concerns about Dalits asserting more power. The worlds that emerged through these interviews revealed the labyrinth of bias and discrimination that makes justice for women who are raped so challenging.

All conversations and interviews were conducted in Hindi, in which I am fluent, and lasted between one and two hours. At times, if the conversations were in Haryanvi (which while proximate to Hindi uses particular phrases and terms that I was unfamiliar with), I would ask one of the activists or lawyers to translate for me. The most intense period of research began in the spring of 2016, lasting from March until August. Subsequent visits were shorter and continued intermittently through January 2020. Throughout this period, I would visit the families and victims each of the six times I came back to India. Through my work with the victims and their families, I also deepened my relationships with the activist groups and lawyers who dealt with some of their cases. Over the years, I have become imbricated in a network of interactions between victims, lawyers, and activist groups. I remain in touch with them even when I am not in India, and I continue to be a part of their ongoing conversations. Where possible, I have drawn on the research for this book to help provide analysis and support for the activists I collaborated with in Haryana. Yet I am aware that leaving Haryana and Delhi comes with profound privileges and disadvantages.

As I research and write about rape in rural Haryana, several concerns shadow my work. First, I aim to write about gender-based violence in a way that expresses the voices and complex subjectivities of the women on the receiving end of violence, but that is careful to not appropriate their voices. I aim to develop an analysis that does not overshadow the complexity and contradictions of my empirical work rooted in the complex lives of the women I'm concerned with. Second, narrating such stories while located within the academic circuits of the Global North presents an ethical and epistemological dilemma about what to say and how to say it. Despite my efforts to be as attentive as possible to these issues as I produced this work, I am aware that the contradictory implications of this narrative may prove my efforts insufficient. I remain concerned about reproducing grave differences in power and the risk of adding to the authority that dominant castes have historically yielded, particularly over whose stories to tell and how to tell them. It is therefore with some trepidation that I recount empirical work from Haryana, at the risk of again reproducing serious power imbalances. And finally, I recognize the risk of writing about brutal violations against women in the Global South. Narrating such stories comes with the peril of reinforcing congealed constructions of brutality and excess that fuse people with place.

CONCLUSION

In January 2018, Haryana witnessed ten rapes in ten days, eliciting outrage (*Hindustan Times* 2018c). One of these cases involved two teenagers who went missing after their tuition classes. I was doing research nearby when news about this case broke, and along with activists and lawyers, I scrambled to go to the village and meet with the families of the missing teenagers. The young girl and boy belonged to different Dalit subcastes from the village. When we got there, the body of the girl had just been recovered from a water canal in another district. The postmortem report revealed that she had nineteen injuries on her body, and the medical examiner suggested that she had been gang-raped (*Scroll.in* 2018). Four days later, the body of the boy was found. The brutality of the rape and murders generated tremendous publicity, drawing local and state political figures to the village to console the family and offer support. A few weeks later, once publicity had waned, speculation about the teenagers began, suggesting they were in a relationship, had gone away together, and were kidnapped and killed by unknown persons. By this time, I had become familiar with the pattern of how this tragic story would unfold: the rumors, the police obstruction, the making and breaking of promises by the state, and over all of it, the immense grief of two families that had lost their children.

While this book recounts these stories based on empirical research in rural Haryana, the analysis that stems from it is not confined to Haryana but resonates in other parts of the country. The narrative of "false cases," the impunity of police officers, the atrocities against Dalits, and the efforts to suppress women's complaints are depressingly commonplace across India. The extensive scholarship by feminists in academic writing as well as in reports and fact-finding documents provides a dense and rich archive of this material.

My choice to look at sexual violation in rural Haryana, however, was deliberate. I wanted to understand what rape does to the complex web of thick relationships in village life. How does it animate structural relationships between castes? What does the claim of *marzi* in false cases do? And why does life after rape bother domestic sexuality? The pace of change in rural Haryana was, and continues to be, dramatic and tragic. In every interview, the changes in Haryana were expressed through helplessness, anger, depression, and frustration. Familiar ways of life were giving way to the strange; old structures were being dislodged but were not necessarily being replaced by more open or equitable ones. The unrelenting struggle to make a living under conditions of neoliberal devastation saturated all the stories.

The following chapters on consent, compromise, land, and death all craft a landscape where the fallout from rape weaves together a wide range of issues. Land is evoked in stories of violation as the reason behind the violence. Land also allows those who have it to threaten and exert power over those who do not. Compromise for money, as one attorney said to me, has become a *dhandha* (business transaction), and one that the poor are often forced to engage in. *Marzi* (consent) anchors the false rape story, based on the narrative that women consented to the relationship. The specter of women's sexual subjectivity generates a broader narrative about women's immorality and functions to discredit them. Meanwhile, death gives credibility to the rape charge, while women who survive a rape are expected to live a social death.

Violence in this study was everywhere, not only in terms of the devastation experienced by the women who were raped, but also in the harm suffered by their families. Violence was not just evident in the spectacular, such as in the deaths that followed certain rapes, but also pervaded the mundane. Violence was evident in the brutal immiseration of the rural caused by the withdrawal of the state, and in struggles for caste power, featuring Jats seeking the restoration of their dominance by making violent demands to get reservation in the category of OBC. Violence was generated by attorneys and judges, by police officers and constables, and by families and communities who all suspected young women of uncontained, unruly sexuality. These women entered young adulthood shrouded with guilt and shame, bearing the charge that any unsanctioned feelings of attraction or love that they might have constituted proof of their immorality and corruption.[18] Violence was what Sanjay experienced when his mother and brother told him that he had ruined their family and devastated his mother's hope in him.

On the day we first met, Sanjay sat with his head bowed while his mother and brother talked about the case and the threats their family suffered.[19] They recalled how Sanjay's father and brother were taken to the police station and detained while efforts to find and capture the couple were underway. Police commonly detain family members as a tactic to pressure runaway couples into returning. Our conversation was interspersed with their accusations about Sanjay's irresponsibility, and stressed how his love affair had jeopardized their family. After a while, Sanjay and I were left alone to talk, which was when I asked about his tattoo. While initially shy and reticent, after a while he talked about the case and his relationship with Kavita. He said they met while at school and would meet in secret when she went for her tuition classes. One day he brought Kavita flowers while they sat at the bus stop. His grief at what had transpired was etched on his face as he struggled with the loss of his relationship and the anger of his family. Toward the end of our conversation, I ask if the jail allowed tattoos. He looked up at me and said that it was not a tattoo. He said he had etched the letter *K* into his skin, using a splinter from a broom.

The last time I visited Sanjay and his family, his brother had called to ask if I could help him find a job. The family had spent a lot of money on the trial and Sanjay's father was no longer able to work. Sanjay's niece was almost a year old and needed clothes and medicines. It was late in the afternoon in winter and the sun was going down. Sanjay offered to walk me to my car. I asked what he planned to do and if he was looking for a job. He had remained quiet through my visit, barely speaking. I asked if he had heard from Kavita or her friend, and he said that he knew that she was now married.

We stopped on the side of the road, just before we reached my car. I asked if he were to see Kavita again, what would he say? In a quiet voice, he said he would ask, "mera saat kyu chorda?" This phrase literally translates to "why did you leave my side?" but means to convey betrayal. In her initial testimony, Kavita had said that she had gone willingly with Sanjay. She subsequently changed her statement twice, and in later testimonies claimed that she had been drugged and taken from place to place by Sanjay and his friend, and that they had both taken turns raping her. Sanjay had heard these horrific accusations in court; his plaintive question was directed at them.

As we reached my car, I felt like I should try to reassure him, and said, "App abhi javaan ho, mohabbat phir se ho gayegi" (You are young, and you'll fall in love again). He turned to me, and with quiet resolve, said, "Nahi hogi" (it will not happen).

1. Consent

On a late winter afternoon in 2017 I go to see Pooja Devi, the station house officer of the *mahila thanna* (women's police station) in Rajgarh, Haryana.[1] I am directed to wait in a room where she is adjudicating a marital dispute between a middle-aged couple. She is forceful yet compassionate, determined and patient, and tries hard to arbitrate a complicated situation. Throughout the hour-and-a-half wait, the men and women gathered occasionally appeal to me, trying to enlist my assistance on their behalf. When Pooja Devi finally turns to me, apologizing for the delay, I briefly explain that I am researching rape in Haryana. She sighs and says, "Nabbe pratishat toh farzi hai" (Ninety percent of rape cases are false).[2] I am not particularly surprised to hear this stark claim. After all, the dominant narrative about rape cases is that they are false, meaning that they are typically filed by women in consensual relationships that have either soured or been made public, as retaliation, as a way to mitigate reputational harm, or as a way to extort money from the defendant or his family.

These claims concerning the frequency of false cases are one of the reasons for the overwhelming hostility women face from the police when attempting to file a rape charge (Bhalla and Vishnu 2012). In recognition of the systematic obstruction that many women face when trying to lodge a police complaint, Human Rights Watch generated a report documenting startling breaches in police conduct and in the rule of law (Human Rights Watch 2017). Despite amendments to the 2013 Code of Criminal Procedure, which holds the police accountable for failing to file a First Information Report (FIR), Human Rights Watch found that the police resist filing cases, especially if the accused is from a dominant caste or community.

Filing an FIR is an intimidating process that requires a woman to recount her rape in front of the police and other strangers in the room. *Mahila thannas*, which opened in 2015, were meant to create less intimidating environments and to facilitate more women coming forward to report crimes. In Haryana, these women's police stations are located in urban centers serving the surrounding rural areas. Haryana is 60 percent rural, and according to one of the police officers I interviewed, there were more complaints from villages than urban areas because village people were more aware of their rights. Women seeking to lodge a complaint first come to these *mahila thannas* accompanied by members of their families. At the *mahila thanna*, they meet with uniformed and plain-clothed police officers in small stark rooms that are sparsely furnished with a desk and a couple of chairs. Filing a complaint is a process that takes several hours, and that requires the victim to repeatedly retell the story of her rape. It is in these thick, daunting encounters that police reports of sexual violations are either crafted or negated.

The considerable challenges a woman faces in filing a rape report compound exponentially if the target of her accusation is someone from a powerful community or caste. Dominant castes and classes have long enjoyed a level of impunity for perpetrating both routine and spectacular violence against those in positions of diminished power (Geetha 2016). Multiple feminists have pointed to the numerous forms of oppression that Dalit women face and the ways in which they are imperceptible to the dominant-caste structures of the police and state (Manorama 2008; Paik 2018; Still 2017; Tamalapakula n.d.; Yengde 2013). If a woman from such a community should even attempt to file a complaint, she is likely to face outrage and even violence by members of the police, the majority of whom are from dominant communities with vested interests in maintaining the social hierarchy. An attempt to file a rape charge, especially against someone from a more dominant caste or class, is understood as a challenge to the existing hierarchy and is strongly resisted.

And yet despite the tremendous adversity women face while lodging complaints, statistics suggests that a growing number of women are filing cases nationwide (Mallapur 2017). So what does Pooja Devi's claim that "90 percent of rape cases are false" mean in the context of a dramatic increase in reported crimes against women? While Devi is specifically referring to rape cases in Haryana, the false case narrative is not uncommon beyond Haryana, where it is also deployed to dismiss the growing number of reported cases as based on false allegations.[3]

In this chapter, I engage with the sexual subjectivity of raped women in rural Haryana by looking at how the claim that these women had consented to these relationships affects rape cases. I propose that this claim about consent has two primary functions. First, it forms the basis of a script about false cases that police officers and other authorities aggressively advance as a hostile response to the growing credibility that women's claims of violation are beginning to receive. While women's claims are being taken more seriously in ways that remain limited and contingent, the fact remains that women have gained ground, both in the discursive realm of public opinion and in the structural realm of the law, and that their gains have triggered a reaction that seeks to undermine them.

Since the late 1970s, the credibility of women's rape claims has been debated and argued in Indian jurisprudence, centering around the question of whether the woman consented. Marks on her body, evidence of verbal or other forms of protest, her manner of dress, and her presence after dark are, according to the law, no longer relevant to the rape charge (for a detailed examination of this history, see Baxi 2014). Since the rape and murder of the young physiotherapy student in Delhi in 2012 and the countrywide protests that followed, women's claims of violation have found further purchase. In 2013, a series of amendments instituted structural changes to criminal law by expanding the definition of rape and by defining consent, while also holding public servants such as the police responsible if they were to "knowingly disobey any direction of the law" (Criminal Law [Amendment] Act 2013). If, both discursively in the public and structurally in the law, a woman's accusations of rape are seen to be at least somewhat credible, then her charge that she was violated has to be taken seriously. Indeed, as a consequence of three decades of judicial and feminist activism, women's testimonies in rape trials are now considered paramount, and women are coming forward in larger numbers to report rape.

However, while an increasing number of women are reporting crimes committed against them, not all categories of women are accorded credibility. The law does not recognize marital rape, and both sex workers and women who have had prior sexual relationships are considered unreliable.

Dalits, sexual and religious minorities, and the poor have an astronomically difficult time having their claims accepted and heard. Miranda Fricker (2008) has called this "testimonial injustice," describing it as "a prejudicially deflated degree of credibility from a hearer . . . it wrongs the subject in his capacity as a giver of knowledge" (69). And yet since 2012 there has been a 35 percent increase in the reporting of crime (Priya 2015). In a context in which women are discouraged from filing a case, their very attempt to lodge a complaint is itself an act of defiance. And it is in response to this defiance that the false rape charge makes an appearance, claiming that a rape never occurred because the woman consented.

My second claim hinges on the question of consent. I heard over and over again that rape charges are false because "woh apni Marzi/sahamati se gayi thi" (she went of her own will). Consent is key to the structure of rape because the charge of violation rests on its absence. However, consent in this context is not about the recognition of an autonomous subject giving permission. Rather, I argue, consent here plays the role of discrediting women as corrupt. A woman who consents to a sexual relationship is stigmatized as unvirtuous and unreliable, rather than respected as a sovereign person exercising her right to choose how she expresses her sexuality. Consent is thus perverted, effecting two simultaneous maneuvers: it discredits legitimate rape charges while also constructing women's autonomy as immoral. It functions as a disciplining device that seeks to bring the straying woman back into the libidinal boundaries of the patriarchal home and state.

While this story of consent is drawn from empirical specificities of rural Haryana, through this case I make three broader claims. First, while consent is key to the architecture of a rape charge, it is also more broadly about sexual subjectivity and agency. Feminists have long advocated for women's sexual autonomy as part of subjectivity. Linda Alcoff (2018) writes that sexual violations have a profound impact on sexual subjectivities in that they alter our capacities and relationship with our selves (110). Second, by drawing on consensual relationships, I aim to dislodge narratives that consider women in rural areas and those in the Global South to be "trapped" by their culture and unable to exercise agency and autonomy. Finally, as this case illustrates, consent can be manipulated to function as a disciplining maneuver.

In this chapter I closely follow the case of Vineeta, who was in a consensual relationship and was made to file a rape case against her lover, Pradeep. This case ended in an out-of-court settlement or compromise, despite the fact that compromise is technically unlawful, if common, in criminal proceedings. In the chapter that follows I lay out the implications of compromise in some detail. By deliberately choosing a case that seemingly aligns with police claims about women in consensual relationships filing false rape allegations, I aim to excavate what the claim of a false case helps animate. How did consent play out in this case, and what are the implications of such constructions of consent for women's sexual subjectivity? I draw on the richness of Saidiya V. Hartman's (1997) *Scenes of Subjection* to offer a theoretical scaffolding to unpack how we might think through subject formation under conditions of coercion. I begin by situating my arguments within feminist theorizing on consent.

THEORIZING CONSENT

Drawing from the historical precursors of the story of consent, I argue that while rape is a profoundly intimate violation, it has both structural and political antecedents and consequences that go beyond the victim and the perpetrator. Two historical events were particularly central to formulating conceptions of consent and the raped woman that would have significant consequences. The first concerns the British formation of colonial laws about the age of consent in the late nineteenth century. The second concerns the brutal violence—including sexual violence, mass abductions, and tens of thousands of rapes—that followed independence and partition in 1947. The newly independent Indian government passed laws about abducted women that would have a lasting impact on how rape and consent are understood and treated. The tentacles of these historical moments continue to have significance as we think about rape and consent to this day.

Let me begin with the colonial-era laws and the story of consent that emerges in the context of British officials' adjudication of rape. During the nineteenth century, the sexual violation of native versus English women registered very differently and served to mobilize different concerns of imperial rule. Jenny Sharp (1991) looks at the specter of the rape of English women in the context of the 1857 Indian mutiny against British rule as "a crisis of colonial authority" (29). During this period English women were transformed into an "institution" that "selectively drew on the Victorian ideal of womanhood." It was this transformation, Sharp argues, that "permits a slippage between the violation of English women as the object of rape and the violation of colonialism as the object of rebellion" (34). While they took the rape of English women by Indian men seriously, colonial authorities viewed the rape of native women with suspicion. Their racist attitudes toward native women and men alike translated into doubting their claims and left their credibility perpetually in doubt.

Colonial society's deep suspicion of the colonized shaped juridical formations, which had a lasting impact in postcolonial India. The infamous "Hale warning," for instance, based on the treatise of the seventeenth-century jurist Sir Matthew Hale, was a caution employed by judges during rape trials, even until the 1980s, which claimed that rape was an accusation easily made but difficult to prove. It served to cast doubt on any woman making a rape claim, requiring her to provide elaborate proof for her complaint to be considered credible. In her detailed examination of rape trials in colonial India, Elizabeth Kolsky (2010, 111) shows that the Hale warning "effectively established a judicial condition in which there were two defendants on trial: one charged with rape and the other charged with the presumption of consent." While Indian laws were based on English law and its patriarchal presumptions about women making false rape claims, native women faced the additional challenge of colonial-era racist attitudes that considered natives to be particularly unreliable witnesses.

Consequently, a series of "scientific" methods were employed to gain knowledge about native character, since the assumption was that the subcontinent was "teeming with perjurers, forgers, professional witnesses and a general population that did not value truth" (Kolsky 2010, 112). Concern with the unreliability of natives was further informed by colonial-era attitudes that considered all Indian women potential prostitutes (Mitra 2020, 62). Such attitudes about Indian women's sexuality were, as described by Mitra, key to governing social life and law.

These concerns with Indian women's sexuality led to the watershed set of criminal laws in 1860 covering rape (in sections 375 and 376) and other crimes under the newly established Indian Penal Code. And it was in the context of these laws that the issue of consent makes an appearance at the end of the nineteenth century and began generating tremendous ferment. The debate on consent pivoted on the issue of personhood, since consent assumed that the person granting it inhabited the locus of autonomy. It emerged in the context of the story of Rukhmabai, a very young bride who on attaining puberty refused to cohabit with her husband (Geetha 2016, 42). When her husband sued in the Bombay province for restitution of conjugal rights, Rukhmabai refused and claimed that the marriage was not of her choice, and eventually went to jail for her stance. The case drew sharp divisions between the reformist elites, who were on Rukhmabai's side, and the nationalists who claimed that the colonial government should not interfere in "native" custom. This debate intensified in the wake of the death of eleven-year-old Phulmonee after she suffered marital rape by her husband in 1890. Phulmonee died, while Rukhmanai did not. V. Geetha notes this acute difference, and how "it is the dead wife who became the measure of justice deliverable by law, and it is the dead wife who drew public attention to the harm caused by a husband exercising his 'natural' right over his wife" (51). The deliberations that ensued from both cases led the colonial government to propose a bill that would raise the age of consent from ten to twelve. But in so doing it differentiated between the age of marriage (in which the colonial government felt it could not interfere) and age of consent. Changing the age of consent led to amending section 375 of the Indian Penal Code that dealt with rape. Despite constructing a difference between marriage and consent, the bill generated vicious debate steeped in the caste politics of Hindu marriage. The concern over the bill was ultimately about women's autonomy outside of community and kin.

The "real issue," Tanika Sarkar (2000) says, "was whether the woman . . . was, in fact, legally and politically a person at all whose claim to life would be self-authenticating because of her personhood" (605). In nineteenth-century colonial Bengal, Sarkar explains, Indian women were not considered autonomous subjects separable from kin and family relations. "A woman was not seen, as yet to be in possession of an individuated identity" (601). It was not until the end of the nineteenth century that women's autonomy came to be fiercely debated in public, specifically a women's right to life. "This was an important and contentious beginning," Sarkar writes, "and the long nineteenth century was in a way a long debate over the claims of a women's community/family/caste to the right to inflict death on her" (602). The tragedy of course is that it took the death of young Phulmonee for the injustice to be recognized. In chapter 4, I consider why death after rape allows for recognition that is otherwise withheld.

While the Age of Consent Bill was ultimately passed in 1891, because it conferred on young women the ability to consent, it was forcefully opposed by various social forces invested in safeguarding the status quo. Prem Chowdhry (2007) writes that the Bill was condemned since it was thought to encourage "love marriages" by recognizing the subject getting married and the requirement of her consent, rather than the consent of her male guardian.

The contention among men who strongly objected to the bill was that consent in marriages always belonged to the male guardian of a potential bride, and not to the bride herself (40). Feminists have long understood that patriarchal control over marriage alliances is at least in part about controlling a series of lucrative arrangements, including the charging of a bride price. As Chowdhry explains, the colonial government's legal recognition of a male guardian's right to consent "made the right to arrange a girl's marriage into a much-coveted one" (41). Chowdhry goes on to elaborate that the colonial government's legal recognition of selling land in order to procure a bride "was enforceable in court," and "reinforced this 'consent' in many cases as lucrative" (41). The relationship between men, land, kin, and consent was reinforced by British colonial law, which in effect reinforced the notion of men as guardians over woman. This notion of male guardianship would reemerge during the Central Recovery Operation of the government of India between 1949 and 1956, and would this time focus on abducted women.

During partition, thousands of women were abducted across the divide between a newly independent India and Pakistan, and a dominant public question after partition in 1947 became how to recover these women. On either side of the divide, the governments of India and Pakistan set up several committees for the recovery and rehabilitation of these women. In 1949, the Indian government enacted the Abducted Persons (Recovery and Restoration) Act, which defined the responsibility of the state toward abducted women, their rights, and the rights of their children born from illegitimate sexual unions, including rapes. Government and public concern with abducted women became inextricably intertwined with ideas about national honor. Veena Das, in *Critical Events* (1995) and *Life and Words* (2007), investigates the question of violence through the story of abducted women after partition. In *Life and Words* she explains how "the figure of the abducted woman allowed the state to construct 'order' as essentially an attribute of the masculine nation," affirming a "sexual contract in which women as sexual and reproductive beings are placed within the domestic, under the control of the 'right' kinds of men" (19). As with the case of Phulmonee and the Age of Consent Bill passed by the British under colonial rule, the issue of abducted women after independence was not confined to concern over family and kin, but animated debates about the very meaning of the nation. In *Critical Events,* Das writes that "the woman's body . . . became a sign through which men communicated with each other" (56). In both the case of Phulmonee and the cases of the thousands of women abducted during partition, the state and other authorities sought to establish "order" by determining the place of women in the home and in the nation. In a different and oft-cited essay, Das (1996) theorizes how the grammar of law understands the violation of women at the "intersection of the discourse of sexuality and the discourse of alliance" (2422). She argues that the law serves to uphold the alliance between men to classify women as marriageable and nonmarriageable.

Independent India inherited these colonial and postcolonial legacies that indelibly mark contemporary laws. It is not possible to fully grasp the contemporary debate on consent without situating it in its history of colonial and postcolonial era concerns. While there certainly are differences between Indian jurists' attitudes toward rape victims and that of their British colonial predecessors, there are also many continuities (Kolsky 2010, 116). One particular continuity is that a victim alleging rape is assumed to have in fact consented to sex unless all the available evidence can substantiate her claim. In her examination of the three-hundred-year-old history of legal reform in India, Rukmini Sen (2010, 82) notes that between 1956 and 2009, postindependence law commissions were tasked with investigating and highlighting areas of the law that merited concern and needed reform. These law commissions produced 234 reports, only eight of which related to violence against women. Only four law commissions in this 1956–2009 period discussed rape, and only in their forty-second report, which came out in 1971, did they directly address consent (Sen 2010, 83). This 1971 report acknowledged that there was a gap between how consent was understood under section 375 and the way it was defined under section 90 of the Indian Penal Code.[4] This discrepancy remained unchanged from the time it was reported in 1971, until it was again reviewed by a legal commission nine years later, which made "recommendations on the definition [of rape and allied offences], issue of consent, burden of proof, arrest procedures and questions during trial" (Sen 2010, 83).

By directly addressing the issue of consent, the eighty-fourth law commission report in 1980 claimed that consent was the antithesis of rape, and acknowledged that consent had to be given freely, without pressure or duress, to qualify as real consent (Sen 2010, 83). This change in the legal definition of consent emerged in the context of growing political opposition to the status quo, including a public outcry and national campaign against rape following a 1979 notorious Supreme Court judgment that acquitted two police officers for the rape of an adivasi girl named Mathura (Baxi 2014).[5] An open letter written by four well-known law professors slamming this Supreme Court judgment also helped push forward reforms to laws governing rape.

In the four decades since the Mathura case, feminist and judicial activism has sought multiple changes to rape law. Its most recent and extensive alterations occurred after the infamous December 2012 Delhi gang rape discussed in the introduction, and the subsequent amendment to the Criminal Law Act in 2013. In the wake of these changes, the question of consent has remained central to the adjudication of rape. Moreover, marital rape and efforts to make the police and the Indian armed forces more accountable have continued to be areas of feminist and judicial struggle.

A paradoxical arena has formed around rape cases filed in retaliation for failed relationships. Police point to these cases, known as "breach of promise to marry" lawsuits, to fortify their claim that most rapes are based on false allegations, involving consensual relationships that have soured. The other arena where the issue of consent has emerged is in elopement cases involving a couple or a young woman under the age of eighteen.[6] In a recent work on the production of "court marriages" that deals with eloping couples, Rama Srinivasan (2020) looks at how the "drama of consent" was "played out through the protection petition story" in the Punjab and Haryana High Court (137). Srinivasan described cases in which young eloping couples seek the protection of the courts to validate their marriage.

I draw on this rich legacy of scholarship and make two distinct arguments. First, I consider the manner in which the concept of consent is manipulated in rape cases and rendered perverse. The consent decree is perverted because the narrative that "90 percent of cases are false" seeks to invalidate rape cases. Rather than accord sexual subjectivity to the women, consent in these cases is warped into evidence of their immorality. I argue that consent is framed primarily as a juridical condition through which the structure of rape is legible, rather than as permission or as an act of agency. Since consent/nonconsent makes visible the architecture of violation in law, efforts to secure access to women's bodies without their consent make women's consent perverse and their claims of violation invalid.

Second, I shift focus from consent to consider questions of sexual subjectivity. In her recent work, Linda Martín Alcoff (2018) argues for a concept of sexual subjectivity that offers "an alternative to the singular focus on the violations of consent" (111). Consent, Alcoff explains, emerged in response to a liberal feminist push to recognize sexual autonomy as differentiated from seduction laws of the late nineteenth and early twentieth centuries in the United States (126). Seduction laws were put in place to help women with financial challenges after they were abandoned by men who left them pregnant. Sexual subjectivity offers a broader conceptual frame than liberal notions of sexual autonomy allow and is about a person's capacity to create their own meaning and to contribute to their own subject formation (124). Other scholars have more recently added to our understanding of sexual subjectivity. Kristen Campbell (2002) sees evidence of this shift toward sexual subjectivity in a 1995 decision by the International Criminal Tribunal for the former Yugoslavia. She writes about how a local commander of the Croatian armed forces was charged with "serious violations of international humanitarian law" (149) and elaborates that this case was significant because it provided "the first definition of the elements of the crime of rape in international humanitarian law" (150). The acceptance of rape as a war crime signaled the international tribunal's acknowledgment of a change in "international norms," which now recognized harm done to women's sexual lives (153).

Deborah Bergoffen (2003) similarly discusses a landmark judgment by the United Nations Hague war crimes tribunal against three Bosnian Serb soldiers for crimes against humanity for their offense of rape. She argues that the significance of Judge Florence Mumba's indictment was that women's human rights were linked to sexual self-determination (Bergoffen 2003, 117). Bergoffen demonstrates how the court's radical departure is that its ruling did not claim "rapes were a crime against the sexed rights of women." Instead, the court "identified rape as a crime against humanity," and in so doing, "exposed the fallacy of treating the masculine body as the universal/neutral body" (120). The crime against humanity was read as "destroying the conditions under which a woman may exercise her right to assert her sexual integrity" (122). For Lorraine Code (2009, 329), Bergoffen's understanding of the indictment signals a new epistemology of rape in which "the damage to female sexual integrity and consent displaces violence as rape's defining features." All of these sophisticated interventions point to an expansion of the terms by which women's sexual subjectivity is comprehended, allowing women who allege rape to be understood as something other than either victims or promiscuous agents.

This conceptual shift seeks to redraft the rape script so that women are no longer mute victims but agents with rights to sexual self-determination (Marcus 1992). Rajeswari Sunder Rajan (1993), in her reading of Marcus's rape script, in relation to colonial texts, says that "for women to 'speak' rape is itself a measure of liberation, a shift from serving as the object of voyeuristic discourse to the occupation of a subject position as 'master' of narrative" (78). In recrafting rape narratives, these authors seek to challenge the idea that sexual violations only produce one-dimensional, degraded, and powerless victims. This is particularly evident among contemporary Dalit women writers who, as Laura Brueck (2012) writes, "are working to rescue Dalit women's bodies from passive manipulation in perpetuating the casteist rape script in which they serve as transactional objects in a power struggle between men" (234).

In some of the most dramatic and paradoxical articulations of women's sexual agency, Nivedita Menon (2004) and Srimati Basu (2015) draw on cases where women file rape cases against their lovers for breach of promise. Rape in these cases is understood as consent garnered under false pretexts and therefore false. The court, however, sees this as an act of promiscuity (Agnes 1992, WS21). What forms of subjectivities are being crafted by women who file rape cases against their lovers for breaching the promises they made? These sorts of rape cases are not about a violation of consent but about forcing a lover's compliance with earlier promises. Similarly, Basu (2015) shows how section 489A in the Indian Penal Code, the legal provision under which physical and mental domestic violence is prosecuted, was often applied to "obtain civil remedies, rather than to end or reduce violence" (177). Women who file 498A or rape cases and enlist other legal strategies are constructed as vengeful. What is of interest to me is that such use of the law by women casts them as corrupt and unreliable. The argument is that if women deploy mechanisms of the state for their benefit, their claim is somehow sullied. But it is precisely these acts that also force the courts and others to contend with women's sexual subjectivity by recognizing them and by demanding responsibility from them.

Here, I am interested in the forms of sexual subjectivity that are constituted in the wake of a rape charge. I suggest that sexual subjectivity, which emerges in the wake of hard-fought battles, produces deep anxiety for people and authorities invested in keeping or complying with the order of things. Consequently, the perversion of consent in these rape scripts that characterize the consenting woman as unreliable or promiscuous and immoral is in an effort to wrest sexual subjectivity from women back to the home, court, and state. I argue that the perversion of consent occurs in response to an expansion of women's credibility. It is to briefly understand this broadening of credibility that I turn next.

CREDIBILITY IN WOMEN'S NARRATIVES

In early October of 2018, *Time Magazine* published an article reporting that India's #MeToo movement was gathering momentum (Ayyar 2018). Quoting journalist Sandhya Menon, who along with other women in the media had recently come forward to name persons who had sexually harassed them, the essay was titled "People Feel There's a Chance of Being Believed." This widespread belief in women's claims of assault and harassment is what has fueled the #MeToo movement, and as more women come forward, it has generated an expansion in the credibility that women are now being accorded. Alcoff (2009, 126) and others have called this expansion in the belief of women's claims "epistemic credibility," which points to a political and structural shift whereby women's claims of violation are taken—at least somewhat—seriously. Prior to this moment, women's claims of violation encountered what Miranda Fricker (2008) has called hermeneutical injustice, whereby their testimony was met with "the dysfunction of unduly deflated credibility" (69).

This simple act of belief signals a much deeper and more profound shift in according women what men (at least dominant-class and dominant-caste men) have for the most part taken for granted. Acknowledging women's credibility means calling for a shifting of the social landscape so that it is no longer possible to dismiss their word outright. Like any profound shift, this change is still nascent and being realized. It is also not unfolding without systematic and forceful opposition.

In the cases I followed, opposition to women's presumptive credibility in rape cases, both discursively and as sanctioned by the law, has manifested itself in the form of a crisis. With women's testimony now recognized as central to rape cases, there is a small yet significant shift that has made it more difficult for authorities to manipulate cases by bringing up a woman's reputation or her past sexual history to undermine her and to benefit the defendant. This shift emerged after the public outcry following the Mathura rape case I mentioned earlier, and the open letter written by legal scholars critical of the court's decision to acquit her perpetrators, which together led to changes in rape law, the Indian Penal Code, and the Evidence Act.

The Supreme Court's decision, in an effort to save face after its much-maligned judgment in Mathura, in the case of *Bharwada Bhoginbhai Hirjibhai v. State of Gujarat* would play a very important role in making women's testimony central to rape trials. Mrinal Satish (2017) writes that the decision of the Court in this case would become "the primary authority" in cases where courts had to decide "whether an accused can be convicted solely on the basis of the testimony of the prosecutrix" (40). Following this case, a woman's testimony became the primary component for building a rape case, and it was supported by secondary forensic and medical evidence. I am suggesting that the significance of women's testimony in rape trials in India demonstrates that women are now presumed credible, even if the credibility they are accorded is still contingent and limited.

Efforts to undermine the credibility women were being accorded took different forms and particularly perverted logics. It is in these perversions that consent, and the manner in which the police deploy it, makes an appearance. As women were accorded presumptive credibility by having their testimonies recognized under the law, reactionary efforts intensified to challenge these testimonies by undermining their credibility. Since the credibility of a woman's statement could no longer be challenged on the basis of her moral character, her case would need to be discredited. And it is in the very architecture of the rape narrative that women alleging rape are made incredible, or unreliable.

Since the structure of a rape charge rests on the question of whether the woman consented, any evidence that the woman consented to the relationship discredits her charge as false. Saying that the young girl went of her own *marzi* (will) makes her case suspect. If the police claim that she consented to the relationship and was filing a false case because of shame or because the relationship was not sanctioned, then her case is not valid. The false rape charge rests on arguing that no violation took place because the relationship was consensual. It is the linking of the women's consent to discredit her case that I consider perverse. It is perverse because women's consent is put forth not to accord agency and sexual subjectivity to women, but instead to render them unbelievable. Consent is used to undermine the credibility of the claim of violation. Let me elaborate on this through the story of Vineeta.

THE STORY OF VINEETA

I first met Vineeta on a late hot summer afternoon. My contact in her village was Deepak, a young Dalit political aspirant I was introduced to through a Dalit lawyer with whom I was collaborating for my research. When Deepak and I reached the village in the morning the sun was already blisteringly hot, and my first stop was to meet with Dalit village elders at Deepak's home. This was a large village with two panchayats (village councils), and the newly elected *sarpanch* (head of the village council) was a Dalit woman. A woman sarpanch is usually just a figurehead whose father-in-law or husband assumes the actual duties of governance in the village. Vineeta's house is in the Dalit *basti* (neighborhood) and close to a dirty, stagnant pond. We enter the house through a small door that leads into a dark room, slightly cool against the glaring sun. Vineeta's father lies on a *charpai* (woven bed) against a wall that has a rickety floor-to-ceiling shelf filled with boxes of *chappals* (slippers). We are invited to sit opposite him on the other *charpai*. He sits up, and we see that his legs are amputated below the knees. On the corner wall rests a set of prostheses for his legs. We talk for a while, and then we are asked to go inside to meet Vineeta and her mother.

Vineeta is a young woman with a lovely, engaging smile. As we ask her to tell us what happened, she sighs and says she is tired of recounting her story over and over again. According to her initial narrative, the incident happened earlier in 2016. While she was studying for her exams, two young boys knocked on the front door late at night. Thinking it was her uncle knocking, she opened the door. The two boys forced a cloth on her mouth that made her unconscious, and then they kidnapped her. After one of the boys assaulted her, she was dropped back near her house in the early hours of the morning, still not quite conscious, where her sister found her. Vineeta is Dalit, and the boys accused are both dominant-caste Jats from the same village. As she recounts the story with a rhythm that speaks of multiple rehearsals, she at one point stops, and says, sort of confessing, that she was in a five-year relationship with the boy who assaulted her. The other boy was his accomplice and had not, according to Vineeta, done anything. After Vineeta was found in the morning her family lodged the case, and the boys were immediately taken into judicial custody. Soon after the complaint was filed, the boys' families came to offer money in exchange for their freedom. In what was a fairly rapid succession of events, a compromise was reached at 6 lakhs (less than $10,000), brokered by members of the *panchayat,* who also held on to the funds until the boys were freed.

When I first went to Vineeta's house, Dalit village elders claimed that what had happened to Vineeta was wrong and that she was a young girl, saying, "Jis ke saat bahut bura hua" (A bad thing happened to her). Yet the narrative they recounted felt like a kind of performance, and their remorse seemed a bit rehearsed, as if they were performing a familiar script for the benefit of visitors from outside. A few months later, after the compromise was brokered, I met with the village elders again, and on the request of Vineeta and her mother, spoke with them about how Vineeta wished to go to college by using the funds from the compromise.

Initially, they agreed that Vineeta should get on with her life, and that going to college was good. But there was a note of hesitancy in their comments, and they appeared to be agreeing with my suggestion to be polite. Whenever I raised the issue of college, they said that Vineeta should get married. When I suggested that the costs for admission should come out of the funds her family received from the *shamjauta* (compromise), they responded more generally that getting an education is good. After a while, as the conversation persisted, they finally said, "En ka matter kuch alag tareeke ka hai" (Their issue was of a different sort). It was clear by this point that they wanted to say something else. They then said, "Tassali nahi hui us ki" (She is not satisfied). It was not clear what they were alluding to, but their hesitancy about Vineeta going to college was clear. When I asked directly if they thought she would go to college, they said, "Nahi padhe gi yea" (She will not study). "Pehli bhi yea hua tha" (This has happened before), they said, referring to the relationship Vineeta had with the young man. And finally, they exclaimed, "Galti toh eshi ki hai" (She is at fault here!). When I asked how it could have been her fault if she had been unconscious, they responded, "Nahi nahi aisa koi nahi, aisa toh bolna padta hai" (No, it was nothing like that, one has to say these things). They elaborated, "Yea sab toh banavti baate hai" (These things are made up for the case) because "samaaj aisa hai" (the society/village is like that). I understood them to be saying that the rape script had to be crafted in order to be recognizable in society and the courts. In contrast to the script that they had constructed and recited, they revealed that they believe "who khud apni marzi se gayi thi" (she went of her own will). "Azaad hona chahti hai" (She wishes to be independent), they claimed, along with "Galt us mei chal rahi hai uh ladki" (That girl is on the wrong path).

After meeting with the Dalit village elders, I went to meet Vineeta and her mother. Vineeta's mother had asked that I help convince her husband to let Vineeta go to college with the funds from the settlement. I had done some research about where she could go. As I reached the front room, where Vineeta's father was lying on the *charpai*, I began to speak with him about college options. Initially, he nodded, but he then said, dismissively, that Vineeta was not interested in college, echoing what I had already heard from the village elders. As I persisted and pleaded, he suddenly got very angry and exclaimed that Vineeta would not leave the house. During this exchange, Vineeta and her mother were standing behind the door, listening to our conversation. On hearing her husband's objections, Vineeta's mother stormed in and confronted him. He was by this point in a rage, and his anger was palpable. Through it, he blamed his daughter for bringing shame to the family and accused both his wife and his daughter of sexual impropriety. Their argument was loud and very animated, with Vineeta's grandparents also joining the fray as accusations were hurled thick and fast. The allegations were familiar and part of a larger discursive landscape in which inferences about Vineeta had solidified to confirm her as guilty. Both Vineeta's father and the village elders read her desire to go to college as a desire to leave home, not as an intention to pursue further studies. When I explained to Vineeta that she had the choice to go to a college near the village or one in another district, she said she preferred to go to the one further away so she would not have to face the taunts of the villagers.

I returned in the winter to find that Vineeta had not sought college admission and was taking computer classes in a nearby town. As we met one afternoon over tea and snacks, she began hesitantly to tell me what had happened the day before she was found unconscious in front of her home. Pradeep had called her and asked her to meet him at the village school. As in the past, after they had sex, Pradeep gave her some *goli* (medicine) to prevent pregnancy. After a while, she said to him, "Pate mei dard hai" (My stomach hurts). As they were walking toward her house, she noticed that the lights were on and inferred that her family was aware that she was not home. On seeing the lights in her house, Pradeep got scared and began to leave. She then called out to him and said, "Bas etne aukaat hai teri?" (which literally translates to "That's all the status you have?" but is meant as an admonishment). Hearing this, Pradeep turned around and returned to her, and they sat together for a while. Vineeta said she did not recall anything that happened after, and that she regained consciousness a day or two later.

When I asked her, "Jo hua tha aap ke beech mei, woh diwai lene se pehele hua tha ya baad mei?" (Did what happened between you occur before or after you had the medicine?) Vineeta replied that it happened before, referring to the sex they had before she took the medicine. I then asked directly, "Apni marzi se ho chuka tha?" (You were willing for it to happen?). She said yes. Referring to her breakup with Pradeep, which I had understood to have occurred a while before this incident, I asked her why she had agreed to go with him when he called. "Aap itini jaldi raazi kaise ho gaye us ke saat ki chalo es ne break-up bhi kar liya, phir achaanak se aa jaata hai, karta hai phone phir aap us ke saat . . ." (How did you agree so suddenly to go with him after the breakup, and he suddenly comes and calls and then you . . .). Vineeta interrupted me and said, forcefully, "Achaanak nahi! . . . paanch saal ho gaye ji . . . paanch saal hue hai! Insaan mei viswaas ho jata hai paach saal mei toh!" (Not suddenly! It'd been five years, five years! In five years, you have faith in a person!)

There are three aspects of Vineeta's sexual subjectivity worth highlighting here. First, she challenged Pradeep and his masculinity when he turned to leave after noticing the lights were on in her house. Her deployment of the word *aukaat* was particular, and in vernacular Hindi/Haryanvi signals a way to mock and call into question a person's character by questioning their worth. In this case, by calling on her lover to stand by her even when he was afraid, Vineeta disrupts a reading of her as primarily a victim. Second, Vineeta says that she was in a relationship with Pradeep and that their sexual relationship was with her *marzi* (consent). Despite being aware of the censure from her family and village, by continuing her affair, Vineeta demonstrated her autonomy and her subversive defiance of patriarchal control. It is precisely this defiance that her father and the village council sought to rein in. Finally, when I asked her why she had gone with him after they had broken up, she was forceful in her response, claiming that her decision was not *achaanak* (impulsive). She asserted that she had been with him for five years, and in that time, had *viswaas* (faith) in him. Vineeta's sexual subjectivity emerges in her deliberate and clearly articulated position about her choices, her assertion that her decisions had not been impulsive, and her faith in her lover.

But Vineeta's subjectivity was inaudible and the autonomy she demonstrated unacceptable in the village. In her incisive examination of subjection and consent in rape narratives in Bangladesh, Dina Siddiqi (2015) says there is implicit acceptance of sexual activity in the village "but no sanction for women to exhibit desire visibly" (520). So while Vineeta's affair was known and implicitly tolerated, it necessitated and resulted in a narrative of violation once it became public. Siddiqi goes on to say that "sex outside of marriage becomes culturally intelligible and defensible only when viewed through the grid of coercion and rape" (520). Because Vineeta's affair demonstrated her to have exercised choice, it signaled her autonomy from kin and was therefore seen as threatening and unintelligible. Writing about the "jurisdiction of heterosexual love," Pratiksha Baxi (2014) says that it is "made manifest in the domain of the law on rape" (234). As a consequence, she concludes that "the blurring of love and rape, or consent and lack of consent, has a specific manifestation when we look at the right of women to choose their partners" (235).

As I detail in the next chapter in my conversation with the village council members, their narrative about the *shamjauta* (compromise) was about preserving village and community honor. The main reason that the compromise works is that it stops the news about the unsanctioned affair from spreading, and it avoids the involvement of the courts, where others would hear about the shameful and unruly incident in their village. It is important that the matter be resolved within the village itself. The filing of a false case of rape, then, is about restoring family honor, and compromise is about preserving village reputation. The reason that Vineeta's case was filed is because her affair became public. In response, the village and members of her family participated in creating a false case to mitigate reputational harm and restore order. At first glance, Vineeta's story fits the false case narrative championed by police officers and other authorities and seems to reinforce the police's claim that women file rape cases when their affair becomes public or when it ends, and they seek to retaliate against their lovers. What this story about unreliable or vengeful women leaves out, however, is the patriarchal social order in which women cannot openly choose to have sexual relationships outside of sanctioned marriages without suffering grave consequences.

That false rape cases are filed is evident. What needs unpacking, however, is how these cases become proof that women's rape claims cannot be considered credible. The claim that 90 percent of rape charges filed by women are false seeks to discredit most cases of rape by suggesting that women cannot be believed. The police's argument undermines the rape charge by claiming that the sex was consensual, which solidifies the subjective construction of the woman as loose, morally suspect, and therefore someone whose word cannot be trusted as truth. The perversity of the "false case" narrative is that by accusing women of being engaged in consensual relationships, it conscripts the family and community into supporting this police narrative, as the Dalit village elders did in Vineeta's case, by suggesting that she does not wish to study and instead just wants her freedom. In this maneuver, Vineeta is not only discredited but also constituted as irresponsible and shamefully outside the libidinal confines of propriety. Consequently, it is not enough that she is no longer credible; she must simultaneously be redrafted into the familial fold. The restoration of family and community honor rests on the urgency with which she can be reconstituted into the circuits of patrilineal exchange as soon as possible (also see Basu 2015).

In an effort to restore her into the fold of the family and village, the council members were keen on getting her married as soon as possible. The money from the compromise was, as is often the case, specifically marked to help get the girl married. This money is understood as compensation to her family for the loss of her sullied value in the marriage exchange (Das 1996). Often rape cases result in "well-worn legal trajectories [that] turn to marriage as a compensatory solution" (Basu 2015, 165). Through her case and the compromise, Vineeta's sexual subjectivity has no legibility. Indeed, her defiant expression of sexual choice, whether wise or not, is considered intolerable by guardians of the patriarchal social order. They see it as evidence of disrespect and as a threat to their authority, for which she must be disciplined to preserve the village and community honor and order. This is why they act quickly to clip her agency to make sexual choices and decisions, and vest such power away from her and to the "rightful" place of her father.

SEXUAL SUBJECTIVITY, AUTONOMY, AND RAPE

If the commonplace understanding of the "will" implies the power to control and determine our actions and identifies the expressive capacity of the self-possessed and intending subject, certainly this is far afield of the condition or terms of action available to the enslaved. Yet the notion of the will connotes more than simply the capacity to act and to do; rather, it distinguishes the autonomous agent from the enslaved, the encumbered, and the constrained.

—SAIDIYA V. HARTMAN, *Scenes of Subjection* (1997)

Not all women who are raped are enslaved. While Dalits in Haryana and elsewhere in India are subject to indentured or other forms of coercive labor bondage, and while they are dehumanized by those in dominant castes, their conditions are very different from the property relations to which slaves in the United States were subject. I draw on Hartman's work on enslaved people in the United States not because I suggest a neat parallel between them and Dalits, but instead because Hartman offers a frame by which to consider the (im)possibility of autonomy and sexual subjectivity under conditions of coercion. In this section, I argue that the perversion of consent in the false rape narrative is about denying the very autonomy that consent implies.

The word "consent" has no direct translation to vernacular Hindi or Haryanvi. The words that most proximate consent are *marzi* and *sahamati*, which translate, respectively, to "will" and "agreement." In what I call consent in the vernacular, the exercise of *marzi* demonstrates more than the ability to do something. It is, as Hartman argues, an act that demonstrates autonomy. In exercising her *marzi*, Vineeta performs agentic autonomy. Patriarchal authorities consider this threatening and intolerable because it expresses her sovereignty—and the limits of their authority—without social sanction. Flavia Agnes explains, "It appears that choice, or desire, as expressed by a woman is somehow intrinsically illicit when it is against parental diktat and caste or community norms, and therefore needs to be contained and controlled" (2011, 11). Thus, in her exercise of *marzi,* Vineeta demonstrates defiance of subjection and claims sexual autonomy, wresting control from her father. Women's sexuality is not in their purview; it is vested in the home and is the domain of the patriarch, and as Das (1995) has argued, in the case of abducted women, with the nation. Vineeta's relationship with Pradeep upsets this bargain and diminishes her father's power. Restoration, therefore, comes at a price in the exchange of money. This structure of restoration emerges from the paternalistic notion that men are guardians of women, especially of unmarried women who are bargained over like commodities in the relationships between men.

Vineeta's father's rage, I suggest, needs to be understood in the thick context of what her *marzi* animates: Dalit vulnerability, loss of reputation in the village, and in particular, his loss of control over the domestic sexuality.

Consequently, his denying Vineeta permission to go to college was about reestablishing his control. However, by continuing her affair even after it was discovered a few years ago, and in wanting to go to college, Vineeta defies the control her father seeks. It is in this defiance that I identify Vineeta's sexual subjectivity. If raped women are supposed to be abject figures who are shunned, and if shame and stigma is supposed to silence and confine them, then by refusing to be sequestered by the humiliation that the rape case causes her family, Vineeta rejects the script of shame. Her effort to slip out of being quarantined as an abject figure instigates derision by the village elders and is the source of her father's anger. I read her quest to leave the village and go to college as a refusal to abide by the diktat of her father and village elders to acquiesce to domestic confinement. Women's sexual subjectivity and agency outside of marital procreative relationships are read as an indictment of male family members whose masculinity is compromised in the wake of their perceived lack of control over domestic sexuality. Vineeta's subjectivity, expressed through a consensual relationship, is therefore unacceptable and intolerable. The compromise brokered in her case was monetary compensation to her father for her transgression and loss of value. But the compromise fundamentally rested on the assumption that she was coerced, attenuating any consideration of her autonomy. In cases of consensual relationships, compromise is about disciplining the woman's body and erasing her consent to an unsanctioned relationship. Women's sexual subjectivity, then, is rendered illegible.

Regarding the rape of enslaved women, Hartman asks, "What does sexuality designate when rape is the normative mode of its deployment? What set of effects does it produce? How can rape be differentiated from sexuality when 'consent' is intelligible only as submission?" (1997, 85). Hartman is here talking about how the sexuality of enslaved women is rendered invisible because her experience of sex is primarily through rape. Yet Hartman's provocative questions show how sexual autonomy can be rendered invisible, even when consent is given, if it is not sanctioned and goes against the prevailing norms. Within the Indian context, Menon writes that "sexual acts not sanctioned by prevailing codes of conduct are illegitimate regardless of whether consent was given" (2004, 126). Vineeta's consent is illegible and read as rape because her relationship is not sanctioned.

But Vineeta's desire also upends a cultural script of Dalit women as victims. In asserting to us that she went with Pradeep willingly, Vineeta rejects the reading of her consent as submission. In *The Silken Swing* (Franco, Macwan, and Ramanathan 2000), the authors discuss how women of subordinate castes articulated both revulsion and desire for dominant-caste men. In demanding a different audible register to be cultivated, they say, "the emotional configurations of the dispossessed and controlled women suggest that there is another language, perhaps a lower voice, than the one we have understood and heard" (3). The significance of these narratives is that it dislodges the script by which Dalit women can only be seen as victims. Remarking on the paradox that emerges when middle-class Dalit women assert their sexuality, Sowjanya Tamalapakula (n.d.) says that they are rejected by mainstream feminists as well as by Dalit male groups. This is because Dalit women's sexual subjectivity is not easily accommodated outside victimhood. Shailaja Paik (2018) similarly implores rejecting a reading of Dalit women as either victims or heroines (3). What then is being asked for by Vineeta and Dalit feminist scholars is the unyoking of rape and sexuality to account for agency and personhood. But sexual agency outside of procreative marriage alliances is viewed with deep suspicion, and women who exercise it are stigmatized as immoral.

The social legitimacy of sexuality within marriage renders all other forms of sexual agency illegitimate and corrupt. When rape charges are filed in retaliation for a breach of a promise to marry, the case is made that a woman's consent was contingent on the man's promise to marry, a promise which served to legitimize the sexual relationship. The remarkable frequency with which these claims are made in court complicates the question of sexual autonomy and consent. As Basu writes, these cases "cause uneasiness in [their] erasure of female sexual agency and [their] evocation of social status conferred by marriage" (2015, 165). As Nivedita Menon reminds us, these cases should not be viewed as being about rape, because equating a man's breach of his promise to marry with rape only reinforces "a discourse that sets up sex as legitimate only within the framework of marriage" (2004, 124).

Sexual agency outside marriage, then, renders women sullied and unreliable. Thus, women who claim to have been raped are forced to demonstrate chastity and sexual monogamy to be considered credible. Ratna Kapur explains that women were regarded as legitimate subjects of injury, but only if they appeared "chaste, pure, monogamous, honourable, and confined to the private/domestic sphere" (2005, 34). Conversely, Mrinal Satish argues, "if the women's sexual behavior is inconsistent with dominant values and norms, her ability to use the law to protect the infringement of her sexual autonomy is weakened, if not completely lost" (2017, 43). If the credibility of a woman's violation is tied to the manner in which she appears, then her capacity to make autonomous choices is severely constrained and not in her control.

While choices are never free and always circumscribed, Vineeta's choice to leave home and go to college was read by her father and by village authorities as her desire to be free. Her *marzi* was read not only through her prior liaisons with Pradeep, but also in her aspirations to leave home and to pursue an education. These aspirations, which reflect her choices, demonstrate her sexual subjectivity. The village elders, for their part, understood her aspirations as derived from her sexual impropriety rather than her subjective autonomy. In their conception, her impropriety made her a sullied woman who did not deserve support from the patrilineal state. It follows that their efforts to restore her were about bringing her back into the patrilineal fold, and did not allow for the "freedom" that college might offer her. However, since Vineeta's value in the marriage market had diminished, her restoration came at a price. It is in these transactions of patriarchal restoration that compromise makes an appearance and is further claimed as evidence of a false rape case. In other words, a dominant narrative has come to suggest that out-of-court compromises are evidence of an untrustworthy woman's false allegations of rape.

Women have historically not been vested with their own sexual subjectivity. So according to dominant patriarchal narratives, when women exercise sexual choice, they can only be viewed as sullied. A woman's consent or violation does not find purchase within coercive systems of patrilineal dominance such as the law, family, community, and the state. She is for the most part considered unbelievable. As described by Prem Kumar Vijayan (2018, 127), the paucity of narratives by victims of rape has made rape both less visible in the public and subject to doubt. It has resulted in "the relentless refusal of patriarchal formations to recognize women as subjects with voices of their own, as agents in their own right" (126). The existence of unsanctioned, consensual relationships that become public, and the central place now finally accorded to women's words in rape cases, have unfortunately resulted in a backlash in which patriarchal forces attempt to restore the social order by discrediting women. They attempt to achieve this by nullifying legitimate rape charges and simultaneously rendering women's autonomy as corrupt.

DILEMMAS AND PREDICAMENTS

Vineeta's story is not unusual and generates a dilemma for Dalit activists and attorneys by veering away from the script of violation. While her affair was not without concerns or grave power imbalances that made her position precarious in the relationship, she remained steadfast in our conversations that she had participated out of choice. While she did not have a say in the compromise, she was glad that the case was settled without Pradeep spending more time in custody. Similar to the case of Bhagana, activists who supported Vineeta encouraged her to not compromise, thinking that Pradeep's family might have coerced her to settle the matter. But when she said that she was in a relationship and that she went of her own *marzi*, the argument that compromise was an outcome of coercion was not sustainable.

In their effort to have their cases succeed and generate the best outcome for their clients, Dalit lawyers and activists also constructed scripts. These scripts were narratives crafted from layer upon layer of stories, documents, anecdotes, and cases in which atrocities against Dalits are recounted in painful detail. Those narratives, congealed into scripts, craft a way to present cases in a manner that is audible to courts saturated with dominant-caste sensibilities. The strategy deployed in this context tries to make violence and atrocities against Dalits visible to dominant-caste law. This lack of capacity to comprehend or see or hear the injuries borne by Dalit victims is what Miranda Fricker (2008) understands as hermeneutical injustice. She refers to a situation in which a person trying to speak of an injustice they've endured enters into an arena with an already deflated sense of comprehensibility, and in which the listener can only partially apprehend what the speaker is trying to express. In such a scenario, there is a "hermeneutical lacuna to which the subject belongs. Such a lacuna renders the collective interpretive resources *structurally prejudiced*" (Fricker 2008, 69; emphasis in original). Dalit lawyers and activists are deeply aware of this lacuna, and therefore deploy their script as a way to make a victim's story audible.

The construction of rape scripts in Vineeta's case needs to be understood in this context. While the lawyers and activists may have some sense of the messy facts in their cases and a fuller picture of what actually happened, they drafted their scripts with a focus on making their cases comprehensible in court. For instance, as part of the narrative, they may claim that Vineeta was kidnapped in a car. The kidnapping scenario served to establish her vulnerability and that she was forced to go with Pradeep; it sought to lend credibility to her rape case. But as Vineeta recounts in the next chapter, had she been aware of how this narrative was crafted, she would have denied any such embellishment. The fact that the kidnapping did not occur needs to be understood not as a story of deception, but as a story that reveals the strategies that must be taken to advocate for rape victims simply because their stories would otherwise be inaudible. Vineeta's correction exposes the manner in which a script simply has to be crafted in order to do its job. Put differently,

Vineeta, like any woman of her position alleging rape, must appear as a victim, appropriately distressed and vulnerable, for her testimony of violation to receive a degree of credibility. Consequently, rape cases can only be discerned within familiar scripts, outside of which they are subject to suspicion and viewed as lacking credibility. The scripts that lawyers prepare are in response to courts that are hostile to claims of violation, and so must be crafted carefully to even be heard.

The need to establish coercion in rape cases, therefore, generates a set of predicaments around cases where there was consent. Since the prevailing narrative around rape cases from the police and courts is that the majority of the cases are about consent, the struggle of Dalit lawyers and activists against police malfeasance and lack of investigation in cases involving Dalit victims generates a predicament when they have to deal with a case like Vineeta's, which was, in fact, about consent—however suffocated by conditions that would not allow it to freely express itself and survive. In crafting an audible rape script, these lawyers and activists felt forced to subvert the very autonomy and sexual subjectivity that Vineeta was trying to establish. In proceeding with the case as a rape case, the lawyers get drafted into structures of patriarchy that seek to nullify attempts at autonomy and that compel Vineeta's enfolding into domestic sexuality. Women's autonomy is a source of concern and anxiety by guardians of the status quo, and rape cases often become the sites through which such autonomy is adjudicated. Women who become independent in other spheres also cause trepidation. As S. Anandhi and Karin Kapadia (2019) write, Dalit women's political activism and their subsequent independence is often considered intolerable among their kin. They explain that "for many Dalit women, their greatest problem is the resistance of their own husbands and male kin/community to their claims to some degree of autonomy" (20).

Dalit women's autonomy is problematic for a range of actors—from their advocates who seek to help them, to authorities who seek to dismiss and control them—because it runs counter to the dominant narrative that frames Dalit women as victims. Manuela Ciotti writes that "accounts of Dalit women which speak of them as all-round personae and as non-victims are very rare" (2019, 76). Drawing on this work, I suggest that framing Dalit women exclusively or primarily as victims is also a script. It is a script crafted as a consequence of "incontrovertible evidence on marginalization, exploitation, and powerlessness found among Dalit women in history and in the present" (Ciotti 2019, 76). But if this is the *only* acceptable script, then Vineeta's sexual subjectivity becomes unrecognizable. In these rape scripts,

Vineeta and other Dalit women can only be seen as victims, not as complex subjects who seek autonomy to determine their own lives. But because as victims their cases function to establish evidence of injustice against Dalits, when they refuse the role of victim or seek a different outcome, they can end up jeopardizing broader efforts to get justice for Dalit women. The dilemma, then, is how to allow space for Dalit women's autonomy outside an overdetermined framework of victimhood, while also struggling for justice for the community.

Dalit women's lives, as many scholars and activists have pointed out, need to be understood as complex and multidimensional (Paik 2018). Dominant-caste feminists and historians, Dalit scholars argue, have neglected to account for Dalit women's and men's agency and struggles as subjects (Anandhi and Kapadia 2019; Paik 2018; Pawar and Moon 2008). These scholars demand that Dalit women's lives be understood in all their complexity and beyond an "undifferentiated Dalit woman universe" (Ciotti 2019, 78). Primarily constructing Dalit women as victims truncates complex subjectivities (Brueck 2012). While the agency of Dalit women may not appear in recognizable ways, it is precisely these contradictory subjectivities that need to be accounted for. When this does not happen, Dalit lives are flattened, and the sexual subjectivity demonstrated by someone like Vineeta is made to remain invisible.

CONCLUSION

In suggesting that young women who allege rape in fact exercised their will and went of their own *marzi*, the false rape charge is not about accommodating an autonomous subject who is capable of will. It is instead about punishment, where the exercise of the young woman's will is indicative of her dishonor and impropriety. This is why she must be chastised, and why restoration takes the form of compensating her father or male guardian for the loss of her value in patrilineal modes of exchange.

Accusing women of filing false rape charges is also about refusing women access to state mechanisms of redress. That women should file rape cases against men—in their village, community, caste, or filial affiliation—is a demonstration of defiance not tolerated by guardians of the patriarchal societal order, who try to suppress such defiance by discrediting their cases. Siddiqi (2015, 515) writes about women filing rape cases in Bangladesh: "These are not conventional transgressions of the moral code or sharia prescriptions but . . . direct challenges to social hierarchy. They are actions that defy gendered structures of inequality at their core; they are, arguably, indicative of new modes of dissent, sharpening inequalities, and instabilities in the social order." Empirical evidence from rural Haryana also bears this out. I heard story after story from lawyers and activists about how women faced tremendous obstacles in getting their cases lodged by the police. Most often police discourage the filing of cases, especially if the case is against someone powerful. For women, this means that filing a case is met with disbelief and an appraisal of what she might have done to encourage the attack (Shalhoub-Kevorkian 2011). In other words, what she might have done to deserve it. The incredulity with which women who file rape charges are met calcifies and means that an astronomical effort is required to make credible a woman filing a case about an actual rape.

The false rape narrative, then, needs to be understood as a punitive response against women for their defiance of subjection. To support this defiance and redress the gross violations to which women are subject, women's and human rights groups in India have for years been organizing against cases ending in compromise. These efforts have entailed support for families and victims against coercive tactics by dominant-caste families or even from within the family and community to settle out of court. In Vineeta's case as well, women's and human rights groups encouraged her to refuse to settle out of court because doing so would reiterate the structures of domination.

There are few avenues that Dalit communities and young women have to seek redress for violations under conditions of profound collective disenfranchisement. In such a context, rape cases, especially involving a Dalit woman and a dominant-caste man, exceed the boundaries of the particular case. They are motivated by the rare opportunity to tip the scales of justice toward those usually on the receiving end of injustice. In Dalit literature, rapes play a prominent role as "catalysts for revenge narratives enacted by men" (Brueck 2012, 230). But these stories erase women, given that "the victimized women have little voice and are often left by the wayside as the narrative focus turns toward the male agents of the recuperation of honor" (Brueck 2012, 230). Fiction by Dalit women seeks to reverse this trend by drafting themselves as protagonists who seek justice in stories of violation. In so doing, they craft their subjectivity.

While Dalit women's narratives are crafting their subjectivity by rewriting the rape script, according to Laura Brueck (2012), in most of these stories, sexual subjectivity is still navigated primarily through violation and retribution. This means that women's sexual subjectivity can still only be discerned through the dual frames of chastity and impurity. This also means that even with the proliferation of Dalit women's narratives, Vineeta's story, from the perspective of her advocates, can still only be told as one in which her sexual subjectivity is read as a rape script that seeks to redress caste injustice and community dishonor.

Hartman (1997) offers a way to consider Vineeta's defiance. Hartman reads the boundary that Celia, an enslaved woman, erects at her cabin against the violations of her owner as a profound act to reclaim her body. Hartman writes: "The effort to reclaim the body and experience embodiment as full, inviolate, and pleasurable, not as an extension of another's will . . . led Celia to construct a boundary at the threshold of her cabin" (86). Hartman is here writing about the repeated rape that Celia endures at the hands of her owner, whom she eventually kills before being hanged for the crime. The act of erecting a symbolic boundary against the threat of future violence is nevertheless a profound act of embodiment and subjectivity.

Hartman explains, "Celia's declaration of the limit was an emancipatory articulation of the desire for a different economy of enjoyment" (1997, 86). Is there space to read Vineeta's act as an effort to articulate "a different economy of enjoyment"? What does it mean to read Vineeta's sexual autonomy as defilement? Within feminist activism and theorizing, there is a long tradition of reading sexual autonomy as generating liberatory possibilities. And yet in Vineeta's case, this possibility is foreclosed. Vineeta's sexual autonomy is intelligible only as a violation. In erasing Vineeta's sexual subjectivity, her family and village council are conscripted into the efforts of the patriarchal state to effect a restoration that denies her subjectivity. While her choices for sexual relationships may not have necessarily been wise, within the discursive narrative of rape in rural Haryana, there is no space where sexual subjectivity is allowable. It is to understand this subjectivity that I want to tease out the following dilemma for feminist theorizing: Vineeta is either framed as morally compromised by her illicit behavior or as a victim who is duped and coerced by upper-caste connivance into entering a relationship that is otherwise not of her choosing. The possibility for agency, even the possibility to make bad sexual choices, is denied her. Does the need for feminist interventions and desirable outcomes generate an erasure of discursive space for sexual subjectivity (Siddiqi 2015, 518)?

Dominant narratives of Dalit women regard them as mute victims, trapped within systems of patriarchy and caste politics. In their account of how Dalit women perceive their own lives, researchers Fernando Franco, Jyotsna Macwan, and Suguna Ramanathan (2000, 6) write that Brahminical upper-middle-class perspectives see these women as "entirely passive victims annihilated under the combined weight of oppressive structures, to be uplifted only by the benevolent outsider." In narrating stories by women from three marginalized caste groups—the Vankar, Bhangi, and Koli-Patel groups—their book conjures a rich, multidimensional world of desire, ambivalence, and violence. Their book offers a multifaceted chronicle of stories that subvert the sense that lower-caste and Dalit women are passive and have no agency or express no desire. Instead, the women in their book speak of attraction and desire for boys among their *vas* (community or village). According to customary law, relationships between girls and boys of the same *vas* are prohibited because they are all considered as part of the same patrilineal clan, and therefore as siblings. But these women, while aware of the prohibition, continued to fantasize and to be attracted to men within their *vas*. Similarly, while they were deeply aware that dominant-caste men would often use women in their social position for sexual pleasure and subject them to violence, they still engaged in relationships with these men. As the authors explain, "Libidinal desire which is at odds with social sanctions and norms constitutes a mode of individual resistance, even if it remains at a latent level and is not expressed in action" (Franco, Macwan, and Ramanathan 2000, 57).

Much work remains to be done at the level of feminist and human rights interventions to carve out spaces that on the one hand address police apathy and inaction in the face of serious sexual violations, and on the other, hold space for sexual subjectivity. Feminists should not be cornered into supporting rape cases filed by women who seek retaliation against, or compensation from, male lovers who break their promises to marry. Nor should they support rape cases filed to mitigate reputational harm and restore a family's or community's honor when an illicit affair is made public. The challenge is to push back against dominant police narratives that assert that 90 percent of women alleging rape are filing false cases, while simultaneously negotiating against the filing of false cases, which are primarily about efforts to restore male authority over women's libidinal economy.

2. Compromise

In February 2011, the Supreme Court of India heard an appeal of a 1997 Punjab and Haryana High Court judgment on gang rape.[1] The High Court had convicted three men of the rape of a young woman who had gone out of her house to relieve herself.[2] The men were sentenced to ten years in prison and fined one thousand rupees each. By the time the case was appealed in the Supreme Court, the men had served three years in jail and the case itself was fourteen years old. The Court released the men. In its decision, the Court explained that it had received an affidavit asserting that the parties "want[ed] to finish the dispute," and had "entered into a compromise" in January 2007. Since the parties to the case now agreed that "the accused may be acquitted" and that there was now "no misunderstanding between them," the Court saw fit to uphold the conviction but release the men by reducing their sentence to time served. (The Court did, however, increase the fine to 50,000 rupees per defendant.) It based its verdict not only on the fact that the parties had decided to compromise, but also on the fact that the raped woman was now married and had two children.

In response to the judgment, Mrinal Satish, a respected legal scholar who writes on sexual violence and criminal law, argued in a law blog that the Court's reasons for reducing the sentence were deeply flawed and relied on "patriarchal notions of shame, value, and honor" (2011). The judges reasoned that a long time had elapsed since the crime, and that the parties themselves wanted to end the dispute. Notably, they also cited the woman's current marital status as an important consideration in their decision to reduce the sentence of the men who had been convicted of raping her. In so doing, they reflected how courts believe that rape diminishes a woman's value in marriage; since the woman was now married and had children, the Court's concern that the crime would affect her marriageability was mitigated. This is how the Court reasoned accepting the compromise between the adversarial parties, even though this sort of plea bargaining and out-of-court agreement is illegal under Indian law for such criminal cases.

Rape is a noncompoundable crime, which means that an out-of-court settlement or a compromise in rape cases is against the law. Most criminal cases are understood as crimes against society in which the state prosecutes on behalf of both the victim and society. A compromise between the victim and the accused, therefore, undermines the intent of the law and the state's standing in such cases. Despite being expressly forbidden, I found that not only was compromise frequently practiced, but that it was also well recognized by everyone from constables and high-ranking police officers to attorneys and judges, as well as by victims and perpetrators. This "public secret" is fostered and practiced with mundane regularity (Baxi 2010).

This chapter is about compromise in rape cases. I ask: What does compromise do in the wake of a rape charge? Who is involved in the negotiations, and who does compromise benefit? I follow three cases of compromise in three villages in Haryana—Bhagana, Matpur, and Jaswadi. The previous chapter focused on the story of a rape charge that was filed after an illicit affair became public, and that ended in compromise. This chapter takes a closer look at the story of compromise and demonstrates how the pressure to settle a rape case relies on structures of caste and land. I draw again on Vineeta's story in Matpur and on the 2014 quadruple rape cases in Bhagana, but focus on Komal's story in Jaswadi.

During the negotiations for compromise, the parties involved typically construct separate scripts to facilitate the desired outcome. My detailed conversations with different groups of people invested or opposed to compromise revealed a much more complex landscape than one discerned exclusively from the drama that unfolds in court. I argue that the rape script shifts and changes at each scale, animating different publics with investments in particular outcomes. Following how compromise works at different scales and what rape does, I look closely at negotiations in the wake of a rape charge. In keeping with my effort to excavate the sexual subjectivities that are generated, I draw on Audra Simpson's (2014) *Mohawk Interruptus* to consider which forms of subjectivity compromise allows. Simpson theorizes the refusal by the Mohawks of Kahnawà:ke to obtain passports and other forms of state recognition as an effort to claim sovereignty "as peoples who belong to a nation other than the United States or Canada" (2). What would it mean to think of compromise as a refusal to participate within oppressive norms and as an effort to claim sovereignty? In what follows, I trace how the story of rape is constructed in different spaces and at different scales—in mahila thannas and the courts, panchayats, and finally in the home and in the story of the victim. It is in these different arenas that the dispute over who has jurisdiction and sovereignty over particular spaces is most discernable.

THE STRUCTURE OF COMPROMISE

Compromise is an out-of-court settlement between the accused and the victim. Typically, in the cases I followed, the victim is never involved in direct negotiations with the accused. Instead, this process usually involves the families of both the victim and the accused. These negotiations are initiated when either a complaint or the threat of a complaint is made. If a complaint has been filed and the accused has been taken into judicial custody, then the family of the accused will approach the family of the victim to ask forgiveness and initiate a conversation on what can be done to free the accused. The panchayat is usually involved in these negotiations. The sarpanch and *lambardar* mediate the negotiations between the families.[3] If an agreement is reached, then the panchayat also structures the compromise. For instance, if the agreement is over money, then the panchayat and the *lambardar* will hold onto the funds until the accused is freed.

Attorneys for both parties are occasionally involved when a compromise is agreed upon, and the defense attorney for the accused will coach the victim on her testimony in court. In court the victim will turn hostile, meaning she will turn against her own prosecuting attorney. Once the accused is set free, the panchayat and *lambardar* release the funds to the victim's family. The victim is never present throughout these negotiations and her opinion is usually not taken into consideration. It is the elders in the families that negotiate and receive the compromise settlement.

In instances of intercaste rape, if the accused is from a dominant-caste family and the victim is from a subordinate caste, the dominant-caste family and its allies will usually use threats of violence and social boycott to pressure the victim into agreeing to a compromise. In Bhagana, Dalit activists alleged that the families of the victims were effectively forced by Jats in the village to reach a compromise. Since most subordinate-caste families are also poor and depend on Jats for work and access to common land, efforts to coerce them to compromise are usually successful. While more Dalits are claiming their rights and refusing to acquiesce to coercive tactics—a point made by both police officers and members of Dalit castes—the numbers of Dalits who assert their rights by refusing to compromise remains relatively small. Because Jats are in a structurally dominant position, it is easier for them to compel a compromise with those in subordinate positions than it is for those in subordinate positions to refuse.

Even though compromise is illegal in criminal cases, there have been recent instances of high court judges recognizing and agreeing to compromise, especially if the accused agrees to marry the victim. In a move to acknowledge that it both knew about the frequency of this illegal practice and opposed it, the Supreme Court in 2015 admonished the lower courts for being complicit in it. In a strongly worded statement, the Court said, "some of the appellate Judges, contrary to the precedents and against the normative mandate of law, assuming a presumptuous role, have paved the path of unbelievable lacunarity to deal with criminal appeals which, if we permit ourselves to say, ruptures the sense of justice and punctures the criminal justice dispensation system" (Press Trust of India 2015). Despite the Supreme Court's strongly worded statement, compromise continues to be widely practiced. At one of the district court offices I visited, an attorney explained that up until a few years ago, two special sessions judges had frequently used a recently introduced plea-bargaining amendment in the Criminal Law Act to deal with rape cases, even though the amendment was explicitly not meant to apply to rape cases. The implications of this minor amendment to deal with major crimes were first told to me by Sarita Mathur.

Minor Amendment for a Major Crime: Plea Bargaining in Compromise Cases

On an initial visit to the second district in which I was doing research, I met with the head of the lawyer's council, who recommended I speak with Sarita Mathur.[4] He described her as an attorney who frequently dealt with violence against women and rape cases, was on their legal aid panel, and was active in the local women's shelter. I met Ms. Mathur and saw that she was a middle-aged woman with a forthright and direct disposition. Not unexpectedly, she too claimed that the majority of rape cases were based on false allegations. But of particular significance was a practice she spoke about from five to seven years ago, when judges in the district courts used a recent amendment to the Criminal Law Act on plea bargaining to adjudicate compromise cases. The amendment had been introduced as a way to deal with a backlog of cases, but explicitly prohibited the use of plea bargaining in particular criminal cases, including rape. Despite the explicit distinctions in the amendment, Mathur claimed that the practice of plea bargaining in rape cases had become rampant. She said that one of the judges had been very good at mediation and had even started a mediation center in the courts to help people settle their cases out of court. The two male judges for the special sessions court would direct attorneys to reach a *shamjauta* (compromise), drawing on how the plea-bargaining amendment was used to settle land dispute cases. As part of their prevailing narrative that the majority of rape cases were false, police and some attorneys would argue that false rape charges were often filed as a way to expedite civil claims in property disputes. As a consequence, the use of plea bargaining in rape cases crossed over from criminal cases to cases involving property and land, blurring the boundary between civil and criminal law. Rape came to be treated as a civil dispute rather than as a crime against women.

Plea bargaining was introduced in India through a change in the Criminal Law Act in 2005. When the amendment to introduce plea bargaining was passed, it excluded cases that mandated imprisonment for more than seven years, offenses that affected socioeconomic conditions, crimes against women and girls younger than fourteen, and serious crimes such as rape and murder. The law commission of India articulated a detailed structure for plea bargaining in 1991 in its 142nd report, and in its 154th report in 1996, it recommended making plea bargaining applicable. The Supreme Court was against plea bargaining because of concerns that it would usher in coercion and corruption in criminal cases. The significance of plea bargaining was articulated in a 2005 Gujarat High Court judgment in *State of Gujarat v. Natwar Harchandji Thakor*. This case was appealed on three grounds; the first two dealt with the length of imprisonment and the fine allocated to the crime, while the third matter led directly to deciding the significance of plea bargaining. The court had to consider "whether innovative judicial directions and prescriptions . . . for recording [a] plea of guilty of an accused . . . would be competent and legal?" (*State of Gujarat v. Natwar Harchandji Thakor*, 1)

In other words, the issue was whether allowing guilty pleas would usher in reduced sentences at the discretion of judges, and whether such reduced sentences would de facto introduce plea bargaining, which up to that point was considered damaging and illegal.

Ultimately, the High Court judgment navigated between allowing judges to award less-than-minimum sentences at their discretion and, on the other hand, cautioned against awarding automatic reductions just because a defendant pled guilty. It ruled that the reasons for awarding a less than minimum sentence had to be "recorded in writing" and based on the "presence of special and adequate reasons" that were "adequate to the circumstances in a given case and peculiar to the accused in each case" (15). Further, the court ruled that the accused could not enter into a plea of guilt to get a reduced sentence, and suggested procedures to mitigate against such misuse of judicial discretion in sentencing. The court, while cognizant that trial courts took the plea of guilt into consideration in their sentencing, was nevertheless reluctant to make such provisions outright illegal. It cautioned against a plea of guilt leading to plea bargaining: "Every 'plea of guilty,' which is a part of statutory process in criminal trial, cannot be said to be a 'plea bargaining' ipso facto" (23). The judgment restrained the courts from treating the two as equivalent and implored them to exercise care in cases where a plea of guilty is raised. While cautioning against incorrectly conflating the plea of guilty with plea bargaining, the judgment however was not against the practice of plea bargaining. In fact, it argued in favor of plea bargaining to ease the significant backlog of cases, since this backlog meant that a multitude of indigent people who could not afford bail were spending three to five years in judicial custody awaiting trial.

While this case was being litigated in the Gujarat High Court, the legislature was at the same time considering an amendment to the Criminal Law Act to introduce plea bargaining. By the time the amended act came into effect in 2006, it explicitly prohibited the use of plea bargaining in criminal cases such as those involving rape. Despite the law's explicit intent to forbid compromise in criminal cases of rape, Sarita Mathur recalled that judges in the district court drew on its plea-bargaining provisions to settle disputes in rape cases. Since the prevailing understanding among those in the courts is that most rape cases are false and that they invariably end in compromise, plea bargaining became a de facto mechanism for resolving such cases. The practice was curtailed in 2016 when the Punjab and Haryana High Court ordered that plea bargaining, which was used to reach settlements in land dispute cases, could not be exercised for compromise on rape cases. While the judgment generated some caution and led to curtailing the use of plea bargaining in rape cases, it did not stop compromise in such cases altogether.

The current special sessions judge in the district, who was responsible for crimes against women, was very conscious of the misuse of compromise in rape cases and had a reputation for being strict in cases involving crimes against women. When I asked her explicitly about compromise in such cases, she said that when she suspects that a compromise was used to settle a case she charges the complainant, meaning the woman who had initially alleged rape, with section 344 of the Criminal Procedure Code (CrPC). Section 344 indicts witnesses for giving false testimony or for fabricating evidence. Despite the "strict" adherence to the law by some special sessions judges like this one, who prosecute those who turn hostile, compromise continues to occur and people find multiple ways to maneuver such cases through the courts. Whether through tactics of coercion or the exchange of money, compromise in rape cases is commonplace due to a structural context of profound poverty and deprivation, where a crisis in the rural economy has led to massive unemployment compounded by caste-based discrimination. As a result, I heard attorneys and others claim that compromise had become a *dhandha*—a business transaction.

The rest of this chapter is divided into four parts, each dealing with a particular scale: the district, the village, the *basti* and home, and finally, the body. I excavate the story of compromise as it weaves through these four scales to reveal and how the "script" of rape shifts and changes. Here I pay attention to contestations over boundaries and claims of jurisdiction over space. What does the compromise of a rape case reveal in each of these spaces? And how might a woman's refusal to continue with a case allow her to claim a certain degree of sovereignty? Following feminist geographers, I look at the social life of rape at small and intimate scales to examine tensions and challenges that may not be visible at higher resolutions.

Compromise Dhandha Hai *(Compromise Is a Business): Testimonial Injustice and the Production of a Narrative at the District Scale*

Haryana has mahila thannas in each district. To understand the narrative that is crafted in mahila thannas, I spent several hours in these police stations dedicated to dealing with crimes against women. In addition to the thannas, district courts were also where the rape script was generated. Together, the police stations and the courts represented the state at the scale of the district where rape charges are first filed, investigated, and then adjudicated. As spaces recognized and established within the bureaucracy of state governance, they have authority and jurisdiction over civil and criminal matters. As such, they wield tremendous authority and power. The scripts produced here therefore congeal as the truth, and claims that counter these established narratives are usually inaudible. Rape in these spaces was primarily understood through narratives of deception, immorality, and coercion—and compromise, as a way to extort money.

My conversations with police officers in three different districts in Haryana were remarkably similar. They all argued that most rape cases are false, and depending on who I spoke with, the percentage of false cases varied from 50 to 99 percent. The second recurring claim was that up to 70 percent of rape cases were not only false but compromised, and that they were compromised for money rather than because of any social pressure or coercion. Phrases I repeatedly heard from those at the thanna were "Woh apni sehmti se gaye thi" (She went of her own will), "Uske sehmti se ho raha hai" (It's happening because she consents to it), and "Sehmti se paise leti hai" (They willingly take money).[5] In these police stations, the narrative of the false case was rehearsed to argue that rape charges were filed to expedite civil claims such as disputes over land and used to extort money. For them, compromise in rape cases is a form of *dhandha* (business transaction).

The women in these police stations sought to demonstrate the veracity of their assertions by telling elaborate stories of deception, false claims, and love affairs. Through each story they sought to convey female irresponsibility and the loosening of sexual mores, which they held responsible for the increase in rape cases. Sheela Devi, the station house officer at one of these mahila thannas, explained this in the following way: "Yea ladkiya gaon se aati hai, ek class attend kar ke phir park ya café mei beth jati ahi. Ma baap ko kuch nahi pata. Jab crime hota hai tabhi pata lagta hai ke mere ladki ke saat kya hua" (These girls come from the village and they attend one class and then they leave and go to the park or a café. The parents don't know what is going on. When a crime happens, that's when parents find out what happened with the girl).[6] These policewomen, and others also invested in the dominant patriarchal social order, considered the sight of young women in the company of boys in public spaces such as parks and cafes as an unwelcome development, and as a tremendous cause for anxiety. More young women of this generation from villages were attending college than ever before. The influx of groups of women in colleges and out in public, accessing public transportation and occupying the restaurants and shops that have opened to accommodate a growing trend, has led to concern over rising impropriety. Not only police officers in the thannas but also parents and others I spoke with in the villages repeated that cell phones were the biggest problem. While many agreed that men who rape are bad and should be punished, invariably they also claimed that women also need to take responsibility for their actions. Ultimately, in a textbook example of victim-blaming, they primarily blamed the young women out in public, their choice of clothes, and their access to cell phones for the assaults.

At another *mahila thanna*, one of the policewomen recounted a story from the previous year. There were three other people in the room, all avidly listening and nodding at appropriate junctures, generating a discursive space of veracity.[7] The story involved a thirty-year-old woman who had come by to file a rape charge, which they investigated and found to be false. According to the policewoman raconteur, it turned out that the woman had been in a relationship with the seventeen-year-old boy she was accusing now of rape. After their affair ended, the woman filed a rape charge in retaliation. The three other people in the room shook their heads in dismay and exclaimed, "Bataao!" The vernacular translation of the word means "Tell me" but is said as a way to convey exasperation about a circumstance or situation over how such affairs between older women and younger men were even possible. The officer went on with the story, saying that the woman wanted the boy to marry her, or if not, then to give her money. The audience scoffed at the absurdity of the ultimatum as a way to demonstrate their disapproval of the tactic and as commentary on the compromised morality of society.

The commentaries I heard at mahila thannas reserved a particular vehemence against and lack of sympathy for women who filed rape and assault charges. Not only was the claim that most rape cases were false echoed in all the *mahila thannas* I visited, but also the animosity and suspicion reserved for women who file charges stood out. Sheela Devi (a station house officer at one of these mahila thannas, as mentioned previously) confidently asserted that women fabricated their injuries when they came to file a complaint. She argued that these young women inflicted scratches and damage to their "private areas" to show that they were assaulted. Illustrating deviousness on the part of young women, she said that they know what is needed to demonstrate rape. I said that surely not all rape can be fabricated, and what about young girls? She replied that you cannot believe a rape case even if brought by girls as young as fourteen and fifteen because they are "fully developed." She said the phrase in English to mean that these young girls were aware of their bodies and had visible breasts, which she took as a sign of their "maturity" and corresponding responsibility. She then said that these young girls were sexually active, and that when they were forced by their families to file a complaint, they often said that they wanted to go with their boyfriends. Devi asked in exasperation, "Batao hum kya kar sakte hai" (Tell me what can we do)?[8]

It was not the repeated pronouncements about false rape and compromise that were surprising or even novel; it was the certainty with which these were professed. At a *mahila thanna* in another district, while waiting for the station house officer, I struck up a conversation with a couple of women constables and officers.[9] I asked how they knew which cases were false. They explained that they can tell which cases are false or true by a "face index." While the conversation was in vernacular Hindi and Haryanvi, they used the phrase *face index* in English deliberately as a way to signal that this was a legitimate, technical process in which the police were trained. It was not the first time I had heard the phrase; in yet another district, the station house officer had made a similar pronouncement, saying, "Hamari ek face reading hoti hai jis se pata lag jata hai ki kaunsa real hai aur kaunsa false case hai" (We are able to do a "face reading" from which we can tell which are true and which are false cases).[10] Through "reading the face" of the complainant and through *taftees* (investigation), the officers claimed they could extract the truth of a case. The face readings, they said, allowed them to discern a person's true feelings: "Jis se mind feeling pata lag jaata hai" (We can tell the feelings of the person).[11] The repetition of such pronouncements by police officers crafted a cohesiveness among them as a unit that they conceived of as different and apart from the general public; a unit possessing the authority and special "technical expertise" to "face read" and determine a person's "truth."

It was not only police officers who were convinced about the connivance of young women who filed rape charges. Many attorneys I spoke with revealed that they too firmly believed that women were for the most part filing false rape charges in order to extort money. On an overcast, cold winter day, I was visiting Sarita Mathur at the district courts when she recounted an elaborate tale of deception involving collaboration between a woman making false rape allegations, police officers, and attorneys. Mathur recounted a story about a young woman who would entice men to have sex with her, and then secretly record them. This woman would later claim that she had been assaulted. When the woman went to file rape charges at the local thanna, the negotiations over money would begin. Mathur said that this woman's ability to successfully carry out her elaborate deception relied on collaborating with police officers in the local *mahila thanna* as well as attorneys.

Mathur's office window, blurry with dust and grime, looked out toward the chambers of other lawyers on a higher floor. She pointed to an office we could see through the window and said that the attorney who used to occupy that office had been involved in the scam, and had since left and was practicing somewhere in Delhi. The police and lawyers would apparently each get their cut of extorted money once the young woman was able to wrest some from the men she falsely accused. According to Mathur, this racketeering scheme fell apart when, during one of these deceptions, the woman did not get what she considered to be her share of the money and set out to trap the lawyers who had been in on the plot.[12]

I am not particularly interested in the veracity of the claims made by police officers and attorneys about compromised and false rape cases. Rather, I am concerned with the "script" that they generate by repeating these claims. The anecdotal evidence with which police officers and defense lawyers peppered their claims were not fantastic stories, but rather deliberate, repetitious performances that established what can be heard as true and false. They were not absolute fabrications, as so many entirely fabricated stories would be hard to sustain over time. They should instead be understood as carefully selected or cherry-picked stories, stretched and molded into claims that authorities used to build the narratives they sought to advance.

The unrelenting, continuous repetition of stories that fit the narrative of false rape cases filed by unreliable women serves to generate what Miranda Fricker (2007) has called "testimonial injustice." Fricker helps us see how the capacity for a claim to be audible against the overwhelming tide of narratives about women and false cases is severely restricted; the claimant and her testimony is discredited before she can even speak. Fricker says, "Testimonial injustice occurs when prejudice causes a hearer to give a deflated level of credibility to a speaker's word" (1). Here, I identify a particular kind of insidious violence that occurs through bureaucratic indifference and congealed judgment. The violence of the pervasiveness of this discourse is that it is widely dispersed, such that it becomes systemic. While particular police officers and attorneys may suspect claims of violation, my research shows how their articulation of disbelief is symptomatic of structural violence rather than a reflection of arbitrary, individual bias. This is not to absolve those who make dismissive pronouncements about women and their credibility, but rather to identify the dispersion of power that settles as truth. Across the bureaucracy, from the most senior police officer down to lowest-ranking constables in the mahila thannas, the similarity of the narratives was striking, and indicative of how this carefully crafted script about false rape charges and unreliable women served to cultivate compliance within the bureaucracy itself. For a bureaucrat, a police officer, or a court official, there is little to no room to think beyond the hegemony of the script, to say nothing of rejecting it.

The lack of credibility in rape cases is compounded for women who are of subordinate caste. Decades of feminist work on sexual violation has clearly documented that women in lower castes are in diminished positions of power and marked as suspect from the get-go, before making any claims. When these women attempt to seek justice, the effort they must exert to establish themselves as credible is astronomical. The violence of testimonial injustice is that lower caste, Dalit, and OBC women are seen not only as suspect but ultimately as undeserving of justice from the state. The issue then becomes, can we understand compromise in all cases to contradict or undermine justice? In what follows, I suggest that disaggregating how compromise works at different scales makes apparent that what may be just at one scale may not be just at another.

COERCION, REPUTATION, AND AMBIGUITY AT THE VILLAGE SCALE

If the narrative at the district scale congealed around false cases and compromise as a business transaction, then at the scale of the village, the story of compromise was about preserving village reputation and maintaining peace. I met with members of the panchayat and elders who adjudicate compromise cases in the village. There is a theatricality to the transaction of a compromise. It usually involves the performance of genuflection and an apology by the father of the accused to the father of the victim, agreements signed and exchanged in the presence of attorneys, and sometimes, the exchange of money. The drama serves to appease adversarial parties, contain the scandal at the scale of the village, and maintain *bhaichara* (brotherhood). In the village, scripts of maintaining peace (not justice) pervade the reasons for compromise. In contrast, among Dalit attorneys and activists, the script of compromise was primarily understood as a story of coercion. As I show toward the end of this section, in the case of a young woman I call Komal, their story of coercion is turned on its head.

Since compromise is illegal, most lawyers are reticent to say on record that they have participated in facilitating it, even as they acknowledge that it occurs with remarkable frequency.[13] The prevailing understanding is that most attorneys help in facilitating compromise by drawing up "an agreement."

These agreements are not legally binding, but the act of signing a written agreement in front of the panchayat and with lawyers present appears to "formalize" a process between the adversarial parties. Baxi (2014) explains that the panchayat usurps the role of the courts in these transactions. She says, "We see time and again, that *panchayats* attempt to appropriate the court's monopoly to adjudicate crime by treating rape as a social dispute that can be settled within a village or community. Further, the *panchayat* speaks the language of compromise as if it were representative of community consensus about how the victim should behave" (181–82). In doing so, the panchayat reaffirms and solidifies its authority and its decisions, making them appear incontestable and inextricable from the natural order of things. In the village, compromise is a transaction that follows this structure of the panchayat adjudicating the dispute and arriving at a consensus. In the cases I followed that involved compromise, the reasons given for preferring compromise over resolving conflict through the courts were all similar to each other. However, the stories of violation that led to compromise differed in each.

In Bhagana, the script of compromise depended on who was making it. Activists claimed that compromise occurred because of coercion and social pressure, while the mothers of the raped girls claimed that they had not been pressured into compromise. In my conversation with Satish Kumar, an activist who has been protesting atrocity and violation in the village for years, she claimed that the conflict with Jats in Bhagana began because "Dalit ko jo adhikar diya hai us se jatho ko khadkti hai" (the rights that have been given to Dalits vex Jats).[14] The conflict between Jats and Dalits in Bhagana had been brewing for a while and was fueled by a social boycott that erupted in disputes over common land. I recount this story in detail in chapter 3, but these social boycotts entailed Jats refusing to let Dalits access resources critical to their livelihoods. It was in this context of ongoing conflict that the four girls of the subordinate Dhanak caste were raped in March 2014. In the course of this conflict, over a hundred Dhanak families left the village and set up a protest camp outside government offices in Hisar, and even spent weeks in Delhi, demanding justice for the raped girls and restitution of their rights to village resources. Among them were the families of the four girls who were raped. When I went to the village five years later in 2019, all four families had moved back. The mothers of two of the girls said their daughters had married and left the village. According to Arun, an activist with Satish, "unhone phaisla kar liya" (meaning they compromised their cases).

The mothers of the girls who were raped, however, had an alternate narrative to the one expressed by Arun and Satish. On the day we met them,

Savatri, the mother of one of the girls, explained, "Do ladkiyo ne phaisla kar liya" (Two girls compromised).[15] She then said that following these compromises, the other two cases also ended, and "hum bahir aa geye" (we came out of the case). The phrase indicates that they extricated themselves from the cases, and conveys their sense of helplessness at having to stay in the village, too worn down to want to fight anymore.

Satish explained that many of the Dalits in Bhagana were *bhandwa mazdoor* (bonded labor) who worked through a system of debt or barter in which they received a *hissa* (portion) of the crop or were paid a small amount to work the land. Since no Dalits owned land in Bhagana, most worked on Jat land. This system of labor in which Dalits did not have independent ways to earn a living rendered them dependent on Jat landlords for their livelihood. So while Savatri claimed that neither her family nor those of the other raped girls were coerced, and that two of the four families refused to take money to compromise their case, the structure of power in Bhagana makes it impossible for Dalits to make choices independent of Jat influence. While there may or may not have been overt coercion to compromise the case, tacit social pressure, backed by indirect economic coercion, made compromise the only viable choice for most.

Meanwhile, in Matpur village, where Vinetta's case occurs, compromise followed a different trajectory. Here, compromise followed a rape charge that was filed by the girl's family once her illicit affair was exposed and made public.[16] In one of my early meetings with Vineeta, one day she said that she wanted to speak with me in confidence. She took me to a private room at the back of the house, where it was dark and very hot. In hushed tones, she told me that a few days ago she had tried to run away from home because her brother had discovered a photograph of Pradeep in her bag. Pradeep was the young man against whom her family had filed a rape charge. Her brother's discovery had taken place as negotiations for the compromise were underway. On finding Pradeep's photograph, her brother and father had shouted at her and threatened her for bringing shame to their family. Vineeta's family is Dalit and very poor, and Pradeep is Jat, and his family has land. In the previous chapter, I recounted that Vineeta and Pradeep had been in an illicit relationship intermittently for five years. After rape charges were filed, a compromise between the families was quickly negotiated. When I asked about the compromise, Vineeta said that she had not been a part of it, and that her parents had conferred with members of the panchayat and the boy's family. Vineeta said that she had seen Pradeep in the village a few days after the compromise but had not spoken with him.

I met with two other people involved in this compromise, including the *pradhaan* (chief or leader) who was also chairman of the district block and an elder in the Dalit community.[17] As chairman of the block he was part of the local bureaucracy, which dealt with the district administration on matters concerning the village. I had met him on an earlier visit before this compromise case. Since he held an important position, he was key to the proceedings of compromise and close to Vineeta's father, and thus represented the family's interests. He said, "Accha ho gaya, parivar ke sadsaye aur gaon ke mukhya un ke beech me phaisla clear kiya" (It was good, members of the family and the important people from the village came together to settle the matter). Explaining the agreement, he said they decided that "koi harkat nahi hogi and mil bhagath ke sabhi kaam karengi" (there will be no trouble and that everyone will sit together and work it out). He then talked directly about the reasons for the compromise, saying, "Gaon mei jo maan samaan hota hai idhar udhar ke baate na phaile, es sab ka sub kuch detkna parta hai" (We need to preserve reputations in the village so that things don't spread here and there, so we need to see to all these things). Claiming that different places settle matters differently, he continued, "Gaon ka alag sheher ka alag matter hota hai alag alag level hai har cheez ki" (Villages and cities settle their matters differently at different levels).

Vineeta's family's lawyer was also part of the compromise negotiations, the *pradhaan* reported, and had accepted the decision by both families to settle. Sunil, a young man who had recently stood for elections in the village and was a friend of the lawyer, explained, "Who bhi tha saat mei, aur panchayat ne kar liya toh who thodi karega ya" (He [the lawyer] was also there after the panchayat made the decision, he wouldn't . . .). Sunil's response trailed off before he completed his sentence, but his inference was clear. He explained that the lawyer did not orchestrate the compromise but was present for it. Since the panchayat and families had decided to compromise, the lawyer would not interfere with their decision. The *pradhaan* stepped in to say, "Manzoor kar liya uh ne" (He [the lawyer] accepted the decision). Sunil responded, "Panchayat ne likh ke de diya ki aage es tarah ki ghanta na ho. Zyada nei phale toh parashanani hogi samaaj mei bhi . . . toh aage phir koi nan . . ." (The panchayat wrote and said that such incidents should not happen in the future. It should not spread in society and so that in the future . . .). As demonstrated in this case, lawyers occasionally participate in compromise negotiations by drawing up an agreement between the parties involved. Their presence and the formality of drafting and signing papers lend a sense of gravitas to the event, which, while not legal, serves the purpose of easing tensions through the drama of a formal apology in front of important people in the village.

The theatrics of compromise serves to appease the adversarial parties, where one accepts responsibility for wrongdoing while restoring the reputation of the wronged party. The reasons for this are to maintain peace among those who must live in the village and to control the spread of rumors that could sully the reputation of the village. According to the *pradhaan*, district officials also recommended this form of settlement. He explained, "Yea toh Sarkar bhi chahti hai ji . . . zyada jaise koi case bartha hai, gaon mei apradhik mamle barthe hai, sarkar ki bhi puri machinery . . ." (The government/state also wants this, when incidents spread in the village, the state machinery also wants this . . .). He explains that the state recommends compromise because compromises eliminate the need for unnecessary bureaucratic paperwork: "Idher udhar ke kagaz uthana, who karna, idhar udhar ka lamba chauda procedure ban jaata hai ji" (Paperwork is gathered from here and there, to do this and that, the procedure is long drawn out). Since the *pradhaan* was also a part of the bureaucracy that represented the interests of the village, his understanding was that the state recommended and encouraged *shamjauta*. He explained, "Aisa who bhi chahti hai, gaon mei control rakho badhia bhai, yeah sarkar bhi sandesh deti hai ji" (Keep control in the village and keep things calm is what the state also recommends). Sunil added, "Ek toh char paach saal chalke case sulja hai aur ek toh apna jaldi sulaj gaya aur en ki bhi besti nahi hui" (In one instance it takes four to five years to resolve the case and in another, it gets over quickly and reputations are preserved). Resolving issues internally, through the panchayat, inoculates the village against reputational damage. In taking this path, the village and the panchayat turn the crime into a social dispute to be adjudicated through the theatrics of an apology and signing papers, and through *mili bhagat*, or the coming together of the parties to resolve the matter.

While this form of resolving conflict over a violation sidesteps a prosecutorial and carceral system, about which there is a growing body of abolitionist critique, in most instances it also compounds violence. It compounds violence because compromise cases in which the accused are guilty use their power and coerce the victim and her family to have charges dropped, enabling them to evade any form of accountability. It also compounds violence in cases like Vineeta's by operating as a means to uphold a patriarchal order, and to obtain funds that she has no control over in order to arrange a marriage she does not want. However, in a different case involving a young woman

I call Komal, compromise generated an alternative set of issues, exposing unexpected dilemmas.

In Jaswadi, the format of compromise followed the usual script. The case garnered a fair bit of attention when in November 2012 sixteen-year-old Komal was allegedly gang-raped by four men, two Jats and two men who belonged to OBCs from her village. Komal's *tau* (father's older brother) helped register the case and supported the family through the brutal process of lodging a complaint and getting the case to court. When I met Komal, four years had passed and she was over twenty years old, had dropped out of school, and was reluctant to return to her studies. The story of Komal's assault had elicited tremendous support from Dalit lawyers, activists, and human rights groups. In the years since her assault her case had not been resolved, and when I first met her in 2016, there was conversation in the village about resolving the case through a compromise. Eight months later a *shamjauta* was reached.

I met Komal's father a few days after the compromise, and he echoed what the *pradhaan* in Matpur said about who was involved in the *shamjauta*: "Gaam ka numberdar tha ji" (The village's *numberdar* did the compromise).[18] When I asked why the numberdar was present, he explained, "Gaon ke bade ko shamil karna partha hai" (We have to include village elders in the negotiations). Members from the neighboring village were also present during the compromise because their farms were side by side and there was *aana jaana* (coming and going) between the families. He then said, "Un ne maafi maang li hum ne manzoor kar li" (They asked for forgiveness and we accepted). This asking for forgiveness is a key part of the drama of compromise. It is asked of the father of the girl, never of her, since she is never present in these negotiations. Being the recipient of contrition and accepting the compromise establishes the father's role as a broker and the subject who has been wronged. It is his reputation, not his daughter's, that is to be repaired in the compromise.

In Komal's case, the format followed the usual template but also diverged in some significant ways. When I asked if the village and *basti* are happy with the compromise, Komal said, "Sara gaam khush hai" (The whole village is happy). She and her father explained that there was no issue now and that the village did not blame them. Komal then said, "Lugai toh bole hai eb toh beti theek se" (The women in the village say she is a good girl). Komal stressed that none of the women in the village say she is a bad girl, and that all of this only happened because "narazi ki hi ne woh party level mei woh ho gaya tha na ji case ke saat. Faisla se har aadmi raji hai" (there was acrimony at the level of the other group because of the case. Everyone is happy because of the agreement decision). Komal then said that the mother of one of the boys came to her and "pair bhi pakar liye the . . . boli beti mere bete ne baksh de" (touched my feet and said please forgive my son). Touching feet is a commonly recognized act of genuflection which is meant to show respect and also seek forgiveness.

To understand how the village navigated the *shamjauta*, I went to see the sarpanch (head of the village). I was greeted at the door by his wife, Ritu, whom I had met on previous occasions and befriended. She welcomed me with a big smile. I had learned that she was a *khiladi* (sportswoman) before she was married and, in our conversations, she had often advocated that girls should participate in sports and get a job before getting married. Her unusual positions made me solicit her opinion on village matters whenever we met. The sarpanch was more reticent in disclosing the affairs of the village and only said that the *shamjauta* was finished and that things in the village were good. His older brother (*tau*) was a respected elder in the village whom I had met a year before. Since then, he had suffered a stroke and was bedridden. When I had met the *tau*, he explained that things in the village were good and tensions were resolved *aapas mei* (together). He was glad that the matter was resolved and that there was peace in the village.

After his brief explanation of the compromise, the sarpanch left for the district offices. Ritu moved her chair closer and, in a gesture of sharing confidence, said in hushed tones that one of the boys who was accused in Komal's case did not have a good reputation. He was known to have done chedkhani ki harkat (incidents of harassment) with the girl in a saamne wale ka ghar (the house they faced). Of the four men accused, two were Jat, and two were from the OBC community. Ritu was talking about one of the Jat boys. At the same time, she said that Komal was a good girl. The reputation of girls who are raped is often sullied, which makes remarking that Komal is a good girl particularly significant as a way to affirm that the girl is not immoral. It is this restoration of reputation that Komal points to when she says that women in the village say that she is a good girl.

Komal's relief at the fact that the women in the village say that she is good, and Ritu's gesture—defending her while also hinting that one of the accused boys had a bad reputation—point to intercaste politics. I had earlier asked the older brother if there were caste tensions in the village, and he said that there was good *bhaichara* (brotherhood). Yet in previous depositions by Komal, she had claimed that a few days after the rape, members of the dominant caste in the village, including the parents of the accused, had called a panchayat and compelled Komal's uncle to agree to a compromise. Komal's claim that dominant castes had coerced her uncle to agree to drop charges and settle out of court resulted in her prosecuting attorneys adding a charge based on the Prevention of Atrocities Act. At this point, the story turns ambiguous. The narrative I was told shifted based on the interests of the person I spoke with, and also shifted because of the impact of my caste and class position. For the most part, dominant-caste individuals I interviewed claimed that there were no tensions and that things were fine in the village. Subordinate and Dalit caste individuals I interviewed told me the opposite.

On the appointed court date, Komal and the supporting witnesses all turned hostile against the public prosecutor who was representing them. An earlier attorney who had initially helped them file the case had accepted their decision to compromise, but had not wanted to participate further and had passed the case to a public prosecutor to handle in court. On the day of the trial, Komal changed her story and denied that the four accused men had raped her. Her brother echoed her revised claim, saying that he did not know anything and relied on his sister's recollection of the incident. The prosecutor then requested to cross-examine Komal and argued that she, as the state's witness, had turned hostile. When he asked her why she was now contradicting her initial statement charging the four men with rape, Komal responded that her statement had been taken under false pretenses and that the police had made her sign on a blank piece of paper on which her statement was later written.

Dalit activists and several reports of police misconduct document that the police take down statements without the knowledge and endorsement of victims. This is also one of the "scripts" of rape. I want to be clear that by pointing to these scripts, I do not mean to suggest that they are necessarily false or incorrect statements. Rather, I want to stress that they are strategies, based on thick layers of empirical evidence collected over many years, that resonate when they are recounted. I am trying to be alert to what this resonance does in particular spaces and who it serves. In cases of rape involving dominant-caste men and Dalit women, for instance, if charges are filed then Jat members of the village pressure subordinate castes to compromise the case. Scripts such as "statements recorded under pressure" or "tactics of compromise forced onto those in subordinate positions" appear with such frequency that they are recognizable to the courts and to attorneys and activists as strategies that are frequently deployed to favor those who are powerful. The fact that these scripts are tacitly recognized by institutions like the police and courts does not, however, necessarily mean that they are challenged by the authorities. It remains ambiguous if Komal's family experienced pressure to compromise, or if her statement followed a script to make their case. By speaking with members of the *basti* (neighborhood) and those at the scale of the "home" that some of these issues and tensions were revealed.

Sympathy, Suspicion, and Fear: Scale of the Basti *and Home*

Dalit bastis are usually relegated to the outer edges of the village. Most homes are very poor and few families, if any, own farmland. Dalits usually work in the fields of *zamindar*s (landowners) or take land on *theka* (loan), with a few families farming it together. While the Dalit *basti* was physically separated from the rest of the dominant-caste homes in the villages I visited, some bastis were also divided by subcastes. In these intimate domains, the narrative of rape navigated between sympathy, suspicion, and fear. For the members of the Dalit *basti*, when the case was about the rape of a Dalit girl by members of the dominant caste, the script revealed their effort to traverse a delicate balance. On the one hand, they attempted to inoculate themselves against the scandal, and on the other, to express sympathy and anger over the violation of one of their own. But their efforts were always tempered by a calculus that forced them to consider their structural subordination to the dominant caste on whom they had to depend for their livelihood.

I spoke with elders in the Dalit *basti*, some of whom held positions in the district or block and were even members of the panchayat. These elders navigated between their position in the bureaucracy and their sympathy with their caste *biradri* (community). At times, such as with Vineeta's case in Matpur, elders were quite uniformly reserved and suspicious. In contrast, concerning Komal's case in Jaswadi, while some members of the *basti* were circumspect and reticent, some demonstrated anger and sympathy, while others tried to distance themselves from the scandal. While the script in the *basti* was varied, in the home, for both young women—Komal and Vineeta—the script was primarily concerned with the family's loss of *izzat* (reputation). Consequently, the home was, for the girls, a space of violence and threats. In the intimate domain of the home, the rape charge made these women more vulnerable to threats from members of their own families.

The Dalit basti in Jaswadi is large, trespassed with a network of narrow winding gullies. The tall boundary walls of homes on either side of these gullies offered a modicum of relief from the hot sun. It was a very hot day in early June when around twelve women from the Dalit *basti* gathered for a conversation with me.[19] They all knew each other, and the intimacy of their intermingled lives was evident in their banter and familiarity with each other's families and homes. Children and babies filtered in and out of the room while we talked, and older women soothed and admonished the children when needed, regardless of whether they were related or not. The conversation was animated and began with some of the older women saying that things were better now than before, because the *bahus* (daughters-in-law) have more say and better status, and because they now eat better. Met with laughter and humor, they talked about their hopes for their children, and in particular, their hope that their children not follow them in *kheti* (farming).

One of them, an older, middle-aged woman, said that she used to be the sarpanch in the village and continued to work for the village even after her term ended. When women are made sarpanch their title is often only symbolic, and an older male family member usually does the actual work, primarily because the work involves activities not considered appropriate for women, like being in public and meeting male members of the village and district bureaucracy. Women's involvement in such public matters is considered shameful and is discouraged. When I asked if there was *bhaichara* or brotherhood, usually meant to indicate a sense of community between Dalits and Jats, they replied that there was *chai paani* (tea-water), meaning that they would have tea or water in each other's homes, but nothing beyond that. They said that the Jats brought them *roti* (flattened bread) to eat when they worked on their farms as *dehadi* (day laborers), but that there was no *aana jaana* (coming and going) from each other's homes. As the conversation progressed, they opened-up more and told me that while there was no active conflict between them and Jats, the Jats didn't want Dalits to progress, because if they did, then "gobar utthane ka kaam kaun karega" (who will pick up cow dung)? While it falls mainly on Dalits to pick up the dung that is made into patties and used as cooking fuel, the phrase is colloquially used to indicate how Dalits are kept in subordinate positions.

While their collective sense of subordination and struggle lent itself to a common language, tensions within the *basti* were revealed when we asked directly about Komal's case. The women gathered shuffled about, getting ready to leave and resume their work, saying, "Hum ko kya pat ji chedkhani hui ya na hui, hum toh bahar rava haan" (How do we know if she was molested, we were outside). This claim of being "outside" was not only about their spatial distance from the incident, but was also an effort to mark a certain social distance to shield themselves from the taint that followed it. One of the women pointed out that Komal's house was away in the corner, saying, in a dismissive manner, "Inka aakhri ghar se" (Theirs is the last house), and suggesting that Komal and her family were distant from others in the *basti*. They then said, "Badnami toh hui uh ki" (Reputation was sullied). While they expressed sympathy for Komal because she did not have a mother, it was clear that there was discomfort in talking about the incident. They lamented the fact that she would have to deal with this *saare umar* (her whole life). But they also said, "Hamar koi na aana jaani" (There is no coming and going to their place); in other words, they would keep Komal and her family at bay, and would not welcome a close relationship with them. Their effort to distance themselves from the incident was because it was tarnished with *badnami*, a loss of reputation, from which they wished to protect themselves. The intertwined proximity of lives in the village requires that alliances and distances are carefully calibrated against the taint of scandal, particularly so as not to jeopardize the relationships with dominant castes on whom Dalits depend for livelihood.

In Matpur, where Vineeta's case occurred, a different set of concerns were articulated. I met with a group of men Sunil had introduced me to. Sitting under an open shed with a fan that circulated hot air, I was invited into a conversation with them. Four to five men were gathered; all of them were either Dalit or OBC. These public gatherings of men who came together at a bus shelter or under a tree or at a shed, to play cards and to chat, were ubiquitous across the villages I visited. No women gathered in public in the same way; instead, they would get together in homes like the women in Jaswadi. An articulate and opinionated man at this gathering was a respected elder in the village. He commanded attention and was deferred to by others throughout our hour-long conversation. It is at gatherings like these that the discourse of what is acceptable, correct, and false is debated and established. It was here that the script was formed.

The men spoke generally about conditions in the village and what had changed, pointing particularly to the lack of *sharam*. Meaning bashfulness, the word in this context was deployed to express a dense constellation of concerns, including adversely changing social mores, gender trouble, and loss of respect. The *tau* made this statement in the context of a broader conversation about increasing numbers of relationships between boys and girls. He said "Dekho taali ek haat se toh nahi bajti" (See, one cannot clap with one hand), alleging that charges of sexual violation stem from relationships in which the boy and the girl indulge *raazi khushi* (through their own choice).

This was the script of rape that the gathering of men had constructed and agreed on, claiming that most stories alleging rape are in fact stories of *sehmti* (consent) that end in compromise, which is akin to *dukandari* (a business transaction). They disparaged compromise in ways that echoed the police officers I had met at the *mahila thanna*. As the conversation progressed, one of the other men sitting beside me said that it happened with his nephew when a girl from Rajasthan filed a case against him. He was now in judicial custody. The family from Rajasthan were migrants who worked at a brick kiln nearby when the boy and girl began a relationship. According to this man, the girl's parents forced her to file a case against his nephew so that they could extort money from the boy's family.

The men began to talk about how compromise often began at two to three lakhs and at times even went up to nine lakhs (approximately $4,000–$12,000). As our conversation proceeded, it was not clear if they were alluding to Vineeta's case or not. I knew that negotiations for compromise in her case were ongoing, with a settlement yet to be reached. I could not ask directly because outsiders asking about these issues, as I was, renders those in vulnerable positions—in this case, Vineeta and her parents—even more precarious. I needed to tread carefully as concerns about *izzat*, which our questions could impact, were central to how these matters would unfold or be resolved. The importance of izzat was most clearly articulated when the *tau* underscored that, after the exchange of money in compromise cases, "izzat toh nahi aati wapis" (reputation is not restored). Concern with the reputation of the caste *basti* was also echoed in the home, when Vineeta's father accused both his wife and Vineeta of having affairs and admonished them for bringing ruin to their family.

While Komal did not face this kind of suspicion from her father and brothers, her *tau* represented a persistent threat. One morning while we were on our way to speak with a government official, a lawyer-activist called us to say that Komal, her brothers, and her brother's wife (*bhabhi*) had been severely beaten up by her *tau*. We rushed to meet them at the local civil hospital. They arrived with blood streaming down their faces and soaking their clothes and were taken immediately to the emergency room. There they were treated for gashes on their heads and were told that in order to file a complaint of assault they would need a medical-legal report from the medical facility near their village, a forty-five-minute drive from the hospital. Despite our efforts to have the medical-legal report generated right there at the civil hospital, they were refused because of recently enforced jurisdiction laws regarding such cases. After we went and got the medical-legal report we came back to the civil hospital, where Komal and her injured relatives were finally admitted for overnight care. Later that evening, Dalit activists and lawyers arrived to help Komal and recorded their statements to file a complaint of assault against their *tau*. We were concerned for the young sister-in-law, who at that time was five months pregnant and had been kicked in the stomach in the attack by the uncle.

When we asked why he had beaten them up, Komal and her brothers said that they had experienced violence from him since they were young, and their father was ineffective protection because he was usually drunk and often absent. They explained that the *tau* was in a protracted dispute with their father over a small plot of land that was jointly owned by the two of them and the rest of their siblings. The uncle wanted Komal's father to give up his share of the land and let the uncle have the land title in his name alone (I detail some of this dispute in chapter 3).

A few days later, when Komal and her brothers were discharged from the hospital, they were reluctant to return to the village because their uncle had threatened to kill them if they came back. It took intervention by some of us to facilitate their return. We went to the deputy police commissioner to plead their case and to ask them to provide protection for Komal and her injured family. We learned the next day that the *tau* was taken to the police station overnight, following which he approached Komal's father and "naak ragad ke maafi mangi" (he rubbed his nose on the ground and begged for forgiveness). But a few months after the incident, the *tau* filed a case in retaliation against Komal's father and brother, claiming that they had molested his daughter. These threats and counterthreats generated a profoundly stressful situation in the home. When I visited Komal a few months later she was happy about her young niece, who was born unharmed despite her uncle's earlier attack, and participated in her care. But this contentment would not last. Her *tau* continued to harass them all, and the threat of violence was never far away. Her brother, concerned for his young daughter and wife, soon decided to leave the village and move to the city. For Komal, this meant that she would yet again be alone at home and vulnerable to violence from her uncle.

In both Vineeta's and Komal's case, the threat of violence hung over the women in the intimate setting of their homes and neighborhoods, and the ongoing rape cases intensified their vulnerability tremendously. What did compromise of their cases mean to them? As I turn to the personal narratives of Vineeta, Komal, and Savatri, I consider compromise as refusal and ask, What does the refusal to file charges allow them to reclaim?

Intimate Violence: Scale of the Body

Writing about rape from the perspectives of those in the village, police officers and attorneys, and even members of the *basti*, allowed for a distance in talking about intimate violation. That distance was erased when we spoke with the victims directly. These conversations were most challenging, tenuous, and incomplete. My concerns about retraumatizing victims or making them feel like I was prying made me hold back. The very significant differences in power between us made me conscious of how my questions might make those in subordinate positions feel pressured to respond. Consequently, I often hesitated and asked questions that were open-ended and exploratory, instead of pointed and probing. While I repeatedly told the women I interviewed that they did not have to answer my questions and that I could stop asking them if they wanted me to, I was aware that my very presence generated a heightened level of risk for them. Associating with an outsider and researcher asking about the incidents could upset their families and communities, concerned, as we have seen them to be, about the impact these cases had on their honor and reputation. The last thing I wanted to do was to increase the pressure, to say nothing of threats and worse, that the women I interviewed felt at home, in their communities, or beyond.

These challenges were compounded because many of the victims I met were Dalit or OBC. While the activists or lawyers who sometimes accompanied me were themselves Dalit, this did not attenuate differences in power. These concerns made selecting those with whom I could speak extremely circumscribed. All the victims and survivors of rape I met had already been in conversation with activists and lawyers, and it was with these activists and lawyers that I initially went to meet them and their families.

The conversation with victims began with the activists recalling their last meeting, which was usually in the aftermath of the incident. I would then introduce myself, explaining what I was doing and where I was from. These initial conversations were open-ended and broad-ranging discussions rather than interviews about the incident. I would then explain my research and ask for permission to return. In those early meetings we would talk about school, *kheti* (farming), or any aspect of their lives other than the rape case. It was only after many subsequent meetings that we would broach the subject of the case. These conversations emerged in different ways: sometimes the victims talked about their case themselves, at other times it came up in the context of another incident, and on occasion we tentatively asked them about their case. In a few of these encounters, I decided against pursuing further conversation after meeting with the victim and her family, because I felt continuing would cause undue distress.

At this intimate scale, the script of rape differed from other scales and mobilized very different concerns. It is at this intimate scale that I draw most directly on Audra Simpson's (2014) work to ask, What if we see compromise not as a failure—of the case to move through the legal apparatus—but as refusal? What would that allow? In conversations with the victims, I tease out how refusal can be generative of autonomy and an effort at seeking sovereignty. In theorizing Indigenous sovereignty, Simpson writes, "Refusal comes with the requirement of having one's *political* sovereignty acknowledged and upheld, and raises the question of legitimacy for those who are usually in the position of recognizing: what is their authority to do so? Where does it come from? Who are they to do so?" (11, emphasis in original).

Simpson is concerned with the Mohawks of Kahnawà:ke who refuse to belong to either the United States or Canada and insist on the sovereignty of their nation. She is theorizing refusal in order to understand it as an alternative to "recognition" (11). There are vast differences between the refusal expressed by Indigenous communities, of jurisdiction by settler colonial states, and the women I spoke with. Yet I draw on Simpson's work because it allows me to understand and theorize refusal as key to the formation of subjectivities. I understand refusal as an effort by a subject to renegotiate their relationship with law and courts, village councils and elders, domestic patriarchy, and even activists. Among Savatri, Vineeta, and Komal I see refusal as a political stance and an attempt at navigating their subjectivity and autonomy (McGranahan 2016a, 334). I read in each of their refusals a claiming of space and autonomy that "can be generative and strategic, a deliberate move toward one thing, practice, or community and away from another" (McGranahan 2016b, 319). I will have more to say about recognition and refusal in the concluding chapter of the book.

Savatri, whose daughter was one of four girls raped in Bhagana, explained her decision after she and other families returned as a way to deal with the limited choices that victims and their families were left with in the wake of the rape case and the unsuccessful political mobilizations that followed to demand accountability. For Vineeta, the story of compromise unfolds as a consequence of her expression of jurisdiction over her body. And finally, for Komal, the story of compromise allows her to gain some control over the narrative of rape that had been dominated by her uncle. In each case, at the scale of the body, the script is about the struggle over sovereignty and autonomy.

In Bhagana, Matpur, and Jaswadi, meeting with the victims was only possible when they continued to reside in the villages or remained in touch with activists and lawyers. In many instances, after they got married, women severed ties with the groups that had initially helped them with their cases, because dredging up the incident generated tensions and problems for them in their marital homes. In Bhagana, two of the four young women in the rape case had left the village after their marriages and had not remained in contact with activists. While we did not meet with them, their mothers spoke with us on their behalf. Savatri, one of these mothers, insisted that the "do ladkiyo ne kar liya phaisla," two girls, decided. She was referring to the other two women who were involved in the case besides her daughter. When Arun asks why she agreed to the compromise, alleging that she participated in the dismissal of the case, she forcefully responds by saying, "Phaisla nahi kiya, apne aap sarkar ne chordh diya" (We did not compromise, the government stopped supporting us). Savatri makes a distinction here between the allegation that they compromised because of coercion versus what she claims was abandonment by the state.

Her narrative contrasts with activists and lawyers who claim that "charo ladkiyo ne gawahai theek se nahi de" (all four girls did not give their testimony properly) because of "dabav from dabangs" (coercion from powerful men). Savatri, however, recounted, "Do ladkiyo ne uh kaha ki ladko ka koi kasoor nahi, mei meri salah te gaye the, bayan palat diya" (Two girls said that the boys are innocent and that they went of their will, they changed their testimony).[20] Speaking of the pain of the long fight that she and her family had to endure, she said, "Un ladko ko koi saza nahi mile, hum ne ghani sunai" (Those boys were not punished, but we had to bear a lot). She also said that they kept fighting even after two of the four girls agreed to the compromise, but finally gave up because the *sarkar* (government) also gave up on them. When activists insisted that she should have continued to fight, she said, "Haamari badnami hogi" (Our reputation will be ruined).

In this comment, Savatri most directly expresses the constraints of her position that circumscribe her choices. In the manner in which she navigated her limitations I read a deliberate disengagement, which is also a kind of refusal. She explained her disengagement as stemming from her need to arrange a marriage for another daughter. If she were to accrue more reputational damage by continuing to participate in the struggle, it would be very difficult for her to arrange a successful marriage for her other daughter. At one point in the conversation, she lamented, "Hum aakele reh gaye" (We have been isolated). This sense of being abandoned, along with the feeling of being forced to stay in the village because of a lack of other options, were two themes which emerged repeatedly in my conversations with the mothers who returned to Bhagana. For many families the village was not a welcoming place, but it was the only place they could go back to for their livelihoods and survival.

In responding to Arun's allegations that she had compromised and been unwilling to continue to fight, Savatri enacted two forms of refusal. First, in challenging Arun's narrative that she and the other families had agreed to compromise their case, she insisted that they were cast aside by the state which no longer supported them. Refusal, Carol McGranahan (2016a) writes, "is a political stance. It is an effort, at least minimally, to redefine or redirect certain outcomes or expectations or relationships" (334). In redirecting the narrative, Savatri claimed an autonomy usually denied to those impacted by rape cases. She refused to acquiesce to the story that the compromise was the fault of the girls who had been raped and their families, and instead sought to shift the responsibility for failing to secure accountability to the state, by which she felt betrayed.

The second way Savatri refused was by disengaging with the ongoing struggle for accountability in order to refocus her energy on rebuilding and bettering her life in the village. The families from Bhagana that had gone to Delhi after initial mobilizations for justice had since returned. Amid this fight for some modicum of justice there had been a split, with some families agreeing to the compensation offered by the government, brokered by a set of Dalit lawyers. This decision had generated some discord between Dalit groups in and beyond Bhagana. Even though the incident and agreement to accept compensation had occurred four years ago, tensions continued to simmer. These differences were about strategy; while some Dalit groups wanted the families to continue to fight, as many had in Bhagana, others considered the implications of a prolonged standoff, which severely impacted the livelihoods of the families involved. For Savatri and others, the refusal to continue alongside those still fighting was an effort to shield themselves and their families from further *badnami* (humiliation), and an effort to rebuild their lives.

In *Mohawk Interruptus* Audra Simpson asked, "What happens when we refuse what all 'sensible' people perceive as good things?" (2014, 1). Savatri's refusal to continue to engage in the struggle, as activists like Arun would like her to, reveals her effort to reconstruct her life under conditions of severely circumscribed choices. For Savatri, refusal was a move away from continuing to fight and toward rebuilding her and her family's life in a village she cannot leave. Vineeta's case generated a dilemma for activists who were at a loss for a language with which to talk about the relationship between a Dalit girl and a Jat boy. The history of the exploitation and violation of Dalit girls in Haryana by the dominant caste had been the script of rape. How then does one name Vineeta's affair with a Jat boy against an overwhelming history of abuse in such intercaste relationships? The predominant frame for understanding such consensual sexual relationships is to name them rape. But can they be understood as rape? What veracity can be accorded to Vineeta's story, as she conceives of it herself? Where does her subjectivity matter in this instance? When we heard of cases like Vineeta's in which women are forced to file a rape charge, we sought to understand what such charges may mean. Vineeta's story was much more subversive than just an act of defiance against conservative village codes. It was, I suggest, about an expression of sovereignty.

There are layers to Vineeta's story: her disobedient act of having an affair with a Jat boy from the village; being forced to file a rape charge against her lover; the subsequent compromise that her parents and village elders orchestrate; and her regret when Pradeep is charged with rape and relief when he is freed from judicial custody. The compromise generated an unexpected alignment between the outcome Vineeta wanted, which was to let her lover go, and the intentions of her parents and village elders. But the common ground reached between them about her case was not however an acknowledgment of her sovereignty by her parents or elders because while she was happy about the outcome, she was never in a position to refuse the compromise either. But in refusing to press charges against her lover as human rights lawyers and activists wanted her to, Vineeta strayed from the script and constructed a different subjectivity. The script was unable to accommodate someone who chose a dominant-caste lover and hadn't been raped by him. On the surface, Vineeta's refusal to press charges looked like a concession to village and other patriarchal authorities, but as we have seen, a closer look shows us that it was in line with her subjectivity as a woman who chose this unsanctioned affair and refused to repent for having defied strong patriarchal codes by asserting her sexual sovereignty.

We last met with Vineeta on a warm winter afternoon. She had called earlier and said that she wanted to talk with us about college options. It had been several months since the compromise, and Pradeep had been freed from custody.[21] Vineeta did not know if her parents had received the money from the settlement. In the months leading up to the compromise, Vineeta confessed that she had felt bad that Pradeep was in detention. She expressed her regret by talking about the time she regained consciousness in the hospital. She says, "Jab mere ko hosh aaya teen din baad, toh jo vakil tha na, us time vakil ne kaha bhai yeah yeah bayan dena hai aap ne, tab agar mei sahi hosh mei thi, tab mai byaan nahi daan di" (When I regained consciousness three days later, the lawyer told me this is what I have to say in my testimony. If I was fully conscious then, I would not have given that testimony). We asked again to make sure what she was saying: "Jo vakil ne bola aap ne wohi bola?" (Did you give the testimony that the lawyer asked?). She replied, "Yes I said what the lawyer asked me to say." She then said, "Puri baat bataye vakil ne . . . gadi ki baat bhi . . . mere gaddi ki koi who na thi ki gaddi mei le gaye" (The lawyer constructed the narrative, including about the car, that they took me in a car . . . they did not take me in a car).

As she spoke about regretting the testimony she had given, Vineeta expressed being troubled by her role in putting Pradeep in judicial custody. But as our conversation persisted, she made clear that she was not interested in rekindling her relationship with him. Her complicated and nuanced articulation of her story with Pradeep demonstrated how she conveyed her sexual subjectivity. Consider, for instance, what Vineeta said when we asked if she had heard from Pradeep after he was freed. She said that he had called a few days ago and asked her why she was not speaking with him. Her response had been, "Zindagi ek baar toh ho gaye aur bhi ghani barbaad kari ni ho toh besti karwah le mei toh nah kari apni zindagi kharab" (Life has already been ruined, if you want to do even more, then do it; I don't want to ruin my life). Vineeta's relationship with Pradeep generated considerable acrimony within her home. While she did not regret her affair, she was nevertheless troubled by all the rancor and animosity surrounding it. Her frustration with Pradeep formed in the wake of the derogatory comments and anger she had been forced to bear while he had in the main been spared from such reproaches. She told us that she had heard that he had left the village and moved to Delhi. She knew there was no possibility of marrying him because of strict rules against intercaste and endogamous marriages.

Vineeta's refusal emerged in a couple of ways. First, it emerged when she refused established village codes prohibiting intercaste relationships and defiantly forged an affair with Pradeep despite them. Second, Vineeta refused the disciplining injunction to repent and self-isolate that the shame and stigma of her affair generated when it was discovered, by continuing her illicit relationship and later by seeking to go to college rather than being shamed into falling back in line and agreeing to get married. By refusing existing sanctions and efforts to shame and discipline her, Vineeta established jurisdiction over her body. Vineeta's defiance of patriarchal authority over her body and her life was, as we've seen, intolerable to her father and to other authorities in her village invested in protecting the status quo.

The anger and backlash Vineeta faced from her family and community underscored the refusal she enacted: the refusal to be disciplined by shame. When we last met Vineeta that winter afternoon, she said that she was being pressured to get married and that there was talk in the *basti* of quickly finding her a *rishta* (marriage alliance). In chapter 1, I recounted how both community elders and Vineeta's father believed that the funds from compromising her rape case should be used to arrange her marriage—or, in effect, to quash her defiance of their authority and to reassert their patriarchal jurisdiction over her body. The arrangement they sought is a common strategy for disciplining the straying woman back into patrilineal forms of control and exchange. But by defying their dictate to get married and instead seeking college options, Vineeta rejected the disciplining shame she was subjected to. I see her father's rage as a response to her refusal to be disciplined by shame, and as a response to her disobedience of his patriarchal authority. However, months later, despite wanting to go to college, Vineeta was still unable to fulfill her wish to leave the village. We see that refusal does not signify an unchanging agentic position, but rather, that it constitutes a terrain of ongoing struggle.

Vineeta's sexual subjectivity is evident in her clarity around not being interested in rekindling her relationship with Pradeep while also vehemently defending her affair. Her dual positions demonstrate her sovereignty in making decisions that she knew to be risky and illicit. She further demonstrates autonomy when she attempts to defy her father and village elders by expressing her intent to continue studying rather than to get married. Allowing ourselves to understand compromise as a strategy that can destabilize existing patriarchal norms through the act of refusal generates the possibility of excavating subjectivities that might otherwise remain obscure.

Both Vineeta and Komal agreed to dropping rape charges and to settling out of court, even though neither was allowed to participate in the negotiations that led to compromise in their cases. I understood why Vineeta had wanted to drop the case filed against her former lover, who had never assaulted her, but I was perplexed by why Komal so vehemently insisted that the four boys accused of raping her should be set free. Unlike Vineeta, Komal had, after all, been assaulted. One day Komal cleared up my confusion, and explained why she wanted the boys to go free.

We saw Komal about a week after she, her brother, and her brother's wife had returned from the hospital to the village under police escort, when her *tau* had prostrated himself in front of them and apologized for assaulting them. He had been taken into police custody after we met with a senior police officer and told him the story, but had been released soon after. While seemingly chastened by his short experience with the police, he had come home. Since we knew that Komal's uncle was deeply involved in her rape case, we wanted to make sure that there would be no problems as the court date for her case approached. I also knew that there were discussions around compromise and was concerned that she was being coerced to drop charges and settle out of court. I had come to visit because I was on my way back to Delhi for a few days and wanted to make sure that things had settled down. It was early in the day, around ten in the morning, and when we reached her home the sun was already blisteringly hot.[22] We sat in one of the two rooms; there was no electricity, and the fan did not work. As we sat in the shade attempting to cool ourselves with hand fans, we asked about the case. Komal sat in front of us and said in a quiet voice, "Rape nahi hua" (I was not raped). We were surprised to hear her say this, and asked her to tell us what she meant.

As she began to recall the incident, her eyes brimmed with tears and her voice cracked. She said that the boys had come to ask after her brother. She was home from school for lunch and told them that her brother was away in college. She offered to give them his number so they could call him. Her uncle saw her talking to the boys with a phone in her hand, forced her inside, and began to beat her. Home alone that day, with his wife and daughter out, he dragged Komal's slight body into the house, and then, as Komal recounted while sobbing, he dragged her up to the loft. Once there, he took a thick stick, from a particular kind of bush with thorns, and struck her behind. Komal continued to describe the horror that unfolded: how her uncle proceeded to hit and punch her, before using the handle of a shovel to sodomize her. She said she lost consciousness and woke up several hours later in the local hospital, with her uncle right there in the room with her. He had already spoken with the doctors and told them that she had been raped by four boys.

The medical report reflected the story of rape as Komal's uncle had told it. Since it is often a male member of a girl's family who accompanies her to file a complaint, the uncle's version of the story had gone unquestioned. Komal described how circumstances would not allow her to say what had happened. For one, her uncle always made sure to be around when she was questioned about the assault. When the father of one of the boys came to ask what had happened and asked if he could speak with Komal, Komal's uncle had threatened to hurt him. Before Komal and her uncle went to speak with a lawyer, he threatened her with more violence and warned her to repeat the story exactly as he had told her to. Since then, whenever Komal had tried to tell anyone the truth, her uncle had threatened to beat her. She feared him, and so did others. When she sought refuge by going to stay with her aunt, her uncle repeatedly called and threatened her aunt and her family. The threats reached such a peak that Komal was eventually sent back home.

When talk about a *shamjauta* was initiated, Komal was eager to settle the case because, as she told me, "uh ladko ka koi kasoor nahi hai" (the boys are not at fault). When I asked if her lawyer knew about this, she said that she had tried to tell him several times and that he knew the boys were not responsible, but he did not know the specifics because she had felt too embarrassed to tell him the gory details. Komal's insistence on compromise was an enactment of refusal that allowed her to preserve some autonomy over how the violation of her body was used. She did not want to let anyone use the violation of her body to build a case that would keep four innocent boys in detention and that could then send them to prison. She had been most distressed that her assault had been deployed to falsely accuse and detain four boys. In agreeing to the compromise, Komal undermined her uncle's efforts to blame other people for the terrible harm he had caused, while also getting away with his crime. Her refusal defied the violence that his manufactured accusations were inflicting on others. Her refusal allowed her to recuperate autonomy and jurisdiction away from her uncle and back to herself. Komal's story illustrates how important it is to accord her and other victims of assault the capacity to make decisions regarding their cases, rather than assume that others know better or have better judgment.

And yet despite the ways in which Komal was able to claim some autonomy in her narrative, it is significant that she did not understand her uncle's assault as rape, and only talked about the case lodged against the four men as false. When I saw her a few months after the compromise, after she had given testimony in court refuting the assault, she looked like a large burden had been lifted from her. She smiled more, and as we walked through the *basti* to the main road, she stopped to greet her neighbors and introduced me to a friend, telling me she was close to her and wanted me to meet her. Komal looked so very different than the last time I had seen her, and I was relieved to see her more at ease. As we walked back, I asked her how things were with her uncle, and she said that she had not had any contact with him. When I asked her again if she agreed with the compromise and if there had been any pressure on her to accept it, she repeated that the boys were not to blame.

Her evident relief stemmed from the possibility that through the compromise she could wrest a measure of control over the outcome of the incident away from her uncle and back to herself. Through the case and its subsequent compromise, Komal's sexual subjectivity emerged in the complex mix of her relief that the case was over and that the wrongly accused boys were free, her perplexing understanding of the assault by her uncle as something other than rape, and her investment and pleasure in being thought of as a "good girl" by the women in the village. If we understand her compromise as a rebuttal, then we can apprehend Komal's refusal "as genealogically linked to resistance, but not as one and the same" (McGranahan 2016b, 320).

DILEMMAS AND PREDICAMENTS IN COMPROMISE

Komal's case and subsequent compromise resulted in dilemmas and complicated predicaments for Dalit lawyers and activists supporting her case. They were keenly aware of their tenuous position in the legal apparatus and worked tremendously hard to get just outcomes for Dalit victims. So when some of their clients wanted to compromise their cases, it generated immense dilemmas for them. Since compromise is illegal in cases of rape, and since it is a mechanism that is often used by dominant-caste perpetrators to force their victims to drop charges and settle for a monetary payment out of court, lawyers were hesitant to touch it. However, dilemmas occurred when, in particular cases, a compromise was the most just outcome available within the limited possibilities. As we have seen, in cases like Komal's, where, according to her, the four accused men were wrongfully implicated, a compromise was a better outcome than pressing forward to convict innocent people—but it was one in which Dalit lawyers could not participate. The long history of Dalit victims being coerced to compromise in cases where the accused belongs to a dominant caste made Dalit lawyers and activists hesitant—if not outright against—this culture of compromise.

When cases are settled outside the courts it means that the accused are exonerated, and that no one is held accountable for the crime. It also means that the strategy of compromise, which so often serves a coercive elite, is reinforced. Even in cases like Komal's, where compromise allowed four innocent men to walk free, the use of the strategy reinforced it for use in other cases where it will function to coerce victims and help real perpetrators evade accountability. When Komal decided to compromise some of the Dalit activists tried to discourage her, primarily because, informed by too many real precedents, they believed that she was being pressured by the dominant-caste allies of the accused boys to drop her charges. Even if they had known that she wanted to compromise because the boys charged had never hurt her, and because though she could not name her real attacker, she at least wanted the innocent boys to be free, supporting her decision to compromise would have been difficult for them.

Similarly, when Vineeta's parents agreed to a compromise, the Dalit lawyers had to leave the case and let a public prosecutor take over. Compromise, even if it functioned to let an innocent man like her ex-lover Pradeep off the hook, created an impossible conflict and dilemma for Dalit lawyers. Some could not be sure that Vineeta had not been coerced into accepting a compromise, that her case was in fact not a case of dominant castes violating a Dalit woman and getting away with it by pressuring her to drop charges. But again, even if they knew that she wasn't coerced and wanted to drop charges because they were wrongfully targeting her ex-lover to mitigate her family's reputational harm, they could not have stood by her agreement to a strategy that is too often used to harm the most vulnerable victims of crime.

In my conversations with activists and lawyers about these dilemmas, they said that while they understood the range of reasons why compromise might occur, they all deeply opposed the practice. Besides their reasons for opposing compromise discussed earlier, they also stressed that their cases only very rarely reached the courts, and that when they did, they represented an important possibility of justice for the community at large. They therefore considered it very damaging to take on clients who might suddenly agree or acquiesce to a compromise, as their compromise would undermine the rare opportunity to fight for justice. These activists and lawyers pointed out that when a case is compromised, particularly in favor of a dominant-caste person who has been accused of a crime, a system of injustice is reinforced, strengthening dominant-caste beliefs that more powerful castes can always evade accountability and emboldening dominant castes to coerce more vulnerable people into drop any charges they have against them.

These lawyers and activists also stressed that compromise cases jeopardized the already precarious position that Dalit lawyers had in court, a position they had worked so hard to establish and improve. They explained that while police officers and attorneys knew that rape cases were frequently compromised for a range of reasons, they specifically viewed compromise in cases filed by Dalit and other subordinate-caste victims as evidence of corruption. In other words, the authorities had a script about Dalits that saw them as prone to filing false allegations against dominant-caste individuals in order to extort money from those individuals in exchange for dropping charges. The superintendent of police at one of the districts I visited made this clear when he alleged that 90 percent of Scheduled Caste and Backward Caste (SCBC) victims compromised the cases in which they are involved, and that they did so for self-interested reasons that had nothing to do with being coerced by dominant castes.[23]

While activists and lawyers concerned with Dalit rights had good reason to oppose compromised out-of-court settlements, they faced a dilemma in cases like Komal's, in which the accused were not guilty of the crime, and in which having to go along with falsely implicating them generated tremendous torment for Komal herself. As discussed, a related dilemma arises in Vineeta's case, which was not a case of rape, but a case in which her family insisted on filing a rape charge to mitigate the impact of Vineeta's unsanctioned—and in their eyes shameful—sexual autonomy. What is to be done in these cases? What would just outcomes look like? When Savatri in Bhagana did not want to continue with her case because she was tired of fighting and felt abandoned, what would it mean to ask her to refuse a compromise and to continue fighting for the sake of community justice?

CONCLUSION

In 2016, the Supreme Court issued a judgment in an appeal of *Ramesh and Others v. the State of Haryana*. The accused had been convicted by the lower Sessions Court for murder, for collaborating and conspiring to conduct criminal acts, and for subjecting a wife to cruelty. The Sessions Court had sentenced the men to life in prison, and the High Court had confirmed this sentence by rejecting their appeal. When their final appeal was heard all the way up in the Supreme Court in 2016, Justice Sikri made a special mention of compromise in his ruling. He argued that compromise as a consequence of intimidation was an ongoing issue plaguing criminal cases in India, particularly because the length of time between filing a complaint and having it appear as a case before trial was often three or four years. In the interim period, those in weaker positions of power were often intimidated into compromising the case and setting the perpetrators free. Presiding over this case, Justice Sikri rejected the appeal by the four men who had conspired to kill a woman who had been subjected to violence and cruelty her whole life. In recognizing the intimidating tactics often employed by those in power to force their victims to drop charges, his ruling specifically mentioned the need for the state to take responsibility and establish a witness protection program.

It was challenging to meet trial court judges who would talk with me, but the few who I did meet made clear that they were very aware of compromise in their courts and made efforts to guard against it. Their tactics included asking witnesses if they were being coerced and threatening to charge them with false testimony when they suddenly went against their original statements. They told me that their efforts to guard against coerced compromises emerged primarily in their cases dealing with crimes against women, as intimidation of women and their families by those in positions of power had become commonplace.

While some of the compromise cases I followed may have become a sort of *dhandha* (business transaction), other compromise cases involved complex stories that could not be reduced to efforts to extract financial gain. As many legal scholars have demonstrated, the law often reinforces a phallocentric, hierarchical social order rather than meaningfully serve the interests of justice and meaningfully reduce harm. So when extrajudicial strategies like out-of-court compromises are used by a village community to resolve conflicts, it is important to attend to the harm that these strategies perpetuate, while also paying attention to the possibilities that they generate that would not be available through the courts as they are currently structured.

These moments of possibility that panchayats facilitate through their out-of-court compromise settlements make apparent what the law currently makes impossible. While it remains indisputable that most plaintiffs agree to compromise their cases after facing threats, intimidation, and coercion to pressure them to drop charges, what happens when compromise allows for a woman like Komal to reclaim some control over the story of her assault by freeing four men who were wrongly implicated in a crime they did not commit? In Komal's case, justice was partially served in the compromise that freed those men. Compromise also freed Komal from the distress she felt from having her assault used to keep four innocent men behind bars. But the compromise in her case also left justice incomplete because her uncle, who perpetrated the brutal assault against her, remained both unnamed and free. In Vineeta's case, we see how compromise can be a tool to resolve certain conflicts that arise from socially prohibited intercaste relationships. When these consensual but sanctioned relationships are discovered, false rape charges are, with some frequency, filed by the woman's family in order to mitigate the reputational harm that her perceived impropriety casts over them. Compromise becomes a way to perform the theatrics of violation while knowing that such a breach did not take place. In Vineeta's example, the drama of the rape case in court, and the subsequent compromise out-of-court, allowed her family to restore their *izzat*, which had been damaged by what they perceived as Vineeta's impropriety. It also allowed her lover Pradeep, who was innocent and who had not violated her, to be freed, as she herself wanted.

There are no easy answers to the story of compromise. I want to be clear: my intention here is not to advocate for or against compromise in rape cases. Instead, I suggest that paying close attention to stories of compromise, particularly in considering compromise as refusal, may reveal forms of autonomy that would otherwise remain obscured. How might such a consideration of compromise allow us to see different possibilities, for those most vulnerable, to recuperate sovereignty and exercise sexual subjectivity? At each scale, descending from the most bureaucratic to the most intimate—the police and legal apparatus, the district and village, the *basti*, home, and the victim herself—compromise means different things and allows for different outcomes.

Notably, violence is the ubiquitous force that wove through all the stories I traced and followed: not just the violence of profound poverty and caste politics, but also actual physical violence. Vineeta was beaten and abused by her family for daring to enact sovereignty over her body. Komal, who has been forced to endure many years of violence by her uncle, came to understand his horrendous act of violation as an extension of the lexicon of violence to which she had been forcefully habituated, and so could not differentiate what had happened to her as rape. The girls in Bhagana may or may not have been coerced to change their testimony, and the story of whether they were raped remains ambiguous. But regardless, they are now effectively silenced in their marital homes from speaking about what they endured; their marital homes shun discussion about their rape cases, which they view as shameful, and mean that the threat of physical and other forms of violence looms over the women.

Of all the stories that I researched, Komal's was the most heartbreaking. She was so young and, in so many ways, so fragile. She worked tremendously hard, as if she had to justify her existence by doing a lot of work around the home. It was both a joy to meet her as well as eviscerating to witness her story. Six months after the compromise in her case was finalized, I heard that Komal's marriage was being arranged. A prior marriage prospect had been ruined by her uncle, who had remained resentful of the compromise in her case and had threatened Komal, her family, and even her lawyer. When she was finally married, I spoke with her and her husband on the phone and was relieved to hear her sound happy. But like so much in her young life, that happiness was short-lived when, less than a year into her marriage, her brother's wife, with whom she was very close and who had just given birth to a little boy, died. Komal's niece and baby nephew were now living with their maternal grandparents, because given patriarchal marriage arrangements in which Komal had gone to live with her husband, only her father and younger brother were left at her previous home, and they could not take care of the children once their mother died.

This chapter, along with the one on consent that precedes it, investigated the forces set in motion once a rape case is filed and the consequences that follow such a filing. In both chapters, the story of land lurks in the backdrop. Vineeta's case ended in compromise only because Pradeep's family had access to land. Savatri felt that she had no other choice but to go back to the village, where her only source of income was work on Jat land. Even the brutal rape that Komal experienced at the hands of her uncle was linked to the fact that he wanted the small plot of land her father owned. To grapple with how land emerges over and over in these stories, the next chapter focuses on the political and economic terrain in which these cases of rape occur and looks at how structures of caste and land are profoundly intertwined.

3. Land

A network of National Highways connects Delhi to Punjab which pass through Haryana. Within a few miles of crossing the border at Bahadurgarh, the oppressive congestion of Delhi fades. Depending on the time of the year, both sides of the highway are vibrant with yellow *sarso* (mustard) fields or acres of tender green shoots of *dhan* (rice). Haryana is famous for its roadside *dhabbas* (local restaurants), which serve hearty local cuisine to travelers going north and west on these highways. A thriller Bollywood film, *NH10* (directed by Navdeep Singh, 2015), named after one such highway which passes through Haryana, is about a young couple that stops at one of these *dhabbas*. The film follows the story of this couple and their unexpected encounter with a young woman who pleads for their help against a gang of village men pursuing her and her lover. The couple is horrified to witness her murder in an honor killing, and when they attempt to intervene, both are assaulted and one of them is eventually killed. The grief and torment of these experiences propel the lead character, played by popular actress Anushka Sharma, to avenge the crimes by killing the men from the village. The film resonated with the dominant cultural imaginary of Haryana as a dangerous place that is hostile to women, a place where the rule of law is suspended and where justice can only be achieved through vengeance.

Mayyar Gaon is a village in Haryana located just off the highway, about three hours from the Delhi border. It's an unremarkable village, with semi-permanent structures and a few shops on either side of the highway, which cuts through the village. Passing through, one often sees men in white *kurta payjamas* gathered in conversation around a hookah or on tractors and bikes. This unremarkable village, however, is famous as the epicenter of Jat protests that have erupted each year since 2010. The Akhil Bharatiya Jat Arakshan Sangharsh Samiti (All India Jat Reservation Struggle Committee) has demanded reservation in government institutions and jobs under the Other Backward Classes (OBC) category, which would reserve up to 27 percent of seats in government jobs and educational institutions for Jats. As part of their protests, Jats from Mayyar blocked the highway and railways, significantly impacting trade and transport lines. In February 2016, just as I was initiating research for this book, the agitations demanding reservations suddenly turned violent. Highways were shut down, shops and buses were burned, hundreds were injured, and twenty people were killed. The army was called out to restore peace. A Dalit activist lawyer warned me that I should not come to Haryana then and should wait for the agitations to die down. When I arrived in Haryana in March the army was still stationed in some places, and signs of burnt shops and damaged homes were everywhere.

The Jat agitations chronicle a tale about entitlement, caste politics, and neoliberalism. They tell a complex story anchored in land and property relations. As I began my work in the shadow of these protests, the story of land kept popping up as I explored the social life of rape. I came to understand sexual violation as connected to these stories of land and crisis, sometimes directly and at other times tangentially. This chapter is about this interpolation. Following the first two chapters on consent and on compromise, I show that the consequences of a rape charge cannot fully be discerned unless we unpack how women's sexual subjectivity is tied to concerns with land and property in Haryana. I follow cases concerning sexual violence in four villages in Haryana: Bhagana, Jaswadi, Malud, and Rudhi. In each case, stories of compromise and consent reappear, and as I show, disputes over land are either directly or indirectly intertwined with each story. Sexual violation is on its surface not a story about land, but it is in fact almost always about land in some way. It is this paradox, of how the story of land was always present, but not in any linear causative manner, that I seek to unpack here.

This chapter is divided into two main sections: the first deals with changes in the political economy of a newly independent India and the impact these changes had on Haryana. It identifies crucial links between land, gender, and caste; links whose importance became very evident in the cases I followed. Divided into two parts, this section is anchored around two moments: the first from the 1950s and the Hindu Succession Act, and the second revolving around the current demand for Jat *aarakshan* (reservation) in the OBC category. The second section in this chapter follows cases of sexual violation and their imbrication with stories of land. This section is itself divided into three parts, concerning disputes over common land, social boycotts, and private land ownership.

POLITICAL ECONOMY OF HARYANA

"Zameen ko izzat maante hai" (Land is considered our honor/prestige).
—Uncle of sarpanch of Rudhi village

"Jab woh bebass ho jaat hai, tab hi soochta hai bechne ki" (Only when the farmer becomes desperate does he consider selling his land).
—Uncle of sarpanch of Rudhi village

"Zameen ko bahu beti maante hai" (Land is thought of as daughter-in-law and daughter).
—Station house officer of *mahila thanna*

These quotes reflect a ubiquitous narrative I heard in conversations with women and men in the villages I visited. For these people, who were mostly from dominant castes, land held a place of reverence. Jats own 80 percent of land in Haryana, with the remaining 20 percent distributed among other caste groups. Dalits are at the bottom of the hierarchy and own only 2 percent of the land. Unlike in Utter Pradesh, a neighboring state where Jats make up just over 2 percent of the population, in Haryana, they constitute 22 percent. Jats' relationships with their land have a long history; myths, stories, proverbs, and songs offer a rich repository of cultural narratives about land and its deep meaning within peasant life.

There are two political moments around which I organize the story of land in Haryana. The first is from the 1950s, when land ownership and tenancy laws in a newly independent India were changed as part of efforts to redistribute land. Of particular contention was the 1956 Hindu Succession Act, which governed the rights of inheritance. This law codified the rights of daughters, wives, and widows to inherit land. It led to tremendous ferment among landed peasant communities, which understood that solidifying women's rights to property would weaken patriarchal control over land, and by extension, over daughters and wives.

The second moment began with neoliberalism of the 1980s, which led to the fragmentation of land and its decreasing viability as a source of livelihood. Combined with affirmative action efforts and growing educational opportunities among lower castes, the neoliberal economic shifts in peasant communities led Jats to resent Dalits for gaining a nominal degree of mobility and power. These two moments, the first soon after India's independence and the second beginning in the 1980s, are crystallized in the violence and narratives that fuel Jat demands for reservation in the OBC category.[1] The links between these moments and sexual violation cannot be discerned without understanding the significance of land in these stories; this is seen in disputes over common land (as in Bhagana and Malud), family disputes that turn brutally violent (as in Jaswadi and Rudhi), and in the social pressure on Dalits to compromise (as in Bhagana and Malud). In what follows I trace this history, highlighting the impact of these two political moments on gender and caste relations in rural Haryana.

POSTCOLONIAL LAWS AND THE DISENFRANCHISEMENT OF WOMEN

The 174th report to the Law Commission on India, published in 2000, dealt with the property rights of women. Archana Mishra (2015) writes that the report reflected the collusion between the state and patriarchal institutions in not granting women equal inheritance rights. The disenfranchisement of women from property was based on the 1956 Hindu Succession Act (HSA), which itself was a source of tremendous contention and debate in newly independent India. The debate around the drafting of the Hindu Code Bill was deeply influenced by nineteenth-century social reform movements. These reform movements led the colonial government to pass legislation that directly impacted the status of women, including legislation which abolished *sati* (widow sacrifice) in 1829, permitted widows to remarry in 1856, and prohibited infanticide (which generally targeted baby girls) in 1870. While social reform movements and legislation dealt with marriage and custom, they did not address or alter laws related to land and property (Agarwal 1994, 204). But by the early part of the twentieth century, change was on the horizon. With the rise of the independence movement, several women's organizations, including of women from peasant communities, began demanding recognition and change in their entitlements to land.[2]

It was in the context of this political ferment that efforts to reform the Hindu Code bill began in the 1940s. The Rau committee released a draft Hindu Code bill in 1944, which abolished the *Mitakshara* and gave women equal rights to property and inheritance.[3] While supported by various women's organizations, the code was vociferously opposed by conservative male members of parliament. A revised draft of the bill was submitted to the Legislative Assembly four months prior to India's independence. After independence the bill was substantially revised and watered down, particularly with regard to women's rights to land. Opponents expressed concern that women inheriting land would fundamentally imperil the family. In the face of controversy and strong opposition, Prime Minister Jawaharlal Nehru shelved the bill in 1951, leading Law Minister B. R. Ambedkar to resign in protest.[4] Later, after the Congress Party's electoral victory, the bill was split into four parts that were passed separately, of which the HSA of 1956 was the most contentious (Agarwal 1994, 210).

The 1956 HSA marked a significant change in women's access to property by allowing inheritance rights for daughters, mothers, and widows. However, in retaining the *Mitakshara*, the HSA ensured that only male heirs were coparceners at birth in joint Hindu family property, while daughters, wives, and widows were only accorded maintenance rights. The HSA also curtailed other property and residency rights of daughters, wives, and mothers, and allowed fathers to will their property exclusively to their sons, depriving their daughters of their share. Moreover, particular kinds of agricultural property, like those covered by tenancy rights, were exempt from the scope of the HSA. Because tenancy laws differed from state to state, this meant that the rules that governed agricultural land diverged from those that governed property under personal law. Consequently, tenancy laws in states such as Punjab and Haryana still "show a strong preference for succession among agnates, with a priority in favor of agnatic males" (Agarwal 1994, 217).

Since much of Punjab and Haryana was dominated by peasant landowners, not tenants, the inheritance laws in the HSA applied in these states. The act mandated that if the land was not under tenancy, then women could inherit the property. It was this provision, which expanded the possibility for women to inherit property, that generated tremendous opposition from landowners.[5] In 1969, the Punjab Legislative Assembly argued that daughters inheriting land because of the HSA was causing land fragmentation (Agarwal 1994, 222). Contesting legislation that would prevent women from inheriting agricultural land, the president of the All India Women's Conference argued that sons inheriting land also caused land fragmentation. Apprehensions regarding land fragmentation were not superficial. In fact, between 1961 and 1971, the number of small holdings (of land less than five acres) increased fourfold, from 16.14 percent to 45.59 percent (Bhalla 1977, A3). Many argued that the breakup of joint family property was happening because daughters and sisters were claiming their share and causing strife. Paroma Sen's (2015) analysis of case law shows that between 1966 and 1986 there was a dramatic rise in the number of land dispute cases, predominantly brought by men to the Punjab and Haryana High Court (19).

However, while fragmentation was occurring, it was not due to women claiming inheritance. Rather, through the 1950s and 1960s, smaller farms "had a higher value of annual output per unit of cultivated area than larger ones, typically because small farms tended to have higher cropping intensities and a more labour-intensive and higher value crop-mix" (Agarwal 1994, 34). These productive small farms generated circumstances which made the breakup of joint property among sons financially viable. This widescale subdivision of joint property was driven by the Green Revolution, which increased productivity per acreage, yielding higher incomes. Sheila Bhalla (1977) writes, "in Haryana as a whole, nearly three-quarters of those who lost land on balance were reduced in size because of the subdivision of joint family holdings among family members" (A4). Land fragmentation was therefore occurring not because of women's claims, but because with the Green Revolution, larger farm sizes were no longer needed to sustain high productivity and income.

Forty-nine years after the HSA was implemented, it was amended in 2005, creating several advantages for women. In particular, women became coparceners at birth and could inherit agricultural property (Agarwal 2005). The amended act did not generate nearly as much controversy as it did when it was first crafted. This time, the issues that coalesced were different. Landholdings had become too small to make a viable living, the price of pesticides and fertilizers had risen faster than the prices farmers were able to get for their produce, and the negative, long-term side-effects of the Green Revolution, intensified by India's neoliberal policies, meant waning agricultural productivity. The majority of farmers in Haryana now own marginally sized holdings, between zero and two hectares (Agriculture Census Division 2018, 34).

By the late 1990s and early 2000s Haryana began to be cannibalized by the expansion of metropolitan Delhi, generating a real estate boom that valued land for industrial parks and housing rather than for farming (Sen

2015). In this context, more women were claiming inheritance rights based on the 2005 Amendment to the HSA (Chandran 2019). Still, the majority of women continued to practice *haq tyaag*, forgoing their right to land in favor of leaving it to their brothers. My empirical evidence bears this out: not a single woman I spoke with said that she would claim inheritance to her father's property.[6] One unexpected response to shifts in the wake of neoliberal disenfranchisement that I encountered was of young women turning to professional wrestling to secure government jobs through sports quotas (Oza 2019). Change was visible everywhere as the younger generation made increasingly urgent efforts to move out of farming. Amid this despair in peasant communities and the regional shift to real estate and service industries, Jat *aarakshan* (reservation) emerged as a way for Jats to consolidate their weakening position.

NEOLIBERALISM AND JAT *AARAKSHAN*

The eruption of violence in the 2016 Jat agitations must be understood in the context of five decades of changes in the political economy of Haryana. The Green Revolution period in the 1960s and 1970s had been particularly favorable to Jats, who mobilized the agricultural boom into political power and economic sovereignty. The Green Revolution transformed Haryana from a poor state that mainly produced cattle fodder during the British colonial period and was then a subsistence economy postindependence, to a strong grain-surplus economy by the 1970s (Chowdhry 2011, 159).[7] High productivity propelled Haryana into being one of the richest states in the union, a change whose impact was felt at the household scale. (For a detailed evaluation of the impact of the Green Revolution, see Dhanagare 1987.) In addition to the Green Revolution, the area experienced a dairy-based "White Revolution," with a rise in milk and milk-based products. These changes in agriculture and dairy production generated high demands for labor. While women were mostly responsible for dairy labor, some also worked on their farms. Consequently, a series of different labor arrangements emerged—attached, casual, *naukar*, or *sajhis*. However, most landlords still belonged to dominant castes, and most laborers still belonged to OBC or Dalit castes.[8] Ultimately, rather than break down caste norms, the Green Revolution adopted and reinforced them (Chowdhry 2011, 189).

When the economic benefits accruing from agriculture and dairy propelled Haryana to prominence, policies by national and state governments benefitted wealthy Jat farmers far more than any other group. The political prominence of Jats was evidenced in electoral politics, which, since the inception of Haryana as a state in 1966, have resulted in Jat chief ministers at the helm of state power for thirty-three years. These caste politics were therefore baked into the social and political fabric of the state, as these elected officials tended to support their caste *biradri* (community) rather than OBCs or Dalits, whose lives remained precarious and vulnerable. Haryana's powerful community of Jat farmers began to consolidate and mobilize into unions to demand subsidies and higher prices for their produce. Consequently, the new agrarian elite farmer emerged who spoke not only on his own behalf but also for his caste and class, as well as for his village as a whole.

The power that Jats accrued by the 1970s began to change in the 1980s. The productive impact of the Green Revolution declined against the rising costs of pesticides, fertilizers, and electricity to pump diminishing supplies of groundwater to irrigate water-intensive crops. Over the long run, it became apparent that the Green Revolution produced growing and unsustainable ecological damage and financial indebtedness. A. Narayanamoorthy (2006) reports that the annual average expenditure on cultivation was approximately 8,791 rupees, with states such as Haryana reporting the highest expenditures (472). After calculating for net expenditure, farm income was often in the negative. This led to more than half of the agricultural households in Haryana going into debt.[9] In every conversation I had with farmers, they lamented the low price they received for their produce from state granaries. By the mid-1980s, Surinder Jodhka (2012) argues, "the Indian countryside began to show a new kind of restiveness" (5). Old ideologies and relationships between landlord and labor had begun to erode. Systems such as attached labor (where the laborer gets a share of the crop) had faded, and most laborers prized their freedom and were increasingly reluctant to enter such binding arrangements with landlords. Patronage and loyalty gave way to distrust and mounting tensions (Jodhka 1994).

The political prominence farmers had enjoyed up until the 1980s began to diminish as India turned to new economic policies in the 1990s. Agriculture and rural India began to recede from the national discourse of economic prosperity, with industry and service taking their place. Prem Chowdhry (2007) notes that the "income generated in the Green Revolution areas has driven away rather than attracted the younger generation to agriculture" (256). The impact of a receding agricultural sector was visible in villages across Haryana: where previously farming had been the biggest employer, now fewer and fewer people depended on farming, and the new generation sought other jobs. The most coveted of these were government positions, which were hard to come by and usually required payment of an enormous bribe to secure. Many of the young men I spoke with were employed in private industry, which had mushroomed in nearby towns. A conversation I had with eight young men in Malud one afternoon exemplified all these issues.

I met Sunil when I first visited the village; he was the nephew of the *lambardar* (collector of revenue, levies, and taxes) and was also my local contact. He gathered about eight of his friends for a conversation late one afternoon.[10] All the men, except one who was an OBC, were Jats. I asked if they were working; most replied that they were unemployed, worked a bit on their farms, or tried for various entrance tests to secure a government position. Some were employed in private industry in a nearby town. Sunil was employed in a private job and was getting married next month. I asked the group: "Aap kheti karna chahte hai ya naukri "(Do you want to work on your farms or get a job?) They all replied that they'd like to be employed in government jobs, but that this was impossible. Kheti toh hai hi (Farming was there) they said, but it was not something that they were willing to do full-time. They explained that "kissan ke liye yojna kam hai" (farmers have fewer government schemes to support them). While the output from farms is good, it was no longer possible to make a living from *kheti* (farming). They talked about how government jobs received hundreds of thousands of applicants, and how one either had to know someone in power or pay a five- to seven-lakh bribe to get such a job. While they said that their village was near a big bustling town where there were plenty of private jobs, they stressed that those jobs paid less and were not as secure or as prestigious as a *sarkari naukri* (government job).

When the conversation shifted to government schemes such as the Mahatma Gandhi National Rural Employment Guarantee Act (MGNREGA), they complained that Dalits, who are predominantly employed in these schemes, don't do the work properly.[11] They said that *faltu* (unnecessary) and *bekar* (worthless) work happens through these schemes because the government was awash in money it was wasting. When I asked about the Jats' demand for *aarakshan* (reservation) in the OBC category, the young men echoed a script I had heard over and over again: that Jats are the victims and that Dalits take advantage of government schemes, that Dalits don't work because everything is given to them, and that Dalits are not qualified for the jobs they have and only got them because of unfair affirmative action policies.

Three aspects of this conversation echo the sociopolitical concerns that have crystalized in Jat agitations: changing political and economic relationships to land, growing resentment of Dalits, and agitation for reservations in the OBC category. First, the young men stated that farming is no longer a viable option, but none of them wanted to sell their farms. In his study of the agrarian crisis in Haryana, Surinder Jodhka (2012) writes, "even though there is still a strong sense of attachment to land, agriculture is no longer seen as a desirable occupation" (13). The Jat community's relationship with the land is old, and crucial to their identity. Both women and men articulated their relationship with land as *izzat* (honor), and Jat women said that a good *rishta* (marriage prospect) was one with a man who had *zameen* and *sarkari nakuri* (land and a government job). The young men I met were critical of those who sold their land. Rumors about how much land was sold and the price it fetched animated the conversation among them. One of them told a story about the high price of land sold in Sonipat (a district in Haryana), which in one instance led to eighty-four Scorpios (relatively expensive four-wheel-drive cars popular in the area) being sold in a single day. But they also said that the money people had received for this expensive land had led to an increase in *gunda gardi* (disorderly behavior).

The second aspect of the men's conversation worth highlighting is that it reflected a growing resentment toward Dalits. The allegation that Dalits don't do their work properly in government schemes such as MGNREGA is part of a larger discourse that characterizes Dalits as lazy and unproductive people who live off government handouts. While resentment against Dalits is not new, older structures of servitude that had defined relationships between the dominant and subordinate castes and Dalits had begun to weaken.

A series of factors contributed to this attenuation of old structures of servitude. Long-standing credit relationships, in which most rural households borrowed from bigger landlords or from *Banias* (merchant castes), had begun to fade. These relationships of dominance and subordination in class and caste status had served to maintain subordinate castes in a servile position of *ji hazoori*. This vernacular term is used to describe expressions of genuflection that Dalits and those from OBCs demonstrate in their interactions with dominant castes. I heard throughout my research that this pattern of *ji hazoori* had begun to diminish. With alternate sources of credit now available the old systems of money lending had not completely disappeared, but they were no longer as widespread. This shift meant that while Dalits might continue to work on dominant-caste farms, there was increasing awareness that they didn't want to be in relationships of subordination. In his detailed examination of changes in attached labor relationships over thirty years, Jodhka (2012) writes, "Labourers intensely disliked working in an attached relationship and chose to work only when they were in dire need of a relatively large amount of cash and had no other source of mobilising credit" (9).

Jats' resentment toward Dalits also stems from the new degree of social mobility available to Dalits as a consequence of quotas in education and jobs. In the 1970s, the state instituted several reasonably successful education schemes for Dalits (Bhalla 1995, 2631). In addition, the state offered interest-free loans for the purchase of books, industrial training, hostel accommodation, and medical services, along with a clothing allowance for Dalit students. It also awarded merit scholarships to generate incentives for Dalit girls to finish their schooling. These government programs fundamentally changed the structure of relationships between dominant and subordinate castes. No longer was the grip over Dalits that dominant castes had held through their earlier monopoly on credit and employment, and through various other measures of social control, as complete as it had previously been. Prem Chowdhry (2007) writes that Dalits were "not challenging the landownership of upper-caste groups, but providing competition in the services by blocking seats through reservations" (145). As a result, many Dalits entered into new professions and took advantage of reservations in panchayat and legislative bodies, generating a "highly differentiated and layered" Dalit middle class (Chowdhry 2009a, 441). Affirmative action policies aimed at correcting egregious Dalit exclusion coincided with a dynamic rise in political mobilization and electoral political participation of lower castes in both central and state governments from the 1970s onward, leading to what Christophe Jaffrelot (2003) has termed the "silent revolution." These visible manifestations of growing lower-caste and Dalit power led to severe anxiety among the dominant castes, who saw their power diminish over the same period. Anupama Rao (2011) writes that these civil rights entitlements have not only benefitted Dalits, but have also had the "paradoxical effect of presenting Dalits as vulnerable subjects always-already susceptible to injury, thus emphasizing violence as a dominant mode of sociality between castes" (615). In other words, affirmative action for Dalits has had the contradictory effect of expanding opportunity while at the same time enabling dominant-caste resentment and violence.

One of the most repeated laments I heard from various dominant-caste members was that Dalits were now "indulging in fashionable attire" and that as a result it was no longer possible to distinguish them from other castes. These laments insinuated a lack of thriftiness and humility among Dalits, suggesting character flaws among them. Making a similar point, a dominant-caste head constable told me that her neighbor, a Dalit man, had sold six *killa zameen* (unit of land) to spend on a lavish wedding for his daughter and a fancy car.[12] These overt demonstrations of wealth are read as vulgar displays of mobility, which come across as slights against the dominant caste. Jeffrey, Jeffrey, and Jeffrey (2002) point to similar attempts to undermine Dalits by questioning their cultural authority in terms of education and by underplaying the discrimination and inequality they face. The other complaint dominant castes often lodge against Dalits concerns the ways in which Dalits dare to claim public space. I heard of violence against Dalits at public wedding processions and at celebrations of Dalit icons like Ambedkar, and of the backlash against constructing statues of Dalit leaders.

While there are signs of change in the expansion of opportunities available to some Dalits, this expansion has not translated into broad structural transformations, with the dominant castes retaining a resilient hold on power and resources. As will be apparent in the three cases I detail, Dalits continue to face violent backlash, social boycotts, and coercive pressure from dominant castes. The nominal and contingent mobility available to some Dalits was intolerable to dominant castes, and the response by them was swift and violent.[13] Since 2000, according to National Crime Records Bureau data, violence against Dalits has increased sevenfold, while the rate of convicting anyone for these crimes against Dalits has remained at a dismal 12 percent (Manoj 2015).

Jat demands for reservations in the OBC category emerged in 2010, a few months after the Mirchpur atrocity in which Dalit homes were burned and an elderly man and his disabled daughter were killed. This demand for reservations is the third point that I want to amplify from my conversation with the young Jat men. Most peasant farming communities in the north Hindi belt—extending from Rajasthan into Punjab, Haryana, Utter Pradesh, and Bihar—belong to OBCs. The remarkable rise of this caste category to political prominence is a long and fascinating tale that begins in the 1920s. But it would not be until the last decade of the twentieth century that OBCs consolidated power through significant electoral victories (Jaffrelot 2000). Yogendra Yadav (1996), commenting on the assembly elections of the mid-1990s, said, "The most significant trend . . . in this respect was the acceleration of the delayed but inevitable rise of the OBCs to political power in north India" (102). Those classed as OBC constitute a sizable percentage, and perhaps the majority, of India's population.[14]

The maneuvering of caste in the OBC category through the 1990s and into the new millennium became folded into vote bank politics between three political parties that were contesting elections in Haryana: the Indian National Lok Dal, the Congress, and the Bharatiya Janata Party.[15] In their efforts to win the state, these political parties promised reservations to court the Jat vote. Alert to the electoral vulnerabilities of the Congress-led minority government in Haryana, Jats used the political moment of a fiercely contested election landscape to push for reservations in 2010 (Rajalakshmi 2010). Their campaign began with agitations over the death of a young man in Mayyar Gaon, the same village that I referenced at the beginning of this chapter. In 2010, when the Akhil Bharatiya Jat Arakshan Sangharsh Samiti (All India Jat Reservation Struggle Committee) began to mobilize, Haryana's Congress government relented and offered them 10 percent reservation in the Special Backward Classes category. However, this reservation policy was immediately challenged in the Punjab and Haryana High Court by a Haryana-based NGO, the Janhit Social Welfare Society, which found that Jats already held the majority of government jobs in the state. In response to the challenge, the Court stayed the order in July 2015 (Dogra 2012).

As a consequence of the Court's stay order, Jats threatened to agitate every day beginning in July 2015 (Hindu Net Desk 2017). The threat of these protests finally erupted in February 2016, just as I was beginning my research. Over several weeks, large-scale violence flared up in multiple districts across the state, with arson and looting reported. At the end of the agitations, twenty people had been killed and over two hundred injured (Yadav 2016). After the agitation, at a Jan Sunvai (people's forum) I attended about the violence, the predominant feeling of anger was directed toward Jats for splitting the thirty-six *biradri* (caste groups) into thirty-five versus the Jats.[16] There were heated differences of opinion between Gujjar and Jat members gathered on how the violence had started in Hansi. Some alleged that the culprits were not people from the village but miscreants who came from outside, others claimed that the government was responsible, and for still others, it was the alcohol mafia that had orchestrated the violence.

The Jat *aarakshan* violence that erupted in February 2016 was the culmination of pent-up frustrations. The long history I have traced here demonstrates how the entitlement among Jat landlords that had been cultivated by the colonial government congealed into a proud rural agrarian identity, an identity that differentiated itself from the rising urban elite. Bolstered by the economic boom brought by the Green Revolution, this agrarian class became powerful and wealthy. They dictated political power in the state of Haryana and saw themselves as stewards of rural culture. But their power was not to last. By the 1980s, the power that Jats had wielded in previous generations began to wane. By the 2000s, landholdings had fragmented to small, unviable sizes and the ability to make a living from the land had reached a breaking point. And by December 2020, this long history I have recounted came to a head when over one hundred thousand mainly Jat farmers from Haryana, Punjab, and Uttar Pradesh initiated what would turn out to be months-long protests in Delhi against three farm laws that the BJP government at the center implemented which would fundamentally remake Indian agriculture (Bal 2021). At a time when the country was suffering from a global COVID-19 pandemic and rural India had been devastated by decades of divestment, the new laws would get rid of the nominal protections that farmers relied on.[17] In addition, Kancha Ilaiah Shepherd (2021) argues that the farm laws were an opportunity for the BJP to reign in states and the power of Shudras, of which Jats are a powerful segment.[18]

But for the subordinate castes, who don't have access to land and depend on Jats for work, this history and recurring crises meant further vulnerability. In the past few decades, many began to move away from agricultural labor and are increasingly reluctant to acquiesce to relationships of servitude. Government education programs from the 1970s offered a way out for some who were able to get education and jobs. These nominal shifts among those who were historically subordinate were intolerable to Jats, who manifested their resentment through violence and in more mundane ways, such as withholding access to resources designated by government schemes. One of these schemes sought to offer permanent homes to Dalits and OBCs, as well as to those living below the poverty line. It relied on village common lands on which to build these homes, and it became a source of tremendous contention and violence. The weakening of Jat power, while Dalits and OBCs simultaneously gained education and employment, rankled Jats, because they perceived these lower caste groups as undeserving and as rising at their expense. When Dalits were suddenly also entitled to land on which to build permanent homes, land that was to be culled from common land, while Jats' circumstances continued to deteriorate, the tensions became explosive. In the next section, I turn to stories which illuminate how the dispute over land and sexual violation are intertwined. This section draws on the cases I followed and focuses on disputes over three issues: common land, social boycotts, and private land.

LAND AND SEXUAL VIOLATION: COMMON LAND

The road to Bhagana is off NH 9 and goes through the village of Mayyar Gaon. A small sign sandwiched between buildings and parked vehicles in Mayyar, easy to miss, points to a narrow and nondescript road that leads to

Bhagana. Both villages are dominated by Jats, who are in the majority, own all the land, and are politically powerful. Proximity in these stories matters; as neighboring villages, Mayyar and Bhagana often share close relationships of kinship and brotherhood. The central role of Mayyar in the Jat call for reservations gave it prominence, and by association Jats in Bhagana were also *dabang*—a term used colloquially to describe those who have power and control over place and people.

The story of the 2014 gang rape of four young girls in Bhagana, which made headlines, involved a land dispute. To untangle this complex tale I meet Satish, who is one of the key members of the group protesting for accountability. He has been agitating in front of Hisar district's administrative offices under whose jurisdiction village Bhagana lies, for the past seven years, living there in makeshift tents through both the intensely hot and bitterly cold months. It is a warm winter day in mid-January when we sit in the sun and he begins to tell me the story of land and assault in Bhagana, which began with a dispute over a playground.[19] When the Jat agitations began in Mayyar Gaon, Satish told me, it had an impact in Bhagana. While disputes and conflicts between Jats and Dalits in Bhagana had been ongoing, in 2011 the situation changed drastically. That year the Jat agitations in Mayyar turned violent, and a Jat sarpanch was elected in Bhagana. The previous sarpanch, a Brahmin, who was elected in 2005, had supported Dalits against Jats because they had voted for him. The conflicts between Dalits and Jats in 2005 escalated because Jats blocked off a road that Dalits used to access farmland and had initiated a social boycott against them. In this dispute, the Brahmin sarpanch helped the Dalits by offering them passage through his fields. In retaliation, when a Jat sarpanch was elected in 2011, he formed a committee that decided that all the *shamilat zameen* (common land) in the village would be divided in proportion to land ownership. Those who had the biggest plots of land got a bigger share. When even Jats in the village who owned small plots protested the scheme because they would get a proportionally smaller share, the Jat committee placated their concerns by allowing them to seize bigger portions. Their strategy with this land grab was to prevent Dalits and those below the poverty line from getting access to village common land through a government redistribution scheme which would entitled them to 100 *gaj* plots for housing.[20] Satish explained that after 2011 and the Jat arakshan these efforts were part of a larger scheme of harassment that included prohibiting Dalits from drying cow dung and grazing cattle on village common land. It was in the context of these conflicts that Jats took over a playground that Dalits had been using for years. Running their tractors over the space, the Jats destroyed benches and uprooted trees. Jats claimed that Dalits had illegally occupied the land and that it was part of village common land that had been set aside for redistribution.

When the Dalits responded by registering complaints in district offices, Jats escalated the conflict and began to make threats. They commenced a total social and economic boycott against Dalits, including actions such as building walls around a village square that blocked Dalit homes and prevented Dalits from accessing the space. These worsening tensions and the intensifying violence in the village, as well as the growing agitations by Jats in neighboring Mayyar Gaon, shaped the context in which four girls belonging to Dhanak (a Dalit caste) were gang-raped by five Jat men in 2014. Many believed that the Jats had raped the girls in retaliation for the land dispute and as a way to teach Dalits a lesson. The relationship between the land dispute and sexual violation in Bhagana was, at least initially, clearly part of ongoing intercaste conflicts. In other villages I looked at the relationship was not as linear, but it was still part of a larger context involving disputes between Jats and Dalits.

I encountered similar issues with dispute over common land in Malud, where in 2012 fifteen-year-old Sheetal was gang raped by twelve Jat men. The police initially arrested eight men, and eventually convicted four men from the village. The dispute in Malud was about a government scheme, through which Dalits were allocated plots on common land on which to build homes. Over the past few years, the conflict in Malud over plots of land for Dalit homes had resulted in litigation by Jat landlords in the civil courts. The plaintiffs in the case claimed that the *shamilat zameen* in the village was the ancestral property that their families had given to the village panchayat for common purposes. Based on this claim, that land could not be given to Dalits to build homes. This conflict generated resentment between the Jats and Dalits. In my conversation with Dalit elders I asked if Sheetal's gang rape was in retaliation for this land dispute, but they denied it. In my conversation with Sheetal,[21] however, she said that soon after her gang rape, prominent Jat members of the village came and specifically referred to the dispute over common land. She recalled that they told her family that if they were to agree to compromise the case, then they would allow the panchayat to build homes for the Dalit community on *shamilat zameen*.[22] In this way, by holding the land that was owed to Dalit families hostage, efforts were made to coerce not only Sheetal and her family, but also their entire community. The tactic of holding an entire Dalit community hostage to get relief or to try to coerce a compromise out of court is one that is commonly deployed.

Sheetal refused to compromise on the rape case and the litigation over ownership of common land was rejected in civil court. In retaliation for the loss they faced in both instances, Jats in the village ran their tractors over the plots of land where homes for Dalits were slotted for construction. One of the Dalit women I spoke with in the village said that the *haveli wale* (those who reside in the big house) had sat overnight on the land that was marked for Dalit families, carrying rifles and preventing anyone from getting access to it. When I visited the village four years later in 2016, the land remained unused; efforts to claim it to build homes for Dalits had continued to be unsuccessful. One morning, while talking to women who were attending a *sansad* (religious gathering at a temple), a Jat woman conceded that the Jat boys who had raped the young Dalit girl were in the wrong.[23] But she felt that despite this, it was Jats who had borne the brunt of having their reputation sullied, because Jat boys had gone to jail. Under such circumstances, she felt it was not possible to give Dalits what she claimed was "their" (Jat) land.

Jat landlords with extensive holdings claim that *shamilat zameen* in the village is their ancestral property. In one conversation with Satpal Bajwa, who had held a high-ranking position in Haryana's previous administration, he claimed that the common land in Malud all belonged to his family and was given to the panchayat in 1956 to generate income for the village. It was a hot late-spring day when I was invited to visit Satpal Bajwa's home. He lived in a big bungalow in town while his nephew resided in the ancestral property in the village. As I walked through a large gate, five or six village elders were sitting on *charpais* in the veranda smoking a hookah. After I greeted them, I went inside and was ushered into a large, well-appointed sitting room artfully furnished with sofas and carpets, indicating his wealth and political status. Satpal Bajwa and his wife spoke with me in both English and Hindi and proceeded to give us a history of the village, which their ancestors had founded. It was in this conversation that Satpal Bajwa said that there was no common land in the village and that the land was given by his family to the panchayat. Part of this land was given to Dalits to build houses through a government scheme called Indira Awaas Yojana in the 1980s. Dalits had sold those houses, he claimed, and now wanted land again.[24]

The government scheme that Mr. Bajwa referred to was part of an effort to improve rural infrastructure. In 2005, various schemes which dealt with rural housing, electricity, roads, water, and communication were consolidated under a plan called Bharat Nirman. The housing scheme under this plan, Indira Awaas Yojana, was initiated in the 1980s under the Ministry of Rural Development by then Prime Minister Rajiv Gandhi. In 2016 the name of the program was changed to Pradhan Mantri Awaas Yojana-Gramin (PMAY-G) and its scope expanded, but with a continued focus on housing for Scheduled Castes (SCs), Scheduled Tribes (STs), and for those living below the poverty line. In his assessment of this scheme, Arjun Kumar (2014) concludes that SCs and STs are lagging behind all other groups in terms of their access to benefits from its programs.

I repeatedly heard the narrative that Dalits had sold the houses that had been allocated to them in other villages as well. It aligned with broader discourses by dominant castes, which claimed that Dalits were deceitful, irresponsible, unworthy, and undeserving recipients of government handouts. Despite evidence to the contrary, with Dalits living in squalid semipermanent structures, often without basic sanitation facilities in their homes, the narrative about their duplicity had solidified. In the context of extensive land fragmentation among Jat households and the weakening of traditional relationships of servitude between castes, Dalits receiving small plots of land to build homes did not sit well with Jats. In Malud, this was evident in the small gestures of Jat antagonism around the allocation of common land for housing. When the land was allotted and the plots demarcated, before Jats ran their tractors over it, Dalits had invited a Member of the Legislative Assembly (MLA) to inaugurate their housing colony. In my conversation with Mr. Bajwa, he said, if Dalits wanted land, then they should have come to them and asked for it. I had heard a similar sentiment expressed from other elders in the village as well. This reaction by Jats is an instance of the slight they felt when Dalits invited an MLA from outside the village to inaugurate the new colony. This was perceived as an affront by the elders in the village.[25] Of course, it was an affront with material consequences; signaling an attenuation in their power over Dalits that Jats were not willing to accept. Jats' political clout and control over all land, not just common land, allowed them to control the very terms by which this issue of redistributing common land was discussed.

It was the same in other villages I visited. In Matpur village, where Vineeta's case occurred, we visited the block president, who showed us 114 families whose homes had recently been demolished. When we visited the site many of the roofs and walls had been broken, but Dalit families continued to live there, with nowhere to go. This story was about a Jat landlord who had lots of land and who had donated three acres of it to the village to build a school. The village built the school in a different location, on common land, and allotted the land that the Jat landlord had given the village to 114 Dhanak and Chamar (Dalit caste) families for them to build their homes. This reallotment of land, which had been given to the panchayat for its use, troubled the Jat family so much that they took the matter to court to reclaim their land. Had the panchayat used the land for something other than giving Dalits property and homes, the Jat family might not have objected. But because Dalit families had already settled on the land and built homes, the matter went to court and the Jat family won, resulting in an order of eviction for the families living there. The Dalit families then asked the panchayat to compensate them with land elsewhere, but this had not yet happened.

Conflicts over common land have escalated to such a degree that the Punjab and Haryana High Court recently ordered an inquiry into the more than thirty-one thousand acres of common land that have been illegally possessed by various members of the village. When Dalit families are denied housing because of disputes in the village and Jats' absolute control over land, they are disenfranchised from the schemes which entitle them to housing. Additionally, access to employment, whether on Jat farms or through employment guarantee programs, depends on Jat landlords and members of the panchayat. Conflicts in the village jeopardize these sources of livelihood. In Malud and Matpur, the Dalit families I met complained that the Jat sarpanch did not offer them work and that work on Jat farmlands had dwindled. They claimed that this was because they were being replaced by immigrant workers from Bihar, who accepted lower wages for farm work. These structures of Jat dominance over Dalit lives and livelihoods meant that Dalits were often poorly situated to fight on behalf of members of their community. When Dalit women and girls are violated by dominant-caste men, ensuing protests initially strengthen community solidarity in a fight to secure justice for the victims. But as many people said to me, the village panchayat and the state bureaucracy usually collude with the dominant caste and together "woh andolan ko thakkana chahte hai" (they wish to exhaust those who are protesting). In Bhagana, this strategy to wear out the protesting Dalit community worked. After a while, the protesting families fractured. Fifty families accepted the compensation the state offered them, and others returned to the village, claiming, "Gaon mei rehna hai" (We have to live in the village).

SOCIAL PRESSURE AND BOYCOTT

The social boycott of Dalit families intensified in Bhagana in 2012 after they filed complaints in court about the destruction of their playground. Jats demanded that no one employ Dalits or buy anything from them. They also imposed a 200-rupee fine on anyone who spoke with Dalits in the village.

Social pressure and boycott, in addition to ongoing economic disenfranchisement, retrenched Dalits' lack of access to public space. While codes of caste have always differentiated space between dominant and subordinate castes—where people eat, defecate, and reside are all subject to discriminatory rules of ritual purity—the boycott went beyond these controls, prohibiting Dalits from accessing common land critical to their survival. Dalits are often responsible for gathering cow dung, which is dried into patties and used for cooking fuel. The drying of cow dung is usually done on common land. When Jats prohibited Dalit families from access to common land to dry cow dung, these families were forced to store it in their homes. Dalits also use common land for grazing cattle which generated additional problems when they were denied access to these spaces. Jats seeking to subject Dalits to pressure or punishment also block public spaces like crossroads and other avenues which Dalits use to access village life. In Bhagana, Jats retaliated to ongoing disputes by blocking off Chamar chowk (a crossroad in the village named after one of the Dalit subcastes) and cutting off some families from accessing the village. When these tensions escalated, 137 families from the village camped outside the district bureaucratic offices in protest. At the district offices, they were harassed by the police and prohibited from putting up tents for shelter.

Tensions between dominant-caste Jats and Dalits predate the gang rape of the four Dalit girls, and, according to Satish, it was the conflict over land and Dalits' refusal to give up that led to the violent assaults. The gang rape made national news when the families from Bhagana went to Delhi to protest in April 2014. The resulting public pressure led to the arrest of five men. When the case went up for trial, however, all five men were acquitted. Satish claimed that the men were acquitted because of social pressure on Dalits by Jats in the village. In the lead-up to the trial, rumors about a relationship between one of the Dalit girls and one of the Jat men surfaced.

Five years later, I visited Bhagana and was accompanied by two Dalit feminist activists who had been central in supporting victims of rape and caste atrocity in Haryana, and who were present during the initial protests for the Bhagana victims in Delhi. They knew Satish and were familiar with the structure of compromise and boycotts in villages across Haryana. At the village we met Savatri and Punam, the mothers of two of the four women who had been raped, and Arun, an activist who worked with Satish. Savatri explained that "do ka phaisla ho gaya tha, ek ladki ka baap mar gaya tha, phir hum akela reh gaye, phir ko nahi ladya case" (two of the girls compromised, one girl's father died, and we were left alone, we did not want to fight the case).

Savatri and Punam challenged Arun and other activists who implored them to continue the case, each explaining that "manne bhi gaam mei rehna hai" (I too have to live in the village). Their earlier lament of having been left alone, along with their emphasis on having to continue to live in the village, expose the constraints they faced in the choices they could make. Later on Savitri added, "Bhes bandhi hai gaam mei" (Our buffalos are tied here). Savitri and Punam had livestock in the village and needed to go back to take care of their buffalos. For many poor landless families, livestock is an important source of income and their livelihoods depend on it. Owning buffalos was one of the only ways poor villagers had to supplement their living, a reality which was even more urgent after Jats launched their crushing social boycott against them. The phrase "Gaam mei rehna hai" (We have to live in the village) was often repeated among those who compromised their cases by settling them out of court. It was meant to signal that they were tied to the village and had to go back, so they had to find a way to live there.

Savatri and Punam felt that their reputation had been sullied from the case, and that the case was causing them to suffer further isolation in the village. They said there is no *aana jaana* (coming and going) with the families of the other girls, and that the incidents—the rapes and their aftermaths—had led to tensions among the community in the village. Since the gang rape case had ended in a compromise, the girls and their families were followed by a shadow of guilt suggesting that the girls were responsible for what had happened. This *badnami* (disrepute), according to Punam, would make it difficult to secure a good marriage for her daughter. She wanted the whole episode of the rapes and the protests to be in the past, and to move forward with her life. The social pressures of arranging marriages and continuing to live in the village limited the stamina families had for continuing to struggle for their rights and for justice.

PRIVATE LAND AND PUBLIC VIOLENCE

In July 2018 I was following up on a case in Rudhi Gaon from several years prior, which had ended in compromise. When I called to make an appointment with the village sarpanch, he said that he could not meet me because a new case of assault had just occurred in the village, involving a seven-year-old girl. He asked that I speak with the station house officer (SHO) of the *mahila thanna* about the new case. At the thanna, I am accompanied by activists, and we make our way to meet the SHO, Ritu Kaur, who was dressed in a khaki uniform and sat behind a large imposing desk.[26]

When we asked about the case after introducing ourselves, she vehemently said, "I will charge this crime under Protection of Children from Sexual Offences Act—POCSO." She related that since 2012, when POCSO became the law, district magistrates treated these cases more seriously. "They do not accept bail when they see it is a POCSO case. The case is stronger," she explained.

The SHO was forthright and confident, and she illustrated her frustrations with her job with an anecdote. She said that when women who have been abused or assaulted come to the thanna, it takes three to four hours to record their statement. By that time, it is usually late evening or night. After police record the statement and take it to the magistrates and judges, they admonish the police officers for asking permission to apprehend the suspect so late in the day. She recounted the magistrates and judges saying, "Is this any time to come? Come by in the morning!" Ritu Kaur said that the dilemma she faced was that she could not send the woman home at night without endangering her and risking that the woman would be coerced to retract her statement by morning. Kaur continued, "Es liye mai statement ke baad koi bhi mahila ko mere paas hi rakhti hun wapis nahi bhej te" (Which is why after their statement we keep the woman with us, we don't send them home). The police station is equipped with several rooms, one of which contains beds and mattresses where victims are often kept overnight.

When we talked about the new case in Rudhi, the SHO was clear that she would charge the man under POCSO, but she nevertheless expressed skepticism about its legitimacy. Like other police officers I met, her response to this case reserved some disbelief, despite involving a child. She said, "Ched khaani ke case mei toh bahut zyada istamaal hota hai" (The accusation of molestation is frequently used in false cases), and explained that in the village these accusations were often made and leveraged in the context of long-standing disputes. She also said, "Jab bhi gaon mei koi bhi baat—jhagda hoti hai—toh kapda phaad dete hai" (Whenever there is a dispute in the village, clothing is torn). The tearing of clothing, usually of women's clothing, is used to register a convincing case of molestation. She proceeded to explain how the manner in which the clothing is torn makes evident when such cases are fabricated. In concocted cases, the clothes of the alleged sexual assault victims are torn in such a way that they can be easily reseamed. She demonstrated that a *kurta's* (long tunic's) side seam is usually torn so that it can be stitched back together again. These are poor people who don't have many clothes, she explained, and they cannot afford to destroy clothing.

She said that the new case in Rudhi seemed like a story about a land dispute, which she asserted was the case for most such stories of molestation. Recalling a past incident involving an eighty-five-year-old man who was accused of molesting a young girl, Kaur said, "The case came to me and I kept it with me for a while, then when we investigated the case, we found that it was a dispute over land and property." The new case in Rudhi was similar to this old one. It too involved the charge of molestation by a young girl's family against an older male neighbor. We asked if we could accompany the SHO to Rudhi when the police went to investigate the case; she agreed and asked that we attempt to find out if this case also involved a conflict over land.

When we got to the village, we found out that the case involved a shy seven-year-old girl and an older man. They both belonged to dominant-caste pandit families, lived close to each other, and had known each other for years. The little girl referred to the older man as *dada* or grandfather. Cases involving dominant-caste families are extremely difficult for researchers and activists to find because they are usually suppressed within the family or village. We would likely not have heard about this case had we not coincidentally been on our way to the village as it was unfolding. When we got there, many of the villagers had gathered along with elders. The police came in two cars and were taking statements from the families involved. Standing at one side of the crowd that had gathered, the family of the accused vehemently denied the charge and implored us to believe that their father would never do such a thing, and then proceeded to accuse the girl's family of impropriety. The girl's family, on the other hand, were visibly very distressed, and economically weaker than the accused. They spoke about how they would be pressured to compromise because of their subordinate class status.

The wife of the accused said that the girl's family had asked for a plot of land in the gully behind their house and had made a false molestation complaint against her husband because they been had refused this plot. The accused man's daughter was very animated, saying that her father had a good reputation in the village and that all the kids came to him. When we spoke to the girl's family we gently asked if there was a land dispute, and they vehemently denied any such dispute with the family of the accused. The mother of the girl proceeded to tell us that they own five acres of land with a water pump and that they had just bought more land for nine *lakhs*.[27] If they already had land, she reasoned, why would they want the other family's property? It was hard not to empathize with the parents; with tears in his eyes, the girl's father said that since the incident had happened there was mounting tension in the neighborhood. Even members of the young girl's family were pressuring the parents to withdraw their complaint. Saying "bhaichara kharrab ho gayega es se" (brotherhood in the village will be ruined with this), the young girl's father told us that he was being compelled by some in the village to reach a *shamjauta*, a compromise. He had to live in this village and could not afford to have *dushmani* (enmity) with all these people.

In Jaswadi, a land dispute similarly informed a complex and brutal tale of assault. When I first met Komal it was on the farmland where her family grows cattle fodder.[28] I was accompanied at this initial meeting by her friend Sheetal (whose own case of gang rape in Malud I briefly mentioned earlier). I recounted the story of Komal's rape, in which four men were falsely implicated, in chapter 2. It turned out that the real story of her brutal assault, which was perpetrated by her uncle, was rooted in a simmering dispute between her family and her uncle. Komal had offered hints about this dispute during our conversations, but I would only learn the full story much later. Komal and her father would recall that the dispute with the uncle had been ongoing for many years and had to do with the land they own.

On a hot summer day in May, I got a call from Komal asking me to come by and see her. She said that her uncle was harassing them. When I got to the village, Komal explained that the uncle had stopped the water from coming to their land. He had blocked its flow by putting in *kapas* (cotton) behind their backs and was insisting that the land be turned over to his name. He claimed that he had spent a lot of money for Komal's brother's wedding and her rape case, and that they owed him. In exchange for the sum of money he said he had spent for their benefit, he wanted the land converted to his name. The *khata* (land revenue record) for the land had been in the name of Komal's grandfather and then divided among his seven sons and daughters. The land totaled seven acres; Komal's father tilled one and a half acres. Among the four brothers and three sisters, the sisters all supported their eldest brother in his contest over Komal's father's land. We filed a complaint against this uncle in the District offices to challenge his most recent efforts of coercion which involved stopping the water from flowing to their farm. Each time I returned to find out what had happened to this complaint, I saw that not much had changed over the course of two years and that the hostility and threats remained.

Komal's uncle's hostility and occasional bouts of violence against her and her family over the years were all aimed at coercing her father to give up his claim on the land. By law, Komal's father was entitled to the land unless he legally gave up his share to his brother. Assaults on women to compel an outcome of such a dispute are not unusual. So while Komal may not have had any control over the land, the brutal attack on her and the occasional, violent attacks on her brothers generated a threat to the family and functioned as pressure to coerce them into acquiescing to the uncle's demands.

CONCLUSION

This chapter has laid out in some detail the historical antecedents that inform disputes over land in Haryana, which infiltrate stories of assault. Beyond direct causal connections between land disputes and sexual assault, like those initially made in Bhagana or speculated about in Rudhi, land anchors social relationships in Haryana. My effort to recount these stories of dispute and violence illustrates what Rana Jaleel (2021) has called "rape's intimacies with property [which are] roughly tethered to expropriations of resources, lives, and land" (24). In these intimacies, caste relations braid together who has access to resources and land. Jats have derived power through a history of access and control over 80 percent of the land in Haryana. Their diminishing power has fueled violence and ongoing agitation to demand reservations in educational institutions and government jobs to secure livelihood options for their future sons. For Dalits, though, who have no land, decades of government redistribution schemes have led to some upward mobility. This shift in the balance of power is intolerable to many in the dominant caste. Rapes of Dalit women in Haryana are often narrated as being about the "need to teach them a lesson." But Dalits are not willing to acquiesce to this violence and are fighting to get cases concerning violence against Dalits registered and taken to court. As one police officer said to me, "Ab log jagrut ho gaye hai" (People are more aware of their rights).

Examining how land intertwines with assault across the three scales of the nation-state, the village, and the intimate helps craft a better understanding of the structures that determine and impede the lives of both the powerful and the vulnerable. Laws governing inheritance that continue to disenfranchise women were shaped in a social and cultural context in which women did not feel entitled to inherit their father's property, even when they had a clear legal right to it. They renounced their right to the property (*haq tyaag*) in order to maintain family relationships and customs. These women usually bear the burden of these dynamics rather than ask for a shift in familial rights and relationships. Long-standing tentacles of tradition inform the entitlement to land displayed by the dominant caste, such that when common land is slated for redistribution among those at the bottom rungs of caste and economy, dominant-caste repression is swift and fierce. In the villages I visited, little if any land was redistributed through these schemes without fierce backlash by those in the dominant caste. As it has done historically, the state colludes with the dominant caste in these instances, because those who fill its rank and file come from these same dominant-caste communities.

Dalits' lack of access to land and their dependence on larger landlords mean that at the scale of the village, those who work on farms are vulnerable to social pressures to compromise, adjust, and acquiesce. The story of compromise in Bhagana is ambiguous and it remains unclear if the young girls' families were coerced to compromise their sexual assault cases or if they did so because of the vulnerability they felt. Either way, the structures of these Dalit families' lives were such that they had to return to their village and figure out how to live within the confines of life there. Whether tacitly or explicitly, the circumstances of their lives produced a limited set of choices that are unlikely to have offered the most just outcomes for their girls and what they had been forced to endure.

At the scale of the intimate, even cases of child sexual assault are tainted with the suspicion that they might involve false charges made to achieve desired outcomes in what are actually land disputes. For the police, land disputes shadow cases of intimate violence and render them unconvincing and implausible. Neither the young girl in Rudhi nor Komal will inherit land, but assaults against them, whether real or potentially concocted by desperately poor families, render them victims of stories emerging from structures that are not of their making. They are the vulnerable collateral damage of disputes about access to property, rooted in vast caste and class inequality. Rape in Haryana is not simply a story about the violation of bodily integrity; it is part of a complex range of structures in which women and girls become vulnerable subjects in a dispute that is ultimately not about them.

4. Death

Mr. Bhalla's cramped office, located in the district court offices near Dantha village, already had about eight people waiting to speak with him when I arrived from Delhi on a late winter morning.[1] The journey from Delhi takes two and a half hours, and I was grateful when he offered hot tea as he invited me to sit. This was my third time meeting him, and he was more candid and less circumspect than our initial meetings. As we began talking about the rape case I was researching, he warmed up, letting local expressions pepper his language while his emphasis and tone changed. He was representing the family of a young girl from a nearby village who was gang-raped in February 2015 and died five months later. The girl's family had been courageously fighting her cases for four years. The two cases—one involving her rape and the other her death—were coming to a close, and Mr. Bhalla anticipated final judgments soon.[2]

During our conversation Mr. Bhalla said, somewhat cavalierly, "Agar ladki ki death nahi hoti toh who logo ko bail ho jata" (Had the girl not died, the men accused of her rape would have gotten bail). Death brought more seriousness to the case, he said. His comment about death was made as a matter of fact, devoid of emotion, as if he were simply trying to explain a legal quandary. And in some ways, that is exactly what death in cases of rape does: it adds gravity to a case that may otherwise be met with doubt. Mr. Bhalla's comment haunted me as I sought to understand why rape is met with deep suspicion in most cases, except when it is followed by death. Women who survive rape are almost always indelibly marked as suspicious, sullied, and immoral. Why are cases of rape taken more seriously when the victim or someone in her family dies? Why does a rape accusation assume more gravity in the wake of death than in the absence of death, however brutal the assault? What does death do? This chapter is about the necropolitics of life and death after rape.

In 2018, the National Crime Records Bureau recorded a significant increase in the number of cases where death and murder followed rape. Such cases were documented to have risen by 31 percent since 2017 (Tiwary 2020). As I scrutinized the weight accorded to rape cases accompanied by death, I saw that this seriousness was notably absent in certain other instances of mortality. The deaths of the poor, Dalits, and other minorities rarely register in these records, and the harm done to them and to their communities is routinely neglected by the state, which is also often complicit in the harm they suffer. So it is very notable, if not startling, when the state, in the form of the courts and the law, is compelled to document and recognize their deaths, when these deaths are accompanied by rape. I deliberately focus on two cases where death follows rape, mirroring the attention and legitimacy the courts accord to such cases precisely because I want to examine why these cases are believed when others are not. The story I track in this chapter is about the lack of accountability for the deaths of those who are routinely neglected by dominant castes, the state, and the law, until a particular type of death forces their recognition.

There are different attachments to women who die or survive rape. When a woman dies, her case is taken seriously and compels investigation; it becomes harder for the perpetrators to receive lighter sentences or bail. Women who survive are not accorded the same respect but are also marked by death; they are relegated to the living dead—*zinda laash*. The victim-survivor is assumed to be fated to a zombie existence, forever tainted, unable to escape the violation that marks her life. A frequently deployed frame through which to view survivors of rape, *zinda laash* signifies that a rape victim's fate is that of a zombie, neither dead nor alive. The state, in the form of the Supreme Court, also adopts this zinda laash frame in its approach to women who have survived rape. Mrinal Satish (2017) cites a 1980 Supreme Court case in which he says, "the Court observed that a rape victim feels 'a deep sense of deathless shame'" (44). The moniker *zinda laash* was repeatedly evoked after a young physiotherapy student was brutally gang-raped in Delhi in 2012. Sushma Swaraj, then foreign minister, lamented in Parliament that "if this girl survives, she will be a Zinda Laash, for the rest of her life" (Kumari and Barn 2017, 2). Jyoti Singh died thirteen days after her assault.[3]

This stigmatization of raped women as doomed to a fate worse than death is anchored in dominant-caste notions tying women's value to their chastity and sexual purity. A raped woman's reputation is sullied, and she is considered worthless. While dominant-caste notions of purity shape this conception of raped women, lower-caste and Dalit women are also subject to similar frames of chastity and morality.[4] First, within the structure of caste violence, dominant-caste men have claimed sexual access to lower-caste and Dalit women (Anandhi and Kapadia 2019).[5] Second, the raped victim is fated to a zombie existence because within dominant heteronormative subjective frames she is unlikely to find a suitable marriage prospect, as she has been despoiled. Her loss in value renders her a burden that her parents must carry, or makes her position, if she is able to get married, precarious in her marital home and subject to derision and abuse. A young woman's life after rape is subject to scrutiny and generates anxiety about women exercising unsanctioned autonomy and choice. The rape survivor whose innocence is perpetually questioned raises the specter of unruly sexuality, which needs to be brought back into the strict confines of domestic patriarchy. This is why efforts to get victims married as soon as possible pervade the afterlife of rape (Deshpande et. al 2013). The death of a raped victim, however, elicits sympathy while attenuating speculation about the victim's innocence or chastity. Suspicion of the raped woman who dies is never absent or completely nullified, but it is less audible than it would have been if she had survived.

This chapter is about life and death after rape. I detail two cases in which death followed rape, examining the perverse legitimacy granted to the rape charge in the wake of death. In the first case, the victim's father committed suicide after a video of his daughter's assault circulated in the village; in the second, the victim died a few months after her assault. I consider death in these cases and the resulting gravity they are accorded, and juxtapose them against the rape cases in previous chapters, in which women who survived rape were met with suspicion and derision. I argue that the zinda laash language reveals a disquiet that survivors of rape generate. Members of the political establishment, local village officials, and even members of a survivor's family are troubled by this figure. Indeed, women who die after a sexual violation elicit more concern and sympathy than those who survive, as if survival is defiance against what ought to be symbolic death.

ZINDA LAASH: THE DISCURSIVE FRAME OF SHAME

When Jyoti Singh's assault became public, responses from political figures and the media predictably rehearsed the tired victim-blaming narratives about "westernization," illicit relationships, women improperly occupying public space, wearing inappropriate clothing, and the influence of sexually explicit media (Rao 2014). The mundane regularity with which some of these statements were regurgitated led the *Times of India*, a leading daily English-language newspaper, to catalog them as "foot in mouth statements" (2013a). The brutality of the assault—combined with both the apathy with which it was initially received and with the rampant victim-blaming it generated—fueled an eruption of protests in the weeks that followed. Anger at the callous reactions and horror at the assault, which had torn open Singh's insides, erupted into rage as thousands took to the street. These protests, which rejected victim-blaming, claimed the right of women to be safely out in public (Phadke 2013).

What does blaming the victim for her assault permit? What is secured and consolidated in grafting blame onto the victim while structural male aggression is essentialized as immutable? While victim-blaming has been thoroughly critiqued by feminists for how it vests responsibility for an assault in women while absolving men and broader structures of misogyny, I am interested in what victim-blaming generates. The architecture of blame rests on an effort to cast women who are raped as responsible for their assaults because they made bad choices. Vesting women with the agency to make bad choices in this way then enables an insidious maneuver to discredit victims as immoral women who should be ashamed. I am interested in the script of shame that is amplified by resurrecting the zombie moniker of zinda laash.

The dominant script of shame after rape follows a particular trajectory in which women are blamed for their assault and then held responsible for the dishonor and burden they bring to their families. Since women, by their very existence, are already considered burdens within structures of patriarchy, any additional shame they bring in the wake of an assault renders them intolerable. Feminists have long rejected this narrative, dislodging the burden on women to prove their innocence and instead placing it at the door of misogynist structures and institutions that support and perpetuate this sexist script. And while this script of shame has been difficult to displace, it did noticeably shift in the winter of 2012. The protests following the attack on Jyoti Singh forcefully rejected any victim-blaming or victim-shaming, cast the police and state as apathetic, and called for reform and change. The remarkable uprising, though, needs to be understood in the context of a decades-long history of feminist activism, which laid the groundwork for the critiques that were articulated, rather than an eruption of spontaneous anger.

The state, which was clearly taken aback by the scale of the protests as they quickly spread outside Delhi, realized that it had to alter its narrative about the rape and its own response to it. In an effort to repair the damage to its legitimacy after its misogyny had been laid bare, the government tried to save Jyoti Singh's life by sending her to Singapore. In the state's quest for damage control, Jyoti Singh was transformed from a shameful figure who brought on her own attack into "India's daughter" (Lodhia 2015, 90). Through this maneuver, she was reconstituted as a "daughter" of the patriarchal state who had failed to protect her against demonic perpetrators. The perpetrators, in turn, were made out to be uncivilized men who came into the city from rural hinterlands and resided in areas where criminal activity thrived. The attack against Jyoti Singh was understood by various media outlets as "an almost inevitable outgrowth of a restless and animalistic masculinity" (92). In contrast, those seeking more nuance and complexity about her assailants, who were all poor migrant men, sought to understand the conditions of disenfranchisement that could generate such brutality, conditions shaped by neoliberalism, migration, and alienation which together produced these "marginalized masculinities" (92).

Singh's death in some ways settled the disquiet that a survivor of rape generates. While rejecting the zinda laash terminology for raped women, some protesters demanded death for the perpetrators (India Today Web Desk 2020). The fact that Jyoti Singh did not survive her assault buttressed their demands; it allowed them to claim that the death penalty was applicable and justified because the perpetrators had exacted the ultimate harm in this "rarest of rare cases." For the state, in the form of the judiciary, avenging "India's daughter" meant that those who defiled her had to be consigned to death, the ultimate punishment for the ultimate crime (Gettleman, Kumar, and Venugopal 2020). She could be avenged fully, and earlier suspicions about how her autonomy and "bad choices" may have elicited her assault were now silenced. But Jyoti Singh wanted to live following her assault.

When she managed to communicate from the hospital, she expressed her wish to live. Five days after her assault, unable to speak because she had a feeding tube down her throat, she scribbled on a piece of paper "I want to live, I want to survive and stay with you all" (Ok and Roberts 2013). Those who survive rape express a wish to live beyond the rape. The zinda laash label is not a self-identification; it is an imposition. In August 2013, the year following the assault on Jyoti Singh, a young photojournalist was gang-raped while she was investigating a story in Shakti Mills, a deserted factory in Mumbai. From her hospital bed, she too rejected the narrative that her survival would be comparable to a living death, and claimed that "rape is not the end of life" (*Times of India* 2013b).

What does the narrative of the living dead allow? I suggest that the power of the zinda laash moniker rests on its ability to mobilize shame. Its currency traffics in the collective agreement that women's virtue is to be protected and that its defilement brings deep shame for the family. The structure of shame brought to the family as a consequence of compromised virtue is vested in caste politics of purity and lineage. Particularly in rural areas, but not exclusively so, the significance of land and of passing it down through customary primogeniture laws means that lineage has to be protected. Consequently, especially among dominant-caste families, women's sexuality is controlled because women are considered to be primarily responsible for maintaining caste purity (Chakravarti 2018, 33). Uma Chakravarti explains that "under Brahmanical patriarchy women of the upper caste are regarded as gateways—literally points of entry into the caste system" (2018, 34). Rape, then, sullies the purity of blood and lines of descent, because it renders the woman no longer virginal and untouched.

The crime of rape is therefore understood within caste patriarchal structures as a crime of dishonor—loss of *izzat*—to the family. Since the raped woman brings shame to the family, she is a defiled figure of no value, and her existence going forward is that of the living dead. A woman's value is primarily constituted through her relationship to her family and community, and she is measured by the honor or dishonor she brings them. Since "women are the repositories of family honor—of their own family as daughter, of their husband's family as wife and mother . . . the implication is that if their conduct is dishonorable, women can ruin their families forever" (Chakravarti 2018, 143). Women's identity in this framework is understood as a relationship, not as an autonomous liberal subject. If constituted through this template, the zinda laash terminology makes sense because she is a dead burden on the family to whom her rape has brought dishonor. Consequently, if she were to die, then shame turns into tragedy, which allows for more maneuverability in structures of caste and family than dishonor.

The protests against the zinda laash narrative after Jyoti Singh's assault attempted to unyoke the relationship between women and family honor. Critiques brought attention to victim-blaming statements that harnessed old yet resilient explanations for women's assault and sought to dislodge the shame that came with alleging assault. The narratives that rely on blaming a victim for her assault adopt two very particular strategies: First, in generating a frame in which women are blamed for their fate, these maneuvers seek to return women to their rightful place within patriarchal family institutions where they can be protected. Straying outside these boundaries is seen to be fraught with danger. For its part, the judiciary—through the courts, the state, and its political statements—endorses this enfolding of women into these structures of alleged protection. Second, blaming victims based on their clothing, their being out in public, and their being in the company of men frames women as making bad choices and then holds them responsible for the danger they face. Both of these maneuvers make assumptions with consequential implications: the first is that the patriarchal structure of the home is a place not of violence but of protection, the only place where women's honor can be safeguarded; second, that women are raped as a result of their bad choices, and that they alone are responsible for the violence they encounter. Shame, therefore, remains women's burden, a thing against which they must be perpetually vigilant in order to avoid being held guilty of bringing it upon themselves and their families.

This is why the desire to live, poignantly expressed by both Jyoti Singh and the photojournalist who was gang-raped in Shakti Mills, is significant: because it rejects the patriarchal caste diktat of shame within which their assault was read, and instead articulates their will. In the chapter on consent, I drew on Saidiya Hartman's (1997) construction of will in the context of the rape of enslaved women. Here, I employ Deepti Misri's (2011) understanding of how will is produced, which she arrives at by studying women who rejected "patriarchal scripting" by protesting in the nude (608). Specifically, Misri examines the 2004 naked protest by Meitei women in Manipur against the Assam Rifles, a military group whose men had tortured, raped, and murdered Thangam Manorama, a female activist from India's northeastern state of Assam, while she was in their custody that year. In response to Manorama's murder, Meitei women staged a naked protest in the streets of Imphal in front of the Assam Rifles headquarters. To understand the significance of their naked protest, Misri draws on Mahasweta Devi's famous story of

Draupadi and its 1988 interpretation and translation by Gayatri Chakravorty Spivak. The story is about a raped tribal woman who stands in front of a police officer, her bare body bloody and matted with the violence of the state. In so doing, Misri argues that "Draupadi refuses the hegemonic script of shame that the wounds of sexual violence are meant to evoke" (608).

The naked protest by Meitei women in front of the army headquarters is a strategy that similarly rejects the state's use of rape to evoke shame and fear. It instead turns the script around by publicly displaying, literally nakedly, that women's bodies are sites of violence sanctioned by the Armed Forces Special Powers Act.[6] The Meitei women's protest included a large banner that read "Indian Army Rape us!," exposing the fiction of the "protective" script of the state by highlighting that the state itself sanctions and legitimizes the use of violence against women. Drawing on zinda laash in response to rape and victim shaming allows patriarchal structures of the state, family, and the law to absolve themselves from their responsibility for violence against women while simultaneously presenting themselves as protectors by constructing poor, lower-caste, and rural men as the unruly ones possessing a toxic masculinity that threatens women. The story of Draupadi and the protest by Meitei women lay bare the fallacy of this claim of protection. In so doing, they turn the narrative of shame around to point to the state as the bearer of disgrace.

On the third anniversary of her daughter's assault, Jyoti Singh's mother similarly called out the state at a protest in Delhi, albeit not directly, by reversing the burden of shame from her brutalized daughter to those responsible for the crime. In an impassioned speech, she said, "I am not ashamed to say my daughter's name, I say to you all as well: No matter what has happened to you, you do not need to hide your name. They are the ones who should be ashamed and hide their faces; they who do repugnant things to us, who trouble our daughters." In a direct allegation implicating the state and the burden of shame it bears, she continued, "They who do not punish these crimes should be ashamed, they who do not make laws for these crimes should be ashamed. We do not need to be ashamed." Finally, she defied the national law that prohibits disclosing the names of rape victims, even by their parents and loved ones, by proudly proclaiming, "I say to all of you that my daughter's name was Jyoti Singh, and from today she should be known as Jyoti Singh" (NDTV 2015; translated from the original Hindi by author). By very publicly rejecting the dominant narrative about how shame attaches itself to the woman who has been raped, Jyoti Singh's mother was able to flip the script and assert that shame fell squarely on the perpetrators and the state. They were the ones who were guilty; they were the ones who should be crushed by shame and held responsible.

SHAME IN STRUCTURES OF CASTE

The rape cases in rural Haryana that I followed, however, featured a story of shame with a different trajectory than in Jyoti Singh's case or in the case of the photojournalist in Mumbai. In the Haryana cases I traced, the discourse of shame was mobilized through subjectivity tied to the community, where rape exceeds the violation of individual bodies to encompasses violence against caste. The victims were not like Jyoti Singh and the photojournalist in Shakti Mills, who by their individual will to live challenged the script of shame. Nor did they inhabit the same locus as Meitei women activists. For Jat, Dalit, and OBC women, their subjectivities are constituted not as individuals but through larger collectives of caste and community. In contrast, while both Jyoti Singh and the photojournalist also belonged to communities and families, their rape was understood as a violation of their personal bodily integrity. In this formulation they were constituted through liberal subjecthood, in which their rape was not about violence against their caste *biradri* (community) but about violence against them as individual women. Even when Jyoti Singh became "India's daughter," she was reproduced as the nation's daughter to reconstitute the Indian state as the good, protective patriarch. Meitei women, however, showed this maneuver to be farcical; their protests revealed that the state that professes to possess a "good masculinity" and to be the protector of women is the very same one that also violates them.

Shenila S. Khoja-Moolji (2017) writes, concerning her empirical work with adolescent girls in the villages of Khyber and Aliabad in Pakistan, "that the autonomous, individual subject of . . . human rights discourse exists side by side with conceptions of being human that traverse the delicate space between individuality and belonging to collectives, be they families, tribes, religious communities, or clans" (378). For those living in agricultural communities, these forms of subject formation are generated as part of a continuum with other people and with land (394). My observation of subjectivities among Jat, Dalit, and OBC communities in the villages was similar. But belonging to a community is not akin to some romantic notion of collectivity; rather, community is a necessary sociopolitical formation among those whose lives are precarious.[7] Chapter 3, which focused on land, detailed the imbrication of dominant and subordinate castes' lives in agricultural communities and examined how their subjectivities were shaped by the collectives to which they belonged. Such collective relationships are sustained through reciprocal rituals generated among rural communities whose lives are vulnerable.[8] These interlocking relationships undergird the structure of compromise in rape cases in the villages. Subjectivities formed in these communities are precarious, so significant effort is made in the wake of rape cases to preserve the reputations of both the dominant and subordinate castes involved. However, caste disparity renders the subjectivities of Dalit or OBC caste vulnerable to dominant-caste mandates.

Dalit literature in particular has documented how the narrative of violence is a story of violating the community, rather than of only violating the individual. Joshil K. Abraham and Judith Misrahi-Barak (2017) write that Dalit literature's "purpose is to *illustrate* and denounce the abominable situation in which Dalits in contemporary India live" (3). Dalit women's place in this literature is particularly significant, as authors writing in vernacular languages narrate their life stories as testimonies of interlocking forms of oppression (Sharma and Kumar 2019). Recent studies about Dalit literature suggest that Dalit autobiographies, such as Bama's *Karukku*, should be treated as testimonials (Nayar 2006). Sarah Beth (2007) observes that "since Dalit autobiographies are meant to be the life story of an ordinary Dalit, to symbolically represent the experiences of every Dalit, the Dalit protagonist is established as the representative of the Dalit community and Dalit identity" (551).

Acts of horrific violence against Dalit men and women, then, are not just confined to bodily harm to the individual but are about retaliation against the caste community. For instance, the massacre of Dalits in Mirchpur, which I detailed in the introduction, or the violence against Dalit women like Surekha and Priyanka Bhotmange, who were raped and murdered in Khairlanji,[9] are about violence enacted on the bodies of Dalit women to teach the entire caste community a "lesson." Scholars have noted that the rape of Dalit women is an assertion of dominant-caste violence and about the emasculation of subordinate-caste men (Anandhi and Kapadia 2019; Rao 2009). Hugo Gorringe (2017) writes that "dominant castes used sexual violence against Dalit women as a means of demonstrating their virility and shaming Dalit men" (6). In this formulation, shame is mobilized by the dominant caste against Dalits and other subordinate castes as a way to humiliate and control the community.[10]

If the rape and assault of Dalit men and women represent violence against the community, then a question arises: Why is there a lack of response to the rape of Dalit women from the larger body politic? Put another way, Anand

Teltumbde (2013) asks why collective national grief was not expressed for Surekha and Priyanka Bhotmange as it was for Jyoti Singh in December 2012.[11] Why was the outpouring of grief and anger over the rape of Jyoti Singh absent when it came to the rape of Dalit women? Just three months before the assault on Jyoti Singh, a young Dalit girl returning from school in Haryana was gang-raped by eight Jat men and left at the side of a canal. Her assault was recorded on a cellular phone, and she was threatened with exposure if she disclosed the incident. A week after the incident, the video circulated in the village and, after seeing it, her father committed suicide. But the incident did not make the papers, nor were any protests in Delhi, a mere three hours away, held in outrage.

The rapes in Khairlanji in 2006 and Sirasgaon in 1963 entailed violent assaults on women, but they were simultaneously and centrally about dominant-caste violence against Dalits as a community. Yet as Meena Gopal (2014) and other feminists have pointed out, sexual violence tends to receive attention only as gendered violence rather than as violence that is simultaneously aimed against an entire caste community. Why is it that the rape of Dalit women can only (and only to a limited extent) be recognized as gender violence but not as caste atrocity (Rao 2009)? Pratiksha Baxi (2014) notes that "judicial understanding of rape as atrocity is thin, and convictions of rape as atrocity are rare" (284). Even in the case of the gang rape of the young Dalit girl in Haryana, the Prevention of Atrocities Act was struck down as one of the charges in the judgment. In the ruling, caste was illegible; its import could not be discerned in the absence of direct evidence that the victim was targeted specifically because of her caste. Baxi explains this incapacity in the law, arguing that "in making a classification between lust and atrocity, judicial interpretation does not construct rape as atrocity, for such forms of sexual violence are seen as isolated crimes against individual women, irrespective of their caste or class" (284). I argue that the law refuses to characterize the rape of Dalit women as caste violence because understanding these rapes as such would implicate larger national public and state institutions. I argue that the very erasure of the rape of Dalit women as instances of caste atrocity is evidence of the state's complicity in the maintenance of dominant-caste violence. How might this erasure of violence against caste communities through the rape of Dalit and OBC women be interrupted? If we understand the rape of Dalit women as mobilizing shame and humiliation against men and their communities, what can interrupt the script of humiliation that this generates for the community?

I suggest that death after rape interrupts the trajectory of this script. I argue that death should not be understood as an abrupt tragic event, but rather as a testimony that has an afterlife, demanding recognition. I propose that death interrupts the script of shame and humiliation by making the institutions of the state, as manifested in the courts and the law, take a case seriously. Because death adds gravity to rape cases, it compels dominant-caste structures to recognize injury. However, this recognition of injury is never complete, and efforts to disrupt it by stoking suspicion about the integrity of the raped woman remain. This is why I deliberately use the word "interrupt," rather than "stem," to describe the trajectory of the script. Death is only able to affect a disruption to the script of shame. It does not dislodge it. In fact, the rape of Dalit women continues to be recognized only as a crime against the individual, rather than understood as also constituting an atrocity against the caste community. Moreover, as we will see in the cases I document in the rest of this chapter, justice in these instances is partial. The stories of death after rape illustrate both the interruption of the humiliation script as well as the ongoing suspicion cast on victims that remains indelibly part of the rape script, rendering justice continually incomplete and out of reach.

DEATH IN RAPE CASES

I draw on two cases in Haryana to unpack the significance of death in rape cases. The case from Malud village is of a young woman I call Sheetal, who was gang-raped in 2012 and left by the side of a canal. I make reference to her case in chapter 3 and where in response to her case, Sheetal and her family were promised land in return for compromising the case. The second case is from Dantha village and involves a young girl I call Ladli who was gang-raped in 2015 and who died a few months later. In analyzing these two cases, I reference Saidiya Hartman (1997) to theorize how death makes subjectivity legible. I am also concerned with the proximity of death for subordinate castes and turn to Ruth Wilson Gilmore's (2007) understanding of race to unpack this relationship between subordination and mortality.

The Story of Sheetal

Malud is a large village, well-known for its big landlords who hold prominent positions in local government and who have family ties to large land developers. Inhabited in the 1800s, the village is close to a large bustling town and accessible by buses and rickshaws. The village is dominated by Jats, with other castes, including Dalits, living there in smaller numbers. Much like the other villages I visited, *kheti* (farming) was in crisis and an increasingly precarious way to making a living. (The conversation with young men seeking employment in the private sector, which I recounted in chapter 3, took place in this village.) Private schools and banquet halls are scattered along the road that leads to the village, offering clues about efforts to engage in private ventures to offset the lack of revenue from farming.

It was late in the morning when I first visited the village, accompanied by a Dalit activist, and it was already hot.[12] We drew curious looks, and I asked a passerby where I could find the sarpanch or a member of the panchayat. It turned out that the person I asked was the *lumberdar* (keeper of records) of the village, and he invited us to his home. At this initial meeting, the lumberdar offered us general information about the village and its history. We were in Malud to speak with members of the village about Sheetal's gang rape, which occurred in 2012. It had been four years since the incident and Sheetal had not been back to the village since. Her case added to the statistics that make Haryana infamous for having one of the largest numbers of gang rapes in the country. She was a young schoolgirl when she was raped, on a late afternoon, as she was walking near a water canal. She recalls that a car pulled up beside her and the men inside pulled her into the car. They drove a distance and took her into the fields. She says that a couple of men on bikes followed the car, and when they all reached the field, some of them began to rape her while others stood watch. She recognized some of the men who assaulted her as part of a gang of Jat men from her village who were involved in a violent incident a few years earlier.

In subsequent years, whenever Sheetal would recount the story of her rape her composure was remarkably different from the other women I met who had been assaulted. Her demeanor was calm, and her recollection flowed like a narrative smoothed by repeated tellings.[13] There was a distance in Sheetal's narrative, as if her many repetitions had created a sort of crust over the tale, hardened against its horror. But while Sheetal appeared composed, she was also a troubled young woman. Over the years I became close to her, and we frequently talked over the phone even when I was back in New York. She was often confused and conflicted about what she wanted to do in the future, even while she claimed that she wanted to go to law school. Like other young women, she was also interested in dance and music and was taking lessons. She was shy and reticent, while also charming and courageous. Her trauma was deep, hidden beneath layers of the demeanor she had crafted to protect herself amid all the attention she received after her assault. The media attention and support from various groups gave her confidence and a sense of self, yet at the same time, she felt lost and unsure. The afterlife of rape left her wounded, and in some ways, adrift. When I first met her, she was recovering from a suicide attempt. She had ingested a bathroom cleaner that had corroded her esophagus and stomach. In the months that followed, she often struggled with eating and speaking.

Sheetal's suicide attempt followed that of her father, who had taken his own life after he saw a video of his daughter's rape. She recalls that after the rape, while she was staying with her grandparents in the city, she fell ill. Distressed by her poor health, her grandparents asked her parents to come from the village and visit her. This is when Sheetal finally told them about her assault. By then it had been nine days since the rape, and she was still experiencing pain in her abdomen. She had delayed telling her parents out of fear; the men had threatened to retaliate if she told anyone what they had done to her. When Sheetal finally told her parents, her father was particularly shocked and aggrieved. On hearing the news, he decided to go back to the village and speak with elders to find out what had happened. Once in the village, he saw the video of the rape that was circulating. Deeply distressed by the video and the assault on his daughter, Sheetal recounts that her father claimed "humare saat anyaye hua hai" (we have had injustice done to us) and committed suicide by ingesting pesticides.[14] On the night of her father's suicide, the news was kept from Sheetal because she had exams the following day; she was finally told four days later.[15] During legal proceedings for her case, Sheetal's mother testified that she held the men who had raped her daughter responsible for the death of her husband, because if it were not for the crime they had committed, he would still be alive. When I ask Sheetal if her father left a suicide note, she said that he did not, but that before his death, he had said that "insaaf nahi milega hume" (we will not get justice).[16]

Sheetal's father's lament echoes in the stories that Dalit families often repeat about the injustice and violence they are forced to endure when they are not believed, when their statements are falsified, and when they are coerced into withdrawing their cases and threatened with boycott if they continue to pursue justice. In Sheetal's own case, she and her family faced threats and intimidation from dominant-caste people in the village. The police, for their part, collaborated in this intimidation by writing in names of Dalit men from the village in the complaint and by distorting Sheetal's descriptions of the Jat men who raped her. Alert to the use of coercion and intimidation in such cases, the Dalit *basti* in the village began to mobilize support for Sheetal and her family. Following the Mirchpur incident in 2010, a network of Dalit and human rights groups had been built in Haryana to respond to cases of atrocity against Dalits. Sheetal's assault and her father's death had generated shock and anger, to which these Dalit organizations and human rights groups responded by coming to the village in support. In the previous section of this chapter, I explained how crime against an individual is recognized within the community as a crime against the caste. In Sheetal's case, the Dalit and human rights groups clearly articulated the threat of dominant-caste coercion and drew attention to her rape and the facts around it.

To resist the coercion Sheetal's family was subjected to by dominant castes in the village and the neglect and hostility they encountered from the police and courts, members of the Dalit *basti* refused to cremate Sheetal's father's body. They sat in protest and said, "Jab tak case darz nahi hoga tab tak dah sanskaar nahi karenge" (We will not perform last rites unless the police file a case and arrest the perpetrators).[17] Their strategy effectively forced the district collector and other members of the bureaucracy to pay attention. In the context of this collective pressure, twenty-four men were finally arrested and twelve were eventually taken into custody. Of these, four were acquitted, four were released on bail, and four were convicted for life, a sentence that carries a twenty-year prison term.[18] Sheetal's rape occurred three months before the Delhi gang rape of 2012; having heightened attention to rape, it helped the latter case quickly garner national and international attention.

The Story of Ladli

The second case I draw on is from Dantha village, involving the gang rape of a fourteen-year-old girl belonging to Kashyap—a subordinate-caste group in the OBC category—by three men from her same caste. The young girl, whom I call Ladli, was assaulted in February 2015 during a wedding celebration in her *basti*. On the evening of the wedding, Ladli had gone outside her house to gather water from a communal tap. There, three men suddenly abducted her and dragged her inside a nearby house. In her testimony, she said that one of the men covered her mouth while the other two lifted her legs and took her into the house, drawing down the metal shutter and gagging her when she tried to shout for help. After they raped her, she was threatened against revealing the incident to anyone. Ladli's grandmother recalled that she had noticed water overflowing from the container at the tap outside their home and called out to her granddaughter.[19] When Ladli finally managed to get home, her grandmother asked where she had been, but she just lay down and went to sleep. The next day she did not wake up despite the attempts by her parents to rouse her. When she finally woke up, her parents saw that her clothes were smeared with blood. She disclosed the incident to them, after which they filed a police report at the nearby thanna, and Ladli was medically examined for rape. On investigating the scene of the crime, the police found liquor bottles and cigarettes at the site.[20]

Ladli's family includes her parents, grandparents, and two younger siblings. When I met this family, they had been fighting to get justice for Ladli for over two years. They are very poor and work as daily wage workers. They had spent an enormous sum of money on the case, and the *daadi* (grandmother) said that whatever they earned, they spent to pay lawyers. The accused are from the same village and reside in the same *basti*. There are four main accused in the case, all of whom belong to the same caste as Ladli: Satish Kumar and Deepak Kumar, who are brothers-in-law, and their friends Tarun Kumar and Ajay. In the various court documents related to the rape case, there is significant variation and inconsistency in who names which accused and when. For instance, in one document Ladli initially names three people: Satish Kumar and the two friends, Tarun and Ajay. But the police investigation only found evidence of two perpetrators and apprehended Satish Kumar and Ajay, claiming there was no involvement of a third person. In the final judgment of the case, Ladli's father's testimony and cross-examination differed from Ladli's. He said that when he went to the police station to file a First Information Report (FIR) with his daughter, she had named two men, Satish Kumar and Deepak Kumar. The father went on to say that Ladli had recognized Satish and Deepak because she had seen them in the village and knew that they were brothers-in-law. In yet another court document, Ladli claimed she knew that the place she was raped belonged to Deepak Kumar's family and that he had stood guard outside while the other three men raped her. According to Ladli's father, he and Ladli's grandfather had filed to add the names of Ajay and Tarun Kumar later on because he realized that these two men had also been involved in the assault on his daughter only when their families came to compel him to compromise the case. These variations in who was named in the case and when served to cast doubt on the veracity of the claims made by Ladli and her family.

After the police investigation led to the arrest of Satish Kumar and Ajay, Deepak Kumar's family began a sustained campaign of terrifying intimidation and serious coercion against Ladli and her family. One day in July, after several months of threats, members of Deepak Kumar's family came into Ladli's house while she was alone and her family was out.[21] They threatened her, telling her to withdraw her complaint or else they would kill her and her family. That evening Ladli was found with extensive burns all over her body. She died shortly thereafter. While her family alleges that Deepak Kumar's family killed her, the court documents claim that she committed suicide because of coercion. The judgment in the case, which was filed after Ladli's death, indicted three people for her death: Deepak Kumar, his mother, and his aunt were convicted on abetment to suicide charges and sentenced to ten years of rigorous imprisonment.[22] A later judgment of gang rape was decided in June 2019, eight months after the abetment to suicide judgment, and relied crucially on both her death and on DNA evidence to prove the assault. The judgment reads, "After being a victim of the gruesome act of gang rape, the victim was shamed by the family members of the accused persons and ultimately she committed suicide by setting herself on fire. Learned counsel argued that the DNA report was supporting the case of the prosecution and that was clinching evidence against the accused persons."[23]

In both Sheetal's and Ladli's cases, death compelled the courts to move forward and to indict the accused. The gravity that death accorded these cases meant, as one lawyer put it, that they became "more serious."[24] The crime of rape is taken seriously when either the victim or someone in her family dies, and thereby gives the case more credibility. Moreover, the fact that both cases involved gang rape, for which Haryana was infamous, added to their weight. But it was the tragedy of Sheetal's father's death and Ladli's death that shifted the tenor of each case, both for Sheetal and Ladli individually, as well as collectively for the community. Consequently, it was the significance of their deaths that was used as leverage to push for justice. But while this strategy worked to get at least partial justice in Sheetal's case, in Ladli's case, it also served to cast suspicion on the legitimacy of the case, as its unfolding revealed discrepancies, conflicts of interest, and prior animosity between the families. I elaborate on these in the "Suspicion After Death" section near the end of this chapter.

RECOGNITION IN DEATH

Death functions as leverage to get a complaint formally registered under the law. The strategy of refusing to perform last rites, which was deployed when protesting Dalits refused to cremate Sheetal's father's body, is an oft-used method to compel authorities to follow the law. There is a perverse violence to this strategy that is worth noting; it is often the finality of death that compels authorities to pay serious attention to those making the complaint, and to follow the most basic of legal procedures. In her recent work on the use of forensic science in cases of torture, Jinee Lokaneeta (2020) similarly remarks on the efforts that police make to avoid the death of a suspect in their custody and evade the unwelcome scrutiny that such death would bring. She says, "The Indian police must avoid causing custodian death, which exceeds the threshold of violence that the state can defend, especially in routine cases" (46). For Dalits in particular, a death in their community, followed by their community's refusal to perform last rites for the deceased, is often the only way to get their complaint heard by the state, as represented by police stations and the village and district bureaucracy. Dalits are effectively forced to forgo their rituals of mourning to meet the urgency of having their basic rights recognized. Even when faced with death, they are effectively denied essential rights.

Here, I draw once again on Saidiya Hartman's (1997) sophisticated analysis of violence directed at the enslaved body to understand the function of death in cases of rape. Hartman carefully crafts an argument about the inability of the law to recognize the enslaved as possessing subjecthood and the capacity to express autonomy. The harm done to the enslaved is not recognized as excessive because it is understood as "necessary to the maintenance of slave relations" (81). This formulation constitutes the enslaved subject as requiring submission, which is why Hartman elaborates that "black submission unmoors the notion of 'force'" (81). In this way, the force and harm inflicted on the Black body because of a "necessity of violence" do not register as harm, unless the violence is exceptional. Then, Hartman rhetorically asks, "What limit must be exceeded in order that the violence directed at the black body be made legible in the law?" (81). The question Hartman poses offers a way to think about why death accords a rape case with a seriousness it would otherwise be denied. Again, I ask, what does death allow?

As I mentioned in chapter 1, my intention in drawing on Hartman is not to construct a parallel between enslaved people and raped women. Rather, Hartman's deft articulation of subjection demonstrates the inability of the law to accord subjectivity to the enslaved. If, per this formulation, we are to consider the enslaved at one end, then at the other would be those who are accorded personhood and subject positions, in the law and elsewhere, such as white men and dominant-caste men. These two positions represent particular extremes: one of recognition and the other of illegibility. Dalit and subordinate-caste women, I suggest, occupy a space in between these two extremes. In articulating the positions at either end of this spectrum, I do not mean to suggest that these subjectivities exist on a linear continuum. Subject formation is not flat and two-dimensional. Instead, I use this framing to help conceptualize how violence directed at the Dalit body is made both legible and illegible.

I propose that the space in between the two poles of illegibility and recognition only becomes perceptible through violence. Anupama Rao (2009), in her understanding of how Dalits are made visible in law, suggests that "Dalits came to be interpellated as injured subjects" through a set of legal measures (173). Dalit and subordinate-caste bodies do not occupy the position of the enslaved, who are not recognized as subjects, nor are they autonomous subjects who are accorded recognition. Somewhere in between, these bodies occupy a liminal space, one that cannot be entirely dismissed nor fully recognized. It is this in-betweenness of the "injured" Dalit female body that I consider to be the source of discomfort and disruption. This body has been crafted through a narrative of excess; she is excessively sexual and promiscuous, akin to how Black women were constituted. This body is a source of both lascivious interest as well as revulsion by members of the dominant caste. Dalit literature is replete with documentation of the manner in which the subordinate-caste female body is "available" to dominant-caste violence. But increasingly, that body is also a source of disruption when it stands as witness and proof of dominant-caste violence. Despite efforts by dominant castes to minimize and dismiss the harm done to subordinate castes, efforts to compel recognition, such as those by the Dalit *basti* in Sheetal's case, are growing.

When the subordinate-caste body reveals that it has been subjected to excessive violence, as when Sheetal's gang rape was recorded and her father committed suicide, or as evident in Ladli's burnt corpse, then the body compels recognition in law, particularly in cases involving rape. In their refusal to perform last rites for Sheetal's father until the injustice he and his daughter had suffered was recognized, a Dalit family and community in Malud forced an acknowledgment that had been withheld by the state, law, and public sphere, all of which are dominant-caste institutions and arenas. Ladli's burnt body compelled the court to press charges, which were ultimately reduced to abetting suicide rather than committing murder. In the judgment, the defense argued that Ladli's suicide was caused by depression. The judge agreed that Ladli's "mental condition . . . had become more fragile" in the period after she had been raped, but insisted that it had been the "constant pressure, torture and threatening by the accused persons . . . particularly on the day of [the] occurrence [of her death] itself" that "drove her to the extreme step of committing suicide." The judge rejected the defense's argument that depression alone had led Ladli to commit suicide and ruled that the accused were responsible for driving her to end her life.[25] The corpses of Ladli and Sheetal's father actually bore witness to the crime, forcing the court to recognize it. Moreover, the brutality of their deaths constitutes testimony in the afterlife of rape, interrupting the script of humiliation and abjection by compelling recognition of injury.

A vicious violence shrouds this strategy, which relies on death to accord recognition. This goes back to the wrenching question Hartman (1997) asks about "the limits that must be crossed for the enslaved body to be recognized" (81). She underscores this recognition by observing that "the slave was considered subject only insofar as he was criminal(ized), wounded body, or mortified flesh" (94). Recognition is only possible for the injured body when death follows. Ladli's burnt body was explicitly recognized in the gang rape judgment, which indicted two people. The judge in the case specifically ruled against leniency by saying, "Due to the effects of [the] gruesome act and conduct of [the] convicts, the life of [an] innocent person was cut short and brought to a ghastly end."[26] Until this point, the victims are neither full subjects nor disposed and allowed to die, as if unnecessary. Rather, the necessity for exploitable labor prohibits a complete refusal to recognize the injuries members of subordinate castes sustain and cannot accommodate an annihilation of their lives. From the perspective of dominant castes, subordinate castes must be made to perpetually live precarious lives, subject to harm and violation, but without recourse to justice.

DERISION AND VIOLENCE AFTER DEATH

When subordinate castes compel the state to recognize them, it is disruptive and offensive to dominant-caste sensibilities. Consequently, when Sheetal's rapists were indicted and sentenced to life in prison, it shocked some dominant-caste elders in the village. Their affront at the verdict was about the ability of a Dalit female body to demand recognition of her bodily integrity and secure punishment for its violation by the state. After her father committed suicide, compounding the violation that Sheetal experienced, dominant-caste efforts to suppress the case in the village by coercion and bribery failed. This inability to suppress the case, which led to the imprisonment of Jat men, generated deep resentment among dominant castes.

When rape cases are decided in favor of the Dalit victim, efforts to discredit the cases and cast suspicion on the women's character are routinely deployed. There is profound intolerance of punishment given to dominant castes for atrocities their members commit against those they consider beneath them. When Sheetal's rapists were sentenced to life in prison, it was a breathtaking reversal of the norm precisely because the state, in the form of the court, recognized the aggrieved and thereby accorded them the subjectivity of personhood, with the capacity to hold rights and defy violation. Members of dominant castes find it deeply troubling to see Dalits inhabit such personhood. When Sheetal's case was filed, there were persistent efforts to discredit it and to coerce her family to retract the charges. Led by a powerful dominant-caste family in the village, who claimed that their ancestors gave the village common land, Sheetal and her family were repeatedly coerced, bribed, and threatened to compromise with the perpetrators.

As I recalled in chapter 3, when I met the powerful landlord Satpal Bajwa at his bungalow in the city, toward the end of our conversation, I asked about Sheetal's rape. It was at this point that he became more animated and spoke disparagingly about what he considered to be illegitimate Dalit claims to village common land. But while his response meandered toward land claims and Jat victimhood, it was for Sheetal that he reserved his more ardent contempt. He said, "Ladki aur us ki ma dhandha karte the" (The girl and her mother were prostitutes). In this display of derision, he made apparent the affront he felt at Sheetal's claim for justice against the Jats who had violated her. Defense attorneys in Sheetal's case similarly impugned her character by suggesting she was sexually promiscuous and by arguing that she was not underage—or young and innocent—like her family claimed.[27]

While he reserved his most acute contempt for Sheetal and her family, Mr. Bajwa was simultaneously frustrated with the accused. At one point in our conversation, he said the "woh ullu ke patthe" (sons of idiots/fools) would not have been caught if they had not recorded the incident. He pointed out that four of the accused men were acquitted because their "faces were not clear in the video." Still, Mr. Bajwa's comments were evidence of the offense he took at a poor Dalit family daring to hold powerful Jats accountable for what both he and other Jats considered not a crime but a social dispute.[28] Because Dalit women's bodies have historically been available for Jats to violate, turning Sheetal's case into a crime jarred Mr. Bajwa and other dominant-caste men and women accustomed to their power and impunity.

As I explained in chapter 3, Sheetal said that her family was told that if they compromised the case, then all Dalit families in their community would receive land.[29] It is precisely this sort of effort to hold the entire Dalit community hostage that exposes how the rape of Dalit women is about caste atrocity. Yet the law is unable to recognize the imbrication of caste relations. The judge in Sheetal's case remarked, "There is nothing on record to show that the prosecutrix [victim on behalf of whom the state is prosecuting the crime] or her family members were ever humiliated or abused by the accused or their family members on the basis of differences in their castes." Therefore, the judgment concluded that the "mere fact that the victim happened to be a girl belonging to a scheduled caste does not attract the provisions of the [Prevention of Atrocity] Act [punishing caste-based violence]."[30] The law only has the capacity to recognize that a rape was motivated by caste violence if this motivation is directly established. It does not have the ability to acknowledge relationships of caste dominance in which Dalit women are assumed to be available to dominant-caste men; so the rape of Sheetal was not, within this paradigm, an aberration. Yet as we will see in the next section of this chapter, the law nevertheless expanded its capacity to speculate about intention when it came to casting suspicion over Ladli's case in favor of the accused, when her side was not consistent in naming suspects.[31] But the law refused to speculate about intention in Sheetal's case. By refusing the script granting dominant-caste men access to Dalit women's bodies, Sheetal asserted her demand that such caste-based violations be seen as a crime. However, the court refused to speculate that the crime against her was at least in part motivated by the desire to maintain caste hierarchies. It rejected charges relating to caste, and remained blind to such caste inferences, even though it routinely makes other types of assumptions.

Sheetal's brave stand against the tremendous pressure to make her withdraw her case not only interrupted the script of humiliation but also exposed the weakening power of Jats in the village. Their effort to hold on to past glory was most evident when I visited Mr. Bajwa's ancestral home in the village. The *haveli* (large house) sits at the corner, with a new private English language school adjoining it. The home showed signs of neglect even though it was inhabited, and the air was heavy and still. Rajeev Bajwa, the nephew of Satpal Bajwa and a respected elder in the village, invited us to sit in the living room while he ordered tea. In our conversation about changes he saw in the village, he told a story that expressed his concern for fading traditions. In a commanding voice, he said that he had seen a young couple out walking during his morning walk to the temple and stopped them to admonish the woman for not covering her head. As he recounted the incident, he lamented that young people do not even greet elders anymore. I am not concerned about the veracity of his story, but his narrative indicates his keen sense of loss of what he considers important traditions and customs. While his story is not itself indicative of caste conflict, I understood his lament about young people's ignorance to be his way of articulating anxiety about the waning power his family once yielded. The inability of the Bajwa family to have the matter of Sheetal's rape resolved internally in the village, and the resulting indictment of the accused, led to a loss of face and to an amplification of Jat concerns about their waning power.

In talking with Sheetal and others about this intercaste conflict between dominant-caste Jats and Dalits, an intracaste fault line was unexpectedly exposed. Sheetal recalled that in addition to Dalits, a few Jat families had supported her. Surprised to hear that people in the Jat *biradri* (caste group) had broken rank, I asked what had led them to support her case. She explained that a few years before her rape, an incident had occurred that involved some of the same Jat men who had assaulted her. An altercation among this gang of men and a young Jat athlete had ended with the athlete dying from his injuries and his killers throwing his body into a canal. To cover up their crime, they colluded with the hospital to which the athlete's body was brought with a story about fake injuries. This is why those in the know referred to the whole incident and scheme as *asli paisa nakli jhoot* (real money, fake injury). The boys were never indicted for their crime because they belonged to powerful families in the village. Distraught at not being able to get justice, the family of the Jat boy who was killed supported Sheetal's case in the hope that, through her, they might finally be vindicated.

The lack of intracaste cohesion among Jats in the village who supported Sheetal was also evident among Dalits. When we visited the village in the summer of 2016, there was a reticence to talk about the case within the Dalit *basti*.[32] Sheetal shared how the caste community had initially supported her while her case was receiving attention, but "jaise he case dheela pad gaya" (as soon as the case lost steam), this support also began to wane. In a conversation with Kapil Banu, a Dalit lawyer who supported Sheetal's case, he recalled that just ten to fifteen days after her rape her *tau* (older uncle) had said, "Das pandhrah din baad hi yea word the . . . ki bahut paise mil gaye . . . hume kya mila?" (You got a lot of money . . . what did we get?).[33] Banu exclaimed that he had been very upset by what Sheetal's uncle had said, and that even after all these years, this comment stood out in his memory. As we sat in the weak winter sun, Sheetal, who joined us in the court complex, said that her family had given her *tau* thirty to forty thousand rupees to compensate him for the costs he had incurred for her case.[34] Her community's reticence to talk about her case can only be understood in the context of the political and economic imbrication of Dalit livelihoods in the village. Rape cases generate tension, and while Sheetal's case had initially generated support in the Dalit *basti*, after the Jat men were indicted that *basti* would have to navigate animosity that even years later still festered among Jats in the village.

The balance between caste groups is a delicate one in which Jats invariably have the upper hand. So when a case like Sheetal's occurs, Jats use their existing power to suppress it. For instance, as soon as the case was registered, the mother of one of the accused came to Sheetal and said that she would give Sheetal's family fifteen acres of land if she were to withdraw the complaint against her son. It was Sheetal's father's death and his belief that they would not get justice that shifted the terrain and allowed Sheetal's family to demand that the case be filed. Death, therefore, is significant in rape cases because it limits the dominant caste's capacity for coercion. The inherent violence in such stories is that the injured families involved must rely on leveraging death in order to have any possibility to be recognized as injured subjects, and in order to have their rights respected.

PROXIMITY OF DEATH

For those who are disenfranchised by caste and class status, death is disquietingly proximate. I consider "proximity" in terms of the structural vulnerability that Dalits and those of subordinate castes have to premature death (Gilmore 2007). I draw on Ruth Wilson Gilmore's often cited understanding of race, which is poignantly echoed by the structural disenfranchisement that those of subordinate caste and class endure. Gilmore argues that racism is "the state-sanctioned and/or extralegal production and exploitation of group-differentiated vulnerability to premature death" (247). Gilmore's definition offers a framework to understand the acute structural vulnerability of Dalits and subordinate castes, whereby premature death generates a possibility for a measure of restitution that is usually foreclosed.

It is a grotesque bargain, in which death generates the space of recognition and compels the law to respond. Understood in this frame, Sheetal's father's dying claim that they would not get justice makes sense. Having lived in the village, he was well aware of the power yielded by the Jats, and of the case of the young Jat athlete who was harassed and killed by the same men who assaulted his daughter. That these men got away with this earlier crime against the child of an incomparably more powerful family than his own made him lose hope for justice. His statement, then, testified to the powerlessness that he experienced. The shame and humiliation that Dalits and others of subordinate castes are made to feel in their encounters with the law and various other institutions, including hospitals, solidify the belief that these institutions are hostile to them. Caste communities construct life histories from daily and intergenerational stories, which have been powerfully documented in Dalit testimonies and prose that demonstrate how shame and humiliation shape the arc of their lives. Sheetal's father's premature death was rooted in the structural vulnerability he experienced as a Dalit man, a vulnerability which rendered it impossible for him to imagine that he would get justice.

Sheetal's father and Ladli both died prematurely, their lives abruptly interrupted by death as if they had been disposable and insignificant. Launching legal cases to give their lives and deaths meaning, along with the failure of the powerful to dismantle these cases in the wake of death, challenged the dominant hierarchy that devalued their lives, and explains why their cases were met with such hostility. Of course, this is not to say that all cases in which death occurs result in recognition by the law. A significant number of cases where death occurs following rape do not end in any sort of justice for the victim. But this is precisely what is at issue here: the few instances in which those in subordinate positions can push for recognition are met with violence. Dominant-caste intolerance toward efforts to seek justice by those who are most often denied it demonstrates the hubris of those who control institutions and structures such as the law. When faced with demands to acknowledge injuries borne by those in subordinate positions, dominant castes often respond with intolerance because these demands are effectively for recognition and legibility within structures that were shaped to protect the powerful over the vulnerable. Notably, while death can force recognition within these structures, it cannot entirely inoculate a rape charge against dominant-caste skepticism and coercion.

SUSPICION AFTER DEATH

Rape cases, I argue, are indelibly marked with suspicion and are sites of persistent coercion. While death in these cases may attenuate some misgivings and limit coercive tactics, it never entirely removes them. In my conversations with attorneys and police officers, there remained a degree of speculation about rape cases, even in instances where the victim or someone close to her had died in the context of the case. This suspicion continued even in cases in which the perpetrators were indicted, as in the two cases I have discussed in this chapter. The overwhelming, hegemonic narrative that the majority of rape cases are false means that astronomical efforts are required to dislodge the suspicion cast over them. Even when there is overwhelming evidence—as in Sheetal's case, where there was video documentation of her rape and other corroborative proof—speculation and coercion against a victim and her family can continue.

I draw on Ladli's case to unpack how suspicion about a case can prolong its violence. I suggest rape cases can remain shrouded with suspicion because they often exceed the boundaries of the case to include other issues. For example, as we saw in chapter 1, rape charges can be filed to mitigate reputational damage once a consensual but socially prohibited sexual relationship becomes public; or they can be filed to expedite or coerce civil litigation, including disputes over land. As with the role that death played in Sheetal's case, Ladli's death was crucial to securing a charge of gang rape. She had to die for a charge to be registered. Yet the judgment in her case only indicted two of the three men who were charged. Tarun Kumar, the third man, was acquitted because the court suspected that his name had only been included in the charges because of prior animosity between his family and Sheetal's family.[35] It was this story of prior animosity, and the weight that the court chose to give it, that animated the violence of suspicion in Ladli's case.

I juxtapose how the court harbored suspicions about the legitimacy of Ladli's case because her family and the family of the accused turned out to have a history of animosity, with how the court refused to consider, to say nothing of suspect, that the Jat perpetrators in Sheetal's case may have been motivated by a long, well-documented history of Jat animosity toward Dalits. The court's bias was evident in its refusal to acknowledge the existence of long-standing, anti-Dalit caste animosity and violence in one case and its ready willingness to acknowledge the existence of prior animosity in the other. The court's willingness to extend itself to speculate about intentions in one type of case but not the other has serious consequences. In Ladli's case, it meant that one of the accused men got off, and that others were charged with lesser crimes. In Sheetal's case, it meant that the court refused to consider that she was targeted because of her caste, which meant that her rapists did not have to face related charges, and that the courts once again helped erase the reality of caste hierarchy and violence.

Tarun Kumar was a lawyer in the district court and known to the judges and other attorneys who worked there. When his name was added to the complaint in Ladli's case, it led to tremendous controversy. Ladli's attorney, Mr. Bhalla, practiced in the same district court as Tarun Kumar, and worried that Ladli could not get a fair trial in a court whose lawyers and judges worked with her accused. Mr. Bhalla urged Ladli's family to appeal to the

Punjab and Haryana High Court to have their case transferred to a different district, citing a conflict of interest. While the case was successfully transferred,[36] it nevertheless did not result in the indictment of Tarun Kumar. Tarun was acquitted because the court believed that his name had only been added to the rape case due to a prior conflict between him and Ladli's grandfather. The court did not believe that Tarun otherwise had anything to do with the assault.

The narrative about how Tarun Kumar had been involved in a legal dispute with Ladli's grandfather was cited in the court's ruling as reason to suspect the charges Ladli's family now made against him. It is not unusual for the legitimacy of rape cases to come entirely under question if it turns out that a history of animosity exists between the parties involved. In his testimony about the case, Ladli's father admitted that when the FIR was lodged after his daughter's rape, she had named only two people: Satish Kumar and Deepak Kumar, who are brothers-in-law. He explained that he and Ladli's grandfather had filed to add the names of Ajay and Tarun Kumar to the complaint later on because he had become aware of their involvement in his daughter's assault only when their families came to coerce him to compromise the case. Ajay's involvement was confirmed through a police investigation and a DNA test that found both his and Satish Kumar's DNA at the scene of the crime and on Ladli's clothes. But Tarun Kumar's DNA was not found. Because his DNA was missing, the reasons for his name being added to the case became all the more suspect, adding fuel to the suspicion that it was because of the earlier dispute between him and Ladli's family. During cross-examination, the attorney for the defense asked specifically about this prior legal case between them.

In the final judgment, this earlier case was referred to as the *Lamberdari* case. It had concerned a dispute between Ladli's grandfather and Deepak Kumar. *Lamberdaris* are record keepers and "holders of numbers" in the village (Hussain 2017). Their position demands respect, and the government of Haryana provides a small honorarium for the person who holds the post (Press Trust of India 2019). I do not have the details of this case, but in my conversation with Ladli's lawyer, she recalled that the *Lamberdari* case involved a dispute over who was appointed to the post. Cases involving such disputes over appointments involve the District Collector's office and are decided in a different court than rape cases. But the *Lamberdari* case was nonetheless presented in Ladli's rape case as relevant evidence indicating prior animosity between her family and the accused. According to the defense, it was only because of this prior history between the parties that the names of Deepak Kumar and Tarun Kumar were added to the rape charge.

The *Lamberdari* case was a conflict between Deepak Kumar, Ladli's grandfather, and a third person; Tarun Kumar was involved as counsel for Deepak Kumar. The defense's allegation, then, was that Tarun's name had been added to Ladli's rape charge as retribution for his having served as Deepak's counsel and for acting, in this capacity, in opposition to Ladli's grandfather. Prior court documents showed that Ladli's father and grandfather had filed applications in the district court to add Tarun and Deepak Kumar's names to the rape case.[37] But while Tarun's name was added to the complaint, and the rape trial proceeded with him as one of the three defendants, the addition of Deepak's name was rejected in an October 2015 order. After the lower court dismissed the petition to add Deepak's name to the case, Ladli's father and grandfather filed appeals with the Punjab and Haryana High court, which were also subsequently rejected.[38] The judge in Ladli's case specifically referred to this history of applications and appeals to add Deepak and Tarun to the rape case as evidence of animosity between the parties. The judgment read:

> In order dated . . . vide which application under section 319 CrPC was allowed, the court did not find any kind of evidence existing against [Deepak Kumar]. Criminal Revision against said order was filed by complainant's father in Honorable High Court of Punjab and Haryana but even that revision was dismissed. . . . Thus, the act and conduct of the father of complainant shows that efforts were made by him to falsely implicate [Deepak Kumar] in the case of his daughter. If that was so, then the possibility of existence of mala fide intention on the part of the complainant party to falsely implicate [Tarun Kumar] through the same application under section 319 CrPC, cannot be ruled out.[39]

The judgment did not rely exclusively on an allegation, but drew on forensic proof to substantiate the argument that Tarun Kumar's name had only been added for mala fide reasons. It pointed to the fact that there was no DNA evidence to corroborate his involvement and that his name was added in July 2015, several months after the sexual assault in February of that year. The court assumed that the delay in adding Tarun's name to the case was due to an effort by Ladli's family to punish him for his involvement in the *Lamberdari* case. The judge's ruling read, "I am of the opinion that the fact that the DNA report has not supported the case of State against [Tarun Kumar], is providing strength to the defense set up by him." Directly referencing the prior *Lamberdari* case, the judgment ultimately acquitted him: "It was argued that in fact [Tarun Kumar] was the counsel for [Deepak Kumar] in the said case of *Lamberdari* and therefore the father of victim was nurturing an enmity with [Tarun Kumar] and therefore he tried to falsely implicate [Deepak Kumar] and has succeeded in false implication of [Tarun Kumar] in this case."[40] The judgment also relied on the discrepancies in the naming of the accused at different times by Ladli and her father, which the court read as mala fide intent to implicate those against whom they had enmity. It was this confluence of issues that led to the acquittal of Tarun Kumar on all charges.

The court's selective concern with potentially illegitimate attempts to implicate others also pervaded the case about Ladli's death.[41] Ladli's mother claimed that when Ladli was being transported from the local hospital to Chandigarh, a larger town with better medical facilities, she gave a dying declaration in which she named the perpetrators who had assaulted her and then later set her on fire. However, the medical evidence in the court documents suggests that Ladli could not have been conscious and able to give a dying declaration. I am less concerned with whether Ladli really made this dying declaration than with the capacity of a dying declaration to mobilize a claim of "truth." A dying declaration is meant to signal that the person on her deathbed, conscious of her imminent demise, would reveal crucial details essential to obtaining justice for her death. But in Ladli's case, the court treated the declaration her mother said she had made with suspicion and chose to try the accused for abetment to suicide rather than the heftier charge of murder, using Section 306 rather than Section 302 of the Indian Penal Code (IPC).

The existence of previous civil litigation between parties is often cited by police officers and attorneys as the reason that people falsely add names to a rape charge. In chapter 3, where I detailed how land was implicated in cases of rape, I referred to a Station House Officer (SHO) I met while we were investigating a case in Rudhi village.[42] This SHO, Ritu Kumar, explained in some detail how women deliberately rip their clothes to be able to file a molestation case. She was emphatic and confident that these cases were about previous conflicts that were being litigated through charges of rape and molestation. While we were in her office, she also referenced Ladli's case in Dantha. At this point, we had been speaking for some time, and she had become less circumspect and more candid. While referring to Ladli's case in Dantha, she leaned forward as if to share a secret, and said in slightly hushed tones, "Es case 302 mei daadi hai" (In this case of 302 [murder] it's the grandmother), alleging that Ladli's grandmother had been involved in her death. While the allegation itself was shocking, what was significant about her comment on Ladli's case was that it was part of her narrative of how there usually are hidden stories behind rape cases. In Ladli's case, the hidden story was that her grandmother had a role to play in her death rather than the perpetrators named in the case, despite forensic evidence and police investigation. So compelling was the script of an alternate truth and made-up allegations that it endured despite overwhelming proof to the contrary.

CONCLUSION

Unlike Ladli, Sheetal survived her rape. But akin to Ladli's case, which was marked with suspicion, the afterlife of rape for Sheetal has also been about constantly negotiating suspicion. Sheetal recalled that after her assault she was scorned by her family members, both near and distant. She faced gibes and sneers from students at her school and later in college. For both these family members and others around her, Sheetal's rape was about her sexual impropriety, and they blamed her for her assault. While she was in school, she complained to the principal about the harassment, but he did little to stem the derision she faced. The moniker of zinda laash with which I began this chapter alludes to precisely these persistent taunts and the shame that a victim is subject to after rape, which make her life akin to the living dead. Having to constantly consider her next steps and whether she would have to deal with new sets of people denigrating her took a toll and led Sheetal to worry about what she wanted to do in the future. In 2017, Sheetal was admitted to a major law program in a district a few hours away from her home. Before joining, she was concerned about what would happen if people there found out about her rape; whether she would yet again face derision and how she would then navigate her life there preoccupied her decision.

This pervasiveness of living under the shadow of rape makes its afterlife harrowing for so many survivors. The constant suspicion and threats, living in fear and subject to humiliating taunts and attacks on your character: this is what zinda laash refers to. It ultimately functions as a disciplining maneuver that pressures survivors to remain under a shroud of shame. The victim is expected to be frozen in time, permanently gripped by ignominy, unable to move on with her life. Her very presence is seen as somehow polluting and threatening. And her attempts at wanting a life after rape are seen as an affront, not only by the perpetrators and those who supported them, but even among her own family. Sheetal's brother has been hostile to her since her rape. When he heard about Sheetal's admission to a law program in a district a few hours away, he beat her up. Since that incident, which involved activists and lawyers coming to her aid, Sheetal's brother married and moved out of the house, taking all their meager belongings. Sheetal's mother, who had supported her, had to move in with her son because she had no income and did not have the means to set up an independent home. Meanwhile, Sheetal's brother prohibited her from moving in with them; she became essentially homeless and was living with Dalit feminist activists in a different district.

When Sheetal's case began in 2012, it drew tremendous attention and support as well as commensurate threats and coercion. During the long battle in the court case, the threats to her and her family were serious enough to warrant police protection. While the case and coercion were ongoing, there was a police van parked outside her family home, and Sheetal has had to permanently retain a police escort. It has been seven years since the judgment in her case, and she continues to have a gunman assigned to her. That she still needs protection demonstrates how the threat of bodily harm and even death remains significant to this day. In part, this is because in her case only four of the accused men were sentenced to prison. The other four were out on bail, and Sheetal said that she had received threats from them.

The continuing threats to Sheetal's life reveal the extent to which her efforts to carve out a life beyond her rape have successfully interrupted the script of shame. She is now completing law school, and over the years she has partnered with Dalit feminist activists in Haryana on cases involving rape. Her life and work is a testament to her efforts at defying the disciplining maneuvers of zinda laash. She does not live in the shadows and while she continues to struggle, her activism demonstrates her defiance against the nomenclature of shame. By tracing the stories of life and death in Sheetal and Ladli's rape cases, I have tried to apprehend how and when subjectivity is formed. What does the granting of subjecthood to someone like Sheetal, whose injury was recognized and considered worthy of prosecution, do? That Sheetal still requires police protection reveals the extent to which defenders of the patriarchal order found her brave fight against injustice intolerable. In both Sheetal and Ladli's cases their fights were not only about justice for crimes to which they were subjected, but also propelled a shift that forced authorities and the law to recognize them as subjects worthy of protection. The grotesque injustice is that this recognition comes only in the wake of death.

Conclusion

On September 14, 2020, in Boolgarhi village in Hathras district, a nineteen-year-old Dalit girl was gang raped by four dominant-caste Thakur men.[1] On the morning of her rape, the young girl and her mother were working in the fields of the Thakurs in the village. As I have shown, for many Dalits and other marginalized castes, working on farms owned by the dominant caste is often their only means to secure a livelihood, a reality which keeps them tethered to relationships of servitude. As a result, any attempt to get justice for those in subordinate positions who have been harmed by dominant-caste individuals is extremely challenging.

The young girl and her family were repeatedly pressured by the Thakurs and their allies to withdraw their rape case against the four men. The police discouraged them from filing a First Information Report (FIR), telling the girl's family to take her away, even though one of the accused men had tried to kill her. After considerable delay, the police finally took the injured young girl to the local district hospital. She was later transferred to a larger hospital where the injuries she sustained during her assault could be better treated. A fortnight later her condition deteriorated, and her life was in peril. Concerns about her impending death forced the police to take the perpetrators into judicial custody. She died shortly thereafter, and the police hastily cremated her body in the middle of the night without the consent of her family (Ara 2020). I end this book with this tragic story because it brings together many of the topics and themes I explored in the preceding pages—rape, brutal violence, dominant-caste power, how the severity of death makes recognition more possible, and how patriarchal forces undermine women's credibility by accusing them of having had a relationship with the accused.

The police who cremated her were well aware that her family and those fighting her case would use her death to compel an investigation into her assault and rape. However, their middle-of-the-night efforts to get rid of her body without the consent of her family drew national attention. Members of political parties as well as Dalit rights groups tried to go to the village to lend support to the family and press for accountability for the crime and police cover-up. In contrast, the police and state government tried to repress public protest and silence the growing outcry by imposing a curfew. When national and international media began reporting on the case and highlighting the brutality of the rape, the coercive exercise of dominant-caste power, and police malfeasance, it compelled the prime minister to appoint a special investigation team. In December 2020, the Central Bureau of Investigation, the country's main investigative arm, which had taken over the case, charged the four men on various counts, including gang rape and murder.

The Hathras case, like others I have described in this book, compels a deeper look at how the subjectivity of women in rape cases is constructed, by whom and for what purpose. In this brief conclusion, I want to dwell on this question of subjectivity from the vantage point enabled by looking closely at three intertwined concepts, namely: refusal, recognition, and justice. While the chapters in this book detailed how in each case the subjectivity of the raped woman was created and contested by various actors, here I attempt to step back from those details and reflect on subjectivity from a different perspective. I suggest that examining subjectivity alongside this sort of conceptual engagement with issues of refusal, recognition, and justice might have considerable transnational implications.

To lay the ground for this conceptual engagement, it's necessary to first recap what Vineeta, Komal, Sheetal, and Savatri, all of whom we met in the course of this book, were able to reclaim as they enacted different forms of refusal. What forms of autonomy and sovereignty were they able to create? In chapter 1 I followed Vineeta's story, tracing how she was forced to file a rape case against her lover when their affair was discovered by her family. I show how over the course of negotiations that led to a compromise Vineeta reluctantly followed a script of rape, but in other candid moments, away from her family, she revealed and defended her relationship with Pradeep. When she proposed to leave the village to pursue further studies, her father was enraged. I have argued that her father's rage was in response to Vineeta's refusal to sequester herself for the shame she was perceived to have brought to her family. Her effort to leave for college away from the village was an act of defiance against village elders and her father. Her quest to leave home was an attempt to escape the humiliation she was forced to endure from the village and her family. By continuing her affair over the course of five years, Vineeta demonstrated autonomy by claiming sovereignty over her body and sexuality in defiance of her father and village elders. That she was reprimanded and prohibited from going to college does not change the fact that she took a political stance, challenging the matrix of power that sought to discipline her, and attempted to recode her relationships with her family and village. Vineeta also refused to be cast as a rape victim, despite having had to play along with that script. She forcefully argued, in her conversation with me, that her decision to go with Pradeep on that last night, before her relationship was exposed, was not impulsive but was based on a five-year relationship she had chosen to have with him. She went on to say that had she been fully conscious when her attorney constructed her side of the story, she would have refused the narrative that others had constructed about what had happened to her; she would have objected to the story that falsely claimed she had been kidnapped and forced into a car. In this way, she rejected a script that cast her as a rape victim and rejected the patriarchal injunction to feel shame for having chosen a prohibited relationship.

Komal's refusal, in chapter 2, emerged in a different fashion. By insisting on compromise, she refused to continue with her rape case and thereby exercised a restricted but significant measure of autonomy. Her expression of independence was particularly significant because it defied her uncle, the man who had brutally assaulted her and who continued to threaten her with violence. In daring to agree to the compromise—and in insisting on it—Komal enraged her uncle, who wanted the courts to convict the four men he had tried to frame for the crime that he himself had committed. In his rage, he even accused Komal's attorney of facilitating the compromise for money. By accepting the compromise, Komal undermined the control her uncle had been able to exert over her and her family. But unlike Vineeta, who had not been raped, Komal had been sexually assaulted by her uncle.

So while Vineeta's refusal to acquiesce to her father's effort to shame and blame her allowed her to reclaim her sexuality, Komal's refusal was not about reclaiming her sexuality. It was about wresting power back from her perpetrator by not allowing him to use the story of her assault in ways that distressed her and to which she objected. Her uncle, who had raped her, wanted to pin the rape on four men who were innocent of this charge. But Komal's refusal to blame these four men for a crime they did not commit allowed her to recuperate a measure of autonomy over her own story and how it was used. Her uncle's constant surveillance and use of terror had prevented her from being able to name him, and he was able to evade being named as her perpetrator. But within the limited sphere of autonomy at her disposal, Komal's refusal was a brave expression of her sovereignty.

Savatri's and Sheetal's refusals generated yet a different set of possibilities. In refusing to continue with the struggle around her daughter's case and refusing to accept the script by activists that she and her daughter had been coerced into compromise, Savatri demands a different interpretation of her story. Even if she was subject to explicit coercion (through direct threats from dominant-caste Jats) or tacit coercion (produced by the fact that dominant-caste Jats owned the land that she was forced to rely on for her livelihood), she asked activists fighting for justice in Bhagana to not characterize her story as a simple story of how she caved to coercion and stopped fighting for justice, but instead to take her subjectivity and vulnerability seriously. She demanded that they acknowledge that the circumstances of her life limited her choices and that by continuing to stay in the village she was actively attempting to rebuild her life, and to survive, against very difficult odds. Refusal here was less about defiance and more about her attempt to live—uneasily—in the village, having nowhere else to go and no other way to make a living. Savatri's refusal was also about shielding herself against more reputational damage in order to protect her second daughter's future and prospects for marriage.

Sheetal was the young woman who had been gang-raped by dominant-caste men in her village and left injured by the side of a canal. Authorities had eventually been forced to take her case seriously after her father, devastated by seeing a recording of her rape, had committed suicide. Despite facing immense pressure from the dominant caste in her village to drop charges, Sheetal had steadfastly refused to compromise her case. She refused when they tried to bribe her with money and land, and she continued to refuse when they repeatedly threatened to hurt her again and even to kill her. Sheetal's brave refusal to drop charges was an immense act of insubordination. As a young Dalit woman, her defiance against powerful Jat families was an insistence that the harm they had inflicted on her be acknowledged. She disrupted the structure of caste power in her village, and she also disrupted the power of the state itself by forcing an investigation. Her refusal to let her rape be buried and dealt with in the village was about claiming her subjectivity as a rights-bearing person. Recall that in his last days, her father had said, with certainty and despair, "Insaaf nahi milega hume" (We will not get justice).[2] I can't help but think that it was partly for him that she refused this predicament, even though it has meant that seven years since the judgment in her case, she continues to have a gunman assigned to her to protect against ongoing threats to her life.

Drawing on scholars who theorize refusal and resistance, I propose that these instances of refusal reveal the relationship these women have with structures of power, and the nature of their struggle against these structures. I understand their refusal as an effort to redefine their subjectivity—their experience and sense of self—within these structures. More than three decades ago Lila Abu-Lughod (1990) reminded us that a careful look at resistance allows for a clearer understanding of how domination works. She cautioned against romanticizing resistance in ways that obscure what acts of resistance can teach us about changing structures of power (53). Carol McGranahan (2016b) builds on Abu-Lughod's work by drawing a distinction between refusal and resistance. Drawing on Audra Simpson's work on refusal, McGranahan (2016a) argues that acts of refusal do not appear as an overt challenge to a particular set of powers in the way that resistance does, but that refusal is nonetheless a "political stance" (334). In other words, acts of refusal concern a subject's relationship with power, and they constitute efforts to redefine or reshape that relationship to power in some way. This is the way in which acts of refusal can be considered political.

Accordingly, I propose that we see the refusals enacted by the women whose stories I've traced as important efforts to redefine their relationship to the structures that have power over them and that seek to define them in terms that are not their own. More concretely, their refusals are efforts to reshape their relationships to structures like the police, courts, and bureaucracy; the village council; the family; and even the scripts and expectations of activists on their side. Their refusals are also efforts to find ways to express their complex subjectivity as they themselves see it, which is different to how these structures caricaturize and define them, principally as unreliable, disreputable, shameful, or, alternately, simply as powerless victims who have succumbed to coercion. By paying attention to the intimate scales in which rape cases are negotiated, we can see how each woman's defiance, efforts to rewrite a script, change a narrative, or ask for a different interpretation is an effort to get out from under these flattening characterizations and their significant consequences. If subjects come into being through structures such as the family, community, caste, courts and the law, then being "recognized" by these structures becomes critically important. For example, courts in India will often only recognize a rape charge as credible if the victim demonstrates sufficient distress and discomfort in the ways that victims are expected to demonstrate distress and discomfort. But if the victim does not appear to be appropriately distraught in the ways that are recognizable to the court, then she is not recognized by the court and is subsequently judged as undeserving of restitution.

Let me draw on a recent court ruling to further illustrate this point. In May 2021, the Sessions Court in Goa acquitted Tarun Tejpal, the prominent publisher of *Tehelka*, a magazine known for its investigative journalism and generally progressive politics, of sexual assault. In her 527-page judgment, Judge Kshama M. Joshi said that "photos show the prosecutrix [plaintiff] to be absolutely cheerful and with a smile on her face and not disturbed, reserved, terrified, or traumatized in any manner" (Asthana 2021). The judged acknowledged, without reservation, that her ruling was informed by the fact that the woman alleging rape did not seem sufficiently distressed in photos taken soon after the incident was to have taken place. This judge's ruling has since come under considerable criticism for relying on the fact that the victim did not appear traumatized enough. The judge refused to recognize the women's injury because she was articulate, conversant with the law, and had demonstrated solidarity with the young girl raped in Hathras. Pratiksha Baxi, a feminist legal scholar whose research has focused on courtroom procedures and sexual violence against women, has noted that this ruling was a "backlash" against growing opposition to patriarchal norms in a case that seemed to not only put the young woman alleging rape on trial, but that appeared to be putting all feminists on trial (Baxi 2021).

The Tejpal case clearly illustrates how recognition by structures such as the court is about the power to identify, or to refuse to identify, a person as a victim who has been harmed and who deserves restitution. Recognition involves a relationship between the structures of power and the subject, which either acknowledges or denies the subject's vulnerability and wounds. However, the terms by which structures recognize and constitute a subject, or the criteria they look for, are not always apparent; they are only revealed when adverse judgments—like the adverse judgment against the woman who accused Tejpal of raping her—bring them to light. The misogyny of the courts and their attempts at protecting caste, class, and gender boundaries are sometimes made visible in such adverse judgments. In the Tejpal case, the terms for recognizing the plaintiff as a victim who could claim protection or restitution from the state were that she should exhibit clear and easily legible signs of distress, and that in addition to that, she should not express sympathy for other young women who had been raped. When the courts refuse to grant recognition, they constitute the subject as undeserving of safety, protection, and the right to recompense. While court rulings like the one in Tejpal's rape case are obvious in their biases and clearly reveal the terms by which they agree to recognize a subject, the terms of recognition are not always apparent in structures beyond the courts. The family, panchayat, district offices, and police stations all generate ways in which they acknowledge or disavow a subject, which then has implications for justice.

I argue that the terms of recognition—the criteria that structures of power demand met in order to recognize subjects—are a *suturing logic* that bind together structures of power and the subjectivities they enable. Let me explain how this logic operates by drawing on the cases I followed. When the panchayat gets involved in rape cases in the village and deals with them as a social dispute, then the terms of recognizing or *mis*recognizing harm are guided by misogyny, caste power, efforts to control the reputational damage sustained by the village, and a desire to not involve the courts. Consequently, panchayats diminish the harm done to the victim in the interest of facilitating reconciliation between the male heads of the families involved. For the young woman harmed, the lack of recognition of her injury reinforces her diminished worth. In the village the panchayat recognizes young women through relations of paternalism, which is why reconciliation is often directed toward her father for her loss of value (Das 1996). So when Sheetal refuses the efforts of her village elders and the panchayat to have her withdraw her complaint, what she calls for in her refusal is a renegotiation of the terms of recognition. In her refusal to withdraw her complaint she exposes the terms by which the village elders and panchayat constitute her subjectivity, and she demands a different outcome, one in which her injury is acknowledged. The consequences of Sheetal's refusal of the terms of recognition put forth by village authorities generates a break with the village; she no longer resides in the village and has not returned to it since her assault. Her break with the village allows her to tentatively forge a different subjectivity that claims autonomy as a person deserving of restitution and justice.

If recognition is a relationship between structures and subjectivity, then refusal by women in rape cases is an effort to renegotiate the terms of recognition. This then leads us to the politics of recognition. One of the most well-known mediations on recognition is by philosopher Charles Taylor (1994), who says, "Equal recognition is not just the appropriate mode for a healthy democratic society. Its refusal can inflict damage on those who are denied it . . . withholding recognition can be a form of oppression" (36). His concern is that diverse and ostensibly liberal democracies like Canada and the United States recognize and respect the "distinctness" claimed by vulnerable or subordinated groups. In particular, his argument focuses on the claim for "distinctness" made by Quebeckers and aboriginal peoples in Canada (52). While democratic institutions are supposed to be guided by a state that grants equal recognition to all groups, the question is, Do all groups want to be recognized by the state?

In his sustained critique of Taylor, Indigenous scholar Glen Sean Coulthard (2014) argues that when "'recognition' is coinceived as something that is ultimately 'granted' or 'accorded' a subaltern group or entity by a dominant group or entity" it "prefigures its failure to significantly modify, let alone transcend, the breadth of power at play in colonial relationships" (31). Coulthard contrasts "recognition" with "sovereignty" and argues that while Indigenous people in Canada seek self-governance, what they instead get from the state is "recognition of Aboriginal rights" (123). Recognition then is how structures such as the state acknowledge a vulnerable or dispossesed group, by granting them rights, while evading the larger challenges and demands that such groups can raise.

When structures like the state recognize an injury and address it by confering rights or making efforts at restitution, they are making gestures that ultimately reinforce their own authority. Coulthard and political theorist Wendy Brown (1995) argue that the recognition of injury by the state does not fundamentally change the fact of its domination. This is why Audra Simpson (2016), who like Coulthard is critical of Charles Taylor, argues that recognition "becomes a political antidote for historical wrongdoing" (20). She means that the state uses recognition to try to erase its past injustices while sidestepping the actual demands of the disenfranchised. For Simpson, the political alternative to recognition is refusal. It is the refusal by Mohawaks to live "tacitly and taciturnly in a 'settled state'" (22). Both Coulthard and Simpson are formulating arguments about recognition and refusal in the settler colonial states of Canada and United States. I draw on them because they expose the fallacy of the belief that justice can be obtained from structures that are invested in dipossession.

While it is clear Coulthard's and Simpson's theorizing is directed at settler colonial states that would never consider aboriginal sovereignty, How might their generative arguments inform our understanding of a different set of structures? Can this lens of recognition and refusal, for instance, help us evaluate modern institutions that have been created to recognize injury? In what follows, I look at how rape comes to be recognized in international arenas as a crime against humanity. This recognition was the result of decades of work by feminist organizations seeking to make visible the harm done to women during war and conflict. Does the recognition of rape at an international scale, and then at more local scales, help secure justice for those who have been are harmed?

According to Taylor (1994), the politics of recognition stems from a "politics of universalism" which stresses "the equal dignity of all citizens." For him, the goal of this politics of recognition is "the equalization of rights and entitlements" between different groups (37). In his account, liberal democratic states enshrined these rights and entitlements in sociolegal practice at all levels, from the local to international covenants and statutes. This is how, through the course of the twentieth century, institutions and practices emerged that recognize harm and make efforts to mitigate it.

As various scholars have described, recognition of harm initiates a process of redress that can take multiple forms and is not limited to a prosecutorial and carceral model.[3] It can include other possibilities like asking for reparations, or demanding an apology.[4] In the international political arena, recognition of harm emerged in the wake of the Balkan wars and the Rwandan genocide in the mid-1990s, when the United Nations issued a report on the "Responsibility to Protect."[5] The United Nations sought to convince member states to commit to protecting their citizens against harm caused by genocide, war crimes, ethnic cleansing, and crimes against humanity. The subsequent years led to extensive debate until 2005, when member states agreed to abide by this mandate.

In order to adjudicate crimes committed during the course of the Balkan wars and to advance its "responsibility to protect" mandate, the United Nations also set up the International Criminal Tribunals on the former Yugoslavia (ICTY) and the International Criminal Tribunal for Rwanda (ICTR). However, according to conversations within international humanitarian law, the tribunals were considered insufficient deterrents against mass atrocities and the call for an international body resulted in the Rome Statute which established the International Criminal Court (ICC). During the tribunals and in conversations and debates that led to the establishment of the ICC, feminists had long been arguing for the recognition of rape in these mass atrocities. Feminist demands to consider rape as a war crime were bolstered by the landmark ICTY judgment that found three Bosnian soldiers who had raped and tortured Muslim women and girls guilty for crimes against humanity (Bergoffen 2003). Janet Halley in *Rape at Rome* (2008) documents in detail the efforts by feminist groups to compel the ICC to recognize rape as a crime against humanity (24). The recognition of rape as a crime against humanity in these landmark judgments, and its enshrinement in the Rome statute, charged states with the moral obligation to protect their citizens against rape. These judgments and feminist organizing led to a shift in international venues by the 2000s, where rape elicited swift international attention and comment.

Kamari Maxine Clarke (2019), an anthropologist whose work focuses on human rights and international law, closely examined the ICC and observed that agreements on the responsibility to protect created the moral justification for international bodies to adjudicate crimes. Yet Clarke, among other scholars and analysts, pointed out that the ICC's call to end impunity by prosecuting heads of states responsible for crimes against humanity was viewed with suspicion by "growing numbers of African and other postcolonial stakeholders" who saw the surge in "the anti-impunity/rule of law discourse as highly biased and uneven" (2). The long history of colonial powers using law as a means to rule over and dominate Africa is well known.

Unsurprisingly, critics and African states view contemporary international bodies with apprehension because "it is clear that the continuity of violence and the plunder of Africa's land and peoples are related to residual colonial inscriptions" (Clarke 2019, 11). Their concern is that the ICC's use of legal instruments to adjudicate harm reproduces African countries' history of colonialism, the effect of which is that "political and economic restructuring made to align earlier forms of effective colonial control" results in "the contemporary management of an international domain within which Africa's violence can trigger ICC action" (259). Clarke is drawing our attention to how countries in the African Union are alert to the vestiges of colonial bias in international bodies such as the ICC. She is concerned that juridical rulings by the ICC that recognize harm and identify perpetrators and victims will equate "justice with the law" (26). She explains how such a narrow equation serves to primarily blame a single perpetrator or group of perpetrators for the harm caused, and generates a response that is predominantly juridical. Consequently, "this new discourse reconfigured the reach of law and located the individual at the center of foreign affairs" (64). As a result, "the figure of the individual was cast in two key roles: the high-level 'perpetrator' criminally responsible for mass atrocities, and the 'victim' to be saved from the perpetrator's violence" (64). This individualization of the perpetrator and victim obscured the "structural underpinnings of institutional violence" (72).

The recognition of harm and the creation of institutions, at the international and local levels, that seek to punish those who perpetuate harm obscures some of the more structural underpinnings of disenfranchisement. Moreover, these efforts at mitigation do not, as Brown, Coulthard and Simpson argue, change the structures in which harm occurs, or offer to shift the terms by which subjects are recognized as deserving punishment or needing restitution. Coulthard (2014) puts it clearly when he argues that "the politics of recognition in its contemporary form promises to reproduce the very configurations of colonialist, racist, patriarchal state power that Indigenous peoples' demands for recognition have historically sought to transcend" (3).

The transactional frame of the legal adjudication of harm means that the responsibility toward victims ends with the punishment of the perpetrators. However, such forms of settlement serve to obfuscate larger structures and their role in perpetuating violence. For instance, in response to the Delhi gang rape, the four accused men were given the death penalty. In response to the atrocities in Yugoslavia and Rwanda, commanders and other leaders were identified and prosecuted for crimes against humanity by tribunals and courts. But as we have seen with the Hathras case, the death sentence given to the men indicted in the Delhi gang rape did not result in structural changes that would mitigate the severe precarity of the lives of Dalit women. Moreover, successful prosecution, manifested in the conviction and severe punishment meted out to these men, strengthens legal mechanisms that are then disproportionately used against Dalits and other groups subjugated by both caste power and the savage inequality produced by the dominant economic order. Abolitionist scholars and activists have compellingly argued, that the prosecutorial, carceral and punitive system of justice not only fails to reduce harm and heal its wounds through meaningful restitution, but will always primarily be used against "excess" populations produced by, in our contemporary moment, the ravages of neoliberalism and its creation of an "unruly underclass" that must be controlled (see among others Kaba 2021; Ritchie 2017). Buttressing their argument, in my view, Kamari Maxine Clarke (2019) suggests that legal technocratic practices constitute "a form of disciplinary power that exists across different scales to classify populations juridically" and serve to "render some deaths acceptable" (16). Recognition of harm by international bodies such as the ICC, and I would add by postcolonial states such as India, whose legal history is drawn from the colonial encounter, tends to reproduce, especially for those who are marginalized, the structures of violence from which they seek relief.

If, as Ratna Kapur (2005) reminds us, recognition by colonial and even postcolonial structures only reproduced the conditions of domination, then what is needed is a foundational break with colonial structures of power. Dubra Mitra (2020) writes that "perhaps no effort for systematization of state practice was as successful as the Indian Penal Code of 1860, a watershed set of criminal laws that shaped the development of penal codes across the colonial world" (68). The Penal Code, along with other laws and legislative efforts, sought to regulate female sexual behavior by giving "the colonial state" the power to define the "monogamous conjugal home as the sole space of legitimate sexual behavior" (69). This legacy filters and informs contemporary understanding of perverse or normal sexual behavior and is reflected in the suspicion with which police officers regard women's claims of rape. What then may we consider as foundation break with these colonial vestiges that continue to impact women's lives today?

And what would justice look like? I want to end by suggesting that when we consider the question of justice from the position of the subjectivities of women in rape cases, then it allows us to see their refusals as efforts at retaining some autonomy over their lives. In this formulation, I understand refusal as a subjectification process rather than a position. That is, refusals are ongoing struggles over sovereignty rather than a definite claiming event. Refusal, as Audra Simpson (2016) writes, "holds on to a truth, structures this truth as [a] stance through time, as its own structure and commingling with the force of presumed and inevitable disappearance and operates as the revenge of consent—the consent to these conditions, to the interpretation that this was fair, and the ongoing sense that this is all over with" (330). For Vineeta, Komal, Savatri, and Sheetal, their "holding onto a truth" is about the struggle over a subjectivity that is not crafted by others. The stories of the brave women I narrate in this book allow us to see a terrain of resistance, where they attempt to make their sovereignty apparent and claim it for themselves in defiance of others. By paying attention to subjectivity, we can grasp and better imagine the range of possibilities for justice that may emerge.

NOTES

PREFACE

1 Bhimrao Ramji Ambedkar is widely considered the father of the Dalit movement in India, and was independent India's first Minister of Law and Justice and a chief architect of the Constitution. Savitribai Phule was a social reformer and educator, and along with her husband Jyotirao Phule, founded the first girl's school in India in 1848. She is regarded as one of the pioneers of Indian feminism. Bhagat Singh is regarded as a revolutionary fighter against British colonialism in India.

INTRODUCTION

1 *Dalit* is the term adopted by those who were formerly known as "untouchable." Crafted by Dr. Bhimrao Ramji Ambedkar, the word literally means "broken people." India is home to over 200 million Dalits, and almost every village has a small, segregated section on the outskirts meant for Dalits. *Jat* refers to the dominant caste in Haryana, an agricultural community that has wielded political and economic power in the state for decades.

2 The charge of kidnapping was deliberate. Prem Chowdhry (2011) writes that it is used in the case of minors because "it is an offence against the right of the parent from under whose guardianship the person is taken away. Consequently, in the case of a runaway woman, a kidnapping case is most often registered to prevent her from exercising her choice in marriage against the wishes of her parents" (299).

3 In 2013 several rape cases were treated as disputes by *panchayats* (village councils) across India, leading the Supreme Court to intervene. In several of these cases, the panchayat forced the girl to marry her rapist. See Deshpande et al. (2013).

4 In their study of dominant-caste violence against Dalits in Andhra Pradesh between 1989 and 1991, Vasant Kannabiran and Kalpana Kannabiran (2003) remark that a source of irritation and violence for the dominant caste, Tsundur, was that Dalit boys dressed extremely well (253).

5 I differentiate between the terms *rape* and *sexual violation*. I use *sexual violation* to indicate a range of violations of bodily integrity and *rape* to indicate the relatively narrow sociolegal category recognized in Indian juridical norms as a specific crime.

6 OBCs refers to a loose category of Shudra castes and subcastes, situated in the lowest rung of the Hindu varna, below the upper castes (Brahmins, Kshatriya, and Vaishya) but above Dalits. The OBCs are numerically significant, representing half the country's population, and have been largely subordinated and marginalized.

7 Field notes, May 27, 2016.

8 I want to be clear that the Judge's verdict to exonerate Sanjay of the rape charge did not stem from a consideration of caste politics that played out in the case. Rather, in my brief meeting with her, I realized that she did not want risk her reputation by participating in a deception. Several times in our conversation she emphasized that she was "strict," an expression I understood to mean wanting to follow the "law."

9 The names of rape victims in India are not revealed in an effort to protect their privacy. The young woman raped in December 2012 was named Nirbhaya, meaning "fearless one," in the press and by her supporters, to acknowledge her brave struggle to survive her rape. She ultimately died from the injuries she sustained while she was raped.

10 Rate of crime is calculated by crime per one hundred thousand people.

11 Khairlanji is the name of the village in the Bhandara district of Maharashtra, India, where members of the Bhotmange family were brutally massacred in 2006. They were one of the few existing Dalit families who owned land and who had been able to acquire an education. They were allegedly killed in retaliation for a land dispute. The women of the family—Surekha and her daughter Priyanka—were paraded naked and gang-raped before they were hacked to death by members of the politically powerful Kumbi caste (which

is classified as OBC). Priyanka's two brothers were also murdered in the attack.

12 Feminist scholars show how Dalit women have been misleadingly portrayed as "more equal" to men in their society, facing less restrictions and possessing more sexual freedoms than most dominant-caste women. Manuela Ciotti (2019) and Shailaja Paik (2018), among others, are critical of this framework. In my own empirical research and in the cases I followed, I found that the sexuality of young Dalit women was always closely guarded, pointing to the resilient patriarchy among Dalit households that Dalit feminists have long critiqued (Manorama 2008).

13 The relationship was impermissible not only because it was intercaste—that is, between a Dalit woman and a Jat man—but also because it was endogamous, which was not allowed in the village.

14 A First Information Report is a document police prepare when they receive information about a crime.

15 These false testimonies are couched and also follow a predictable script, hence their recognition in court.

16 There is a long history, documented by Dalit feminists, activists, and writers about the specificity of Dalit women's vulnerability to sexual violence from dominant-caste men. In her extensive empirical work, Anandhi (2019) explores the experiences of Dalit women resisting practices such as "dedication," in which young Adidravidar Dalit girls were made sexually available to dominant-caste Naidu men (99).

17 Srimati Basu (2015) writes that since the United Nations Decade for Women, women's police stations have been popularly conceived as institutions that could reduce gender-based crimes. Institutionalized in several countries, the assumption that they would reduce harm was based on an essentialized conception of women that imagines women would necessarily be more sensitive to female victims. However, ethnographies of these women's police stations, including my own experience in them, reveals that "policewomen in these units are unsympathetic to feminist approaches to gender violence and enact hegemonic gender and class ideologies" (192).

18 In *Contentious Marriages, Eloping Couples* Prem Chowdhry (2007) remarks that within the peasant communities of north India, the "dominant morality does not expect emotional and erotic satisfaction in marriage and regards love and sexuality with distrust and suspicion" (2).

19 Field notes, May 22, 2016.

CHAPTER 1. CONSENT

Parts of this chapter were shared at the 2018 Religion and the Global Framing of Gender Violence Workshop, Columbia University, New York. An earlier version of the chapter was published as an article in 2020 as "Sexual

Subjectivity in Rape Narratives: Consent, Credibility and Coercion in Rural Haryana" *Signs: Journal of Women in Culture and Society* 46, no. 1 (Autumn 2020): 103–25.

1 In keeping with ethnographic convention, all names of people and places have been changed to preserve anonymity.

2 It must be noted that this figure was made in reference to the rape of adult women, not to the rape of children under the age of twelve.

3 I want to be clear that I have little doubt that false cases are indeed filed. While I have no way to corroborate how many or what percentage of cases are false ones, my argument is not about numeric disparities. Instead, it is about how the claim that most rape cases are false functions as a discursive maneuver to discredit allegations of rape and the women who make them.

4 Prior to the amendments to the law in 2013, section 375 of the IPC defines when a rape is committed. Section 90 of the IPC refers to how consent cannot be given under duress, misconception, by insane persons and children and if the person is intoxicated. However, clauses 3 and 4 of section 375 spell out conditions in which a sexual relationship can still be considered rape, even though consent was obtained. Section 90 cover a different set of grounds of when consent cannot be accepted. The 42nd law commission pointed to the gap between sections 375 and 90 that spelled out the exceptions to consent.

5 *Adivasi* is the term used for people in India who are considered Indigenous. The Mathura case refers to a 1979 Supreme Court case in which two policemen were charged with raping an Adivasi girl named Mathura. The acquittal resulted in outrage and in a national campaign against rape, which in turn brought discourses on rape into the public domain. The defendants in the case had alleged that Mathura had willingly had sex with the police officers and was now loath to admit this in front of her family and lover. The court agreed, and determined that Mathura had consented by pointing to the lack of injury on her body and to the fact that no one reported to having heard any verbal protests from her. In response to the public outcry and a significant open letter by four law professors slamming this ruling, rape law was substantively amended in 1983. The changes included renaming the law's section on rape to "sexual offence, emphasizing the construction of rape as sexual violation" (Baxi 2014, 3).

6 This age of consent is based on the Protection of Children from Sexual Offences Act (POCSO) that was passed by the Indian Parliament in May 2012, raising the age of consent from sixteen to eighteen.

CHAPTER 2. COMPROMISE

1 *Baldev Singh & Ors versus the State of Punjab* in the criminal appellate jurisdiction of the Supreme Court of India.

2 Understanding sexual assault as something that stems from a lack of toilets can lead to a superficial analysis that proposes that violence occurs because

of a lack of facilities rather than because of more fundamental structural inequities and problems (Dutta 2016). Consequently, such different analyses of the root problem result in very different proposals for what needs to change.

3 The *lambardar* is a holder of numbers in the village and was introduced by the East India Company in the early nineteenth century under the Mahalwari system for collecting land revenue (Hussain 2017). The system continues to this day and is recognized as an integral part of the state revenue collection system (*Times of India* 2011). The *lambardar* is responsible for the collection of revenue, levies, and taxes, as well as for demarcating boundaries and encroachments. The Government of Haryana offers a small honorarium to *lambardars* for their work (Press Trust of India 2019).

4 As noted earlier, in keeping with ethnographic convention to preserve the anonymity of the people I interviewed, the names of districts are not revealed and the names of all persons and places have been changed.

5 *Sehmti*: The word *sehamati*, in the vernacular, is pronounced truncated as *sehmti* and means "will" or "consent." Field notes, June 2, 2017.

6 Field notes, January 12, 2017.

7 Field notes, June 2, 2017.

8 Field notes, January 12, 2017.

9 Field notes, June 2, 2017.

10 Field notes, July 24, 2018.

11 Field notes, July 24, 2018.

12 Field notes, January 17, 2017.

13 Pratiksha Baxi (2014) also notes that the culture of compromise consolidates itself after 1983 and 2002 amendments whereby the defense could no longer attack the victim on the basis of her past sexual history (180).

14 Field notes and interviews, January 16, 2019.

15 Field notes and interviews, January 18, 2019.

16 Field notes and interviews, August 9, 2016.

17 Field notes and interviews, August 9, 2016.

18 *Numberdar* and *lambardar* are different words for the same position. Field notes and interview, January 12, 2017.

19 Field notes, June 7, 2016.

20 Field notes and interviews, January 18, 2019.

21 Field notes, January 13, 2017.

22 Field notes, May 23, 2016.

23 Field notes, April 20, 2016.

CHAPTER 3. LAND

1 For more information on the history of the Jat demand for OBC status, see Datta (1999).

2 Efforts to retain control over inheritance and sexuality led to customs that compelled widows to remarry within the family. However, women contested such efforts even at the cost of being labeled unchaste, which indicates their assertion of autonomy over their sexuality and inheritance (Chowdhry 2011, 111–14).

3 *Mitakshara* and *Dayabhaga* are twelfth-century texts that were used by the British to craft Hindu Law. These texts applied to different parts of India and were themselves drawn from an ancient legal treatise called the *Dharmashastras*. For a detailed discussion of these texts and their genealogy, see Agarwal (1994, 84–99) and Halder and Jaishankar (2008).

4 Bhimrao Ramji Ambedkar is widely recognized as inspiring the Dalit movement and was India's law minister and architect of the constitution.

5 In the aftermath of the HSA, instances of sisters claiming their property emerged. In one case from Amritsar in 1960, Chowdhry (2009b) recounts how a sister successfully litigated and won a case for ownership of land against an agnatic relation. Concerns with such cases and the rights that women were now accorded by the act led members of the Haryana political establishment to exclaim that it was fomenting greed among the public and inappropriately promoting marriage alliances with women who did not have brothers and stood to inherit their father's property (xviii-xxii). Concerned with daughters exercising their right to access their own property, the Haryana legislature passed a unanimous resolution to amend the HSA in 1979. The resolution, however, was rejected by the President of India.

6 There is a large body of work that examines the specific contributions of women in peasant communities, critiquing the lack of attention to these contributions in studies (Deere 1995; Razavi 2009). Women's work and social reproductive labor in peasant life and economy were starkly evident in rural Haryana. My effort here is to specifically highlight the gendered history and relationship with land.

7 Punjab (from which Haryana separated into an independent state in 1966) was important to British rule for army recruitment and for the cultivation of fodder. Colonial rulers were loath to interfere with customary laws, as doing so might disrupt their efforts to maintain political control. These efforts to rule meant favoring landowners who wielded considerable power in the area. Attempts to cultivate relationships with these landowners led to crafting legislation that favored them. For example, the 1900 Punjab Alienation of Land Act benefitted Jat landowners and restricted the sale or mortgage of agricultural land. Prem Chowdhry (2011) writes, "The purpose of the act . . . was to enable the persons among favored agricultural castes 'possessing of sufficient capital' to invest in land. . . . Consequently, the swallowing up of petty owners by their caste men or members of other agricultural castes was accepted and encouraged by the British Administrators" (44).

8 The changes to farm labor as a consequence of the Green Revolution is a much more complex story than I offer in truncated form here. Several

scholars have commented on how the changes propelled different kinds of attached and casual labor. Contesting formulations by Tom Brass and Sheila Bhalla, Surinder Jodhka (1994) argue that attached laborers in Haryana were more indebted than their casual counterparts.

9 Surinder Jodhka (2006) writes that more than 78 percent of households were in debt in Punjab. As a neighboring state to Haryana with similar political economic structures and peasant economies, debt in Haryana is commensurate to debt in Punjab. Also see Jodkha (1995).

10 Field notes, April 28, 2016.

11 MGNREGA is the Mahatma Gandhi National Rural Employment Guarantee Act, which guarantees the right to deskilled manual work for rural workers for one hundred days per year. It is part of social programs to help benefit the poor in rural India. For detailed, comprehensive work on the act and its implications see Khera (2011).

12 Field notes, April 20, 2016.

13 On October 12, 2002, five Dalit men were lynched in Jhajjar after it was alleged that they were skinning a cow. Reports of the incident cite that a narrative—explaining how heightened emotions had led to a flare-up of violence—was shaped and circulated in order to cover up what really happened. Dalit activists and others claimed that the five men were actually transporting cattle skin when they were stopped by the police. This was not unusual. However, after the men refused to pay more than a "reasonable amount" of bribe, they were taken to the local thanna and beaten, and one of them died. In an effort to cover up the policemen's crime, the story of mob violence was crafted and publicized (Jodhka and Dhar 2003). Three years later, on August 27, 2005, a mob of Jat men threatened two thousand Valmiki families that lived in Gohana, Sonipat district, after a brief altercation between a Valmiki and a Jat man in which the Jat man was killed. A few days later, 1,500 Jat men torched 50 Valmiki homes in the area (Gatade 2005). On the anniversary of the death of the Jat man the following year, a young Dalit leader, Rakesh Lara, was shot dead. On April 21, 2010, eighteen homes of the Valmiki community were looted, ransacked, and burned by Jat men in Mirchpur, a village in Hisar District. In the fire, a disabled seventeen-year-old girl and her father were burned alive.

14 In 2011 a socioeconomic and caste census was generated, the results of which were never released. According to some, such a census would reveal that OBC groups constitute in excess of 52 percent of the country's population.

15 Vote Bank politics refers to the pattern of voting by a particular community that would as a block vote for a particular party or candidate. These expectations of a community to vote in a favor of one candidate and/or party is rewarded with real or imagined benefits to the community. The promise for OBC status was one such commitment by the Congress government in the state elections to court the Jat vote.

16 The 36 *biradri* refers to different caste groups in the area including Dalits. Field notes, April 5, 2016.

17 After a year of protests, Narendra Modi announced in November 2021 that the farm laws would be repealed. The rare reversal by the BJP government is considered by many commenting on the repeal as an effort to appease farmers in Punjab and Uttar Pradesh, key states where the BJP is contesting upcoming assembly elections, the outcomes of which are seen as an important indicator for BJP's national electoral prospects (*Scroll.in* 2021).

18 The complexity of caste politics and Jat dominance in Haryana and other places in the Hindi belt, is that while they retain their position of power at the local scale by exploiting those in subordinate position to them, they nevertheless also face increasing precarity of their own position and power in the wake of larger neoliberal changes manifest in these farm laws.

19 Field notes, January 16, 2019.

20 The *gaj* is a unit of measurement equivalent to a yard.

21 Field notes, April 14, 2016, and January 15, 2020.

22 Field notes, April 14, 2016 and January 15, 2020.

23 Field notes, April 28, 2016.

24 Field notes, April 29, 2016.

25 Field notes, April 29, 2016.

26 Field notes, July 24, 2018.

27 The *lakhs* is numbering unit for 100,000.

28 Field notes, March 14, 2016.

CHAPTER 4. DEATH

1 Field notes, January 9, 2018.

2 The case involving her death was decided in October 2018, and the rape case was decided in June 2019.

3 Indian law prohibits releasing the names of rape victims to the media in order to preserve their anonymity and to guard against the shame that rape victims encounter. However, as mentioned previously, in 2015, on the third anniversary of Jyoti Singh's assault, her mother said publicly at a protest in Delhi: "My daughter's name is Jyoti Singh" (NDTV 2015).

4 For instance, see Clarinda Still (2017) who writes about the how Dalits have appropriated forms of upper caste patriarchy, "making it their own" (190).

5 Feminist scholar Pratiksha Baxi (2014) argues, "the word 'access' retains the ego as masculine, and therefore the description of what upper-caste men do to women they consider inferior elides the experience of the woman (read: object) by blurring the distinction between rape and seduction" (39).

6 Armed Forces Special Powers Act (AFSPA) give the armed forces the authority to maintain peace in those parts of the country it deems "disturbed areas." It has been documented by Human Rights groups that AFSPA has

enabled violations by soldiers while shielding them from accountability. For Amnesty International's full report see https://www.amnestyusa.org/reports/the-armed-forces-special-powers-act-a-renewed-debate-in-india-on-human-rights-and-national-security/.

7 Also see Surinder Jodhka's (1999) essay on community where he interrogates its use in the social sciences.

8 Some of the rituals that many spoke of are between brother and sister. For a married woman, this relationship secures her bond with her maternal home in the years following her marriage, which is in turn a place from which she expects to receive support. It is this relationship that many women argued would be jeopardized if they claimed their share of their father's land. These rituals are not just found among those castes who have land, but also among Dalit and OBC castes. For further details see Chowdhry (2011, 264–73).

9 Khairlanji is the name of the village in Bhandara district of Maharashtra, India, where members of the Bhotmange family were brutally massacred. They were one of the few land-owning and educated Dalit families and the incident allegedly occurred over a land dispute in 2006. The mother Surekha and her daughter Priyanka were paraded naked and gang-raped before they were killed by members of the politically powerful Kumbi caste (classified under the OBC category). Priyanka's two brothers were also murdered in the attack. For further details see Dutta and Sircar (2013), Paik (2018), and Rao (2011).

10 A similar framework of shame and humiliation was mobilized against Muslim men in Gujarat during the pogrom in 2002 (Sarkar 2002).

11 Suraj Yengde (2013) notes that prior to Delhi protests in 2012, nineteen Dalit women were raped in Haryana.

12 Field notes, April 19, 2016.

13 Field notes, May 8, 2016.

14 Anonymized interview, May 5, 2016.

15 Field notes, May 8, 2016.

16 Anonymized interview, May 5, 2016.

17 Anonymized interview, May 8, 2016.

18 Field notes, May 8, 2016, and court documents (documents with author). The judgment was decided in May 2015. I am withholding identification of the court case in an effort to preserve the anonymity of the victim's family, who are identified in the documents. The court case involved the following charges of the Indian Penal Code: 376 G (gang rape), 363 (kidnapping), 506 (criminal intimidation), and Section 3 (1) SC/ST Act (defines various types of atrocities against Schedule Castes and Schedule Tribes).

19 Interview with grandmother, May 15, 2017.

20 Field notes, May 15, 2017, and court documents. The judgment was decided in June 2019. I am withholding identification of the court case in an effort

to preserve the anonymity of the victim's family, who are identified in the documents. The court case involved the following charges of the Indian Penal Code: 376 G (gang rape), 323 (voluntarily causing hurt), 506 (criminal intimidation), and section 6 of the POCSO Act (Protection of Children from Sexual Offences). Section 6 refers to aggravated penetrative sexual assault.

21 Interview with grandmother, May 15, 2017.

22 They were charged under section 306 of the Indian Penal Code, which is abetment of suicide.

23 Case document with author.

24 Interview with lawyer, January 17, 2019.

25 Document with author. I am withholding identification of the court case in an effort to preserve the anonymity of the victim's family, who are identified in the documents. The court case involved the following charge of the Indian Penal Code: 306 (abetment of suicide). The judgment was decided in October 2018.

26 Document with author.

27 Sheetal was fifteen years old when she was raped.

28 In the village, rape is treated as a social dispute by bringing the disputing families together in discussions arbitrated by village elders and members of the panchayat (Baxi 2014).

29 Field notes, April 14, 2016, and January 15, 2020.

30 Documents with author.

31 I would like to acknowledge Jinee Lokaneeta for drawing my attention to this point.

32 Field notes, May 4, 2016.

33 Field notes, January 15, 2020.

34 These costs, Sheetal said, were for "*chai pani*" (tea and water), which refer to the costs of hosting Dalit and Human rights groups and others that come to the village to support the case.

35 There were four main accused in the case, all of whom belong to the same caste: Satish Kumar and Deepak Kumar (brothers-in-law), Ajay (friend), and Tarun Kumar (friend).

36 An application was filed in the Punjab and Haryana High Court and decided in April 2018 in favor of the petitioner.

37 The applications to the court relied on section 319 of the Code of Criminal Procedure (CrPC), which allows the court to proceed in a case against a person. In essence, this provision in the code allows the complainant to add other persons to a case.

38 In February and March 2018, the appeals to have Deepak Kumar's name added to the rape case were dismissed by the High Court.

39 Document with author.

40 Document with author.

41 This case was decided under section 306 (abetment of suicide) of the Indian Penal Code in October 2018.

42 Field notes, July 24, 2018.

CONCLUSION

1 Hathras is a district in Uttar Pradesh, a neighboring state of Haryana.

2 Interview with Sheetal, May 5, 2016.

3 Carceral forms include the extensive apparatus of the prison industrial complex.

4 Reparations have been discussed in multiple contexts, most prominently to address and repair harm from slavery in the United States as well as in the context of postapartheid South Africa. Apologies include the attempts by the Korean women who are demanding apology from the Japanese government for its role in the sexual exploitation during the Korean–Japanese war. See Sterngold (1993).

5 It has been extensively documented and argued that the "responsibility to protect" is about putting US and US-allied "boots on the ground," and has served to expand US-dominated militarism and hegemony for both political and economic ends (Mamdani 2010; Branch 2011).

REFERENCES

Abraham, Joshil K., and Judith Misrahi-Barak, eds. 2017. *Dalit Literatures in India*. New Delhi: Routledge.

Abu-Lughod, Lila. 1990. "The Romance of Resistance: Tracing Transformations of Power through Bedouin Women." *American Ethnologist* 17, no. 1: 41–55.

Agarwal, Bina. 1994. *A Field of One's Own: Gender and Land Rights in South Asia*. New Delhi: Cambridge University Press.

Agarwal, Bina. 2005. "Landmark Step to Gender Equality." *The Hindu*, September 25. http://www.binaagarwal.com/popular%20writings/Landmark%20Step%20to%20Gender%20Equality%20TheHindu_25sep05.pdf.

Agnes, Flavia. 1992. "Protecting Women against Violence? Review of a Decade of Legislation 1980–1989." *Economic and Political Weekly* 27, no. 17: WS19–WS21, WS24–WS33.

Agnes, Flavia. 2011. "Interrogating 'Consent' and 'Agency' across the Complex Terrain of Family Laws in India." *Social Difference Online* 1, December: 1–16.

Agriculture Census Division. 2018. "Agriculture Census 2015–16." New Delhi: Ministry of Agriculture & Farmers Welfare, Government of India.

Akbar, Amna, and Rupal Oza. 2012. "'Muslim Fundamentalism' and Human Rights in the Age of Terror and Empire." In *Gender, National Security and*

Counter-Terrorism: Human Rights Perspectives, edited by Margaret Satterthwaite and Jayne Huckerby, 152–82. New York: Routledge.

Alcoff, Linda Martín. 2009. "Discourses of Sexual Violence in a Global Framework." *Philosophical Topics* 37, no. 2: 123–39.

Alcoff, Linda Martín. 2018. *Rape and Resistance*. Cambridge: Polity.

All India Dalit Mahila Adhikar Manch (AIDMAM). 2018. "Voices Against Caste Impunity: Narratives of Dalit Women in India." New Dehli: All India Dalit Mahila Adhikar Manch—National Campaign on Dalit Human Rights (NCDHR).

Anand, Jatin. 2021. "Oxygen Langar Breathes Life into Patients." *The Hindu*, May 9. https://www.thehindu.com/news/cities/Delhi/covid-19-oxygen-langar-breathes-life-into-patients/article34517509.ece.

Anandhi, S. 2019. "Gendered Negotiations of Caste Identity: Dalit Women's Activism in Rural Tamil Nadu." In *Dalit Women*, edited by S. Anandhi and Karin Kapadia, 97–130. London: Routledge.

Anandhi, S., and Karin Kapadia, eds. 2019. *Dalit Women: Vanguard of an Alternative Politics in India*. London: Routledge.

Anandhi, S., and Meera Velayudhan. 2010. "Rethinking Feminist Methodologies." *Economic and Political Weekly* 45, nos. 44–45: 39–41.

Ara, Ismat. 2020. "Hathras Gang-Rape and Murder Case: A Timeline." *The Wire*, October 28. https://thewire.in/women/hathras-gang-rape-and-murder-case-a-timeline.

Asthana, N. C. 2021. "Tarun Tejpal Judgment Underlines How Little the Judiciary Has Learnt on Sexual Violence." *The Wire*, May 28. https://thewire.in/law/the-tarun-tejpal-judgement-underlines-how-little-the-judiciary-has-learnt-on-sexual-violence.

Ayyar, Kamakshi. 2018. "'People Feel There's a Chance of Being Believed': India's #MeToo Movement Gathers Momentum." *Time*, October 12. https://time.com/5421509/india-metoo-sexual-harassment-feminism-women/.

Bakhtin, M. M. 1982. *The Dialogic Imagination: Four Essays*. Translated by Michael Holquist and Caryl Emerson. Edited by Michael Holquist. Austin: University of Texas Press.

Bal, Hartosh Singh. 2021. "Mandi, Market and Modi." *Caravan*, February 28. https://caravanmagazine.in/essay/farm-laws-adani-reliance.

Bama. 2012. *Karukku*. Translated by Lakshmi Holmstrom. 2nd ed. New Delhi: Oxford India Paperbacks.

Basu, Srimati. 2015. *The Trouble with Marriage: Feminists Confront Law and Violence in India*. New Delhi: Orient Blackswan.

Baxi, Pratiksha. 2010. "Justice Is a Secret: *Compromise* in Rape Trial." *Contributions to Indian Sociology* 44, no. 3: 207–33.

Baxi, Pratiksha. 2014. *Public Secrets of Law: Rape Trials in India*. New Delhi: Oxford University Press.

Baxi, Pratiksha. 2021. "For the Judge, It Was a Feminist Who Was on Trial, Not Tarun Tejpal." *The Wire*, May 29. https://thewire.in/women/for-the-judge-it-was-a-feminist-who-was-on-trial-not-tarun-tejpal#:~:text=Science%20

About%20Us-,For%20the%20Judge%2C%20It%20Was%20a%20Feminist%20Who,on%20Trial%2C%20Not%20Tarun%20Tejpal&text=No%20one%20can%20oppose%20a,survivors%20deserve%20a%20fair%20trial.

Bergoffen, Debra. 2003. "February 22, 2001: Toward a Politics of the Vulnerable Body." *Hypatia* 18, no. 1: 116–34.

Beth, Sarah. 2007. "Hindi Dalit Autobiography: An Exploration of Identity." *Modern Asian Studies* 41, no. 3: 545–74.

Bhalla, Abhishek, and G. Vishnu. 2012. "Tehelka Investigation: The Rapes Will Go On." *Moment of Truth*. Blog post, April 14. https://mallusviewpoint.blogspot.com/2012/12/tehelka-investigation-rapes-will-go-on.html.

Bhalla, Sheila. 1977. "Changes in Acreage and Tenure Structure of Land Holdings in Haryana." *Economic and Political Weekly* 12, no. 13: A2–A16.

Bhalla, Sheila. 1995. "Development, Poverty and Policy: The Haryana Experience." *Economic and Political Weekly* 30, no. 41/42: 2619–34.

Bharwada Bhoginbhai Hirjibhai v. State of Gujarat. 1983 AIR 753, SCR (3) 280. Available at https://indiankanoon.org/doc/207774/.

Branch, Adam. 2011. "The Irresponsibility of the Responsibility to Protect in Africa." In *Critical Perspectives on the Responsibility to Protect: Interrogating Theory and Practice*, edited by Philip Cunliffe, 103–24. New York: Routledge.

Brenner, Neil. 2001. "The Limits to Scale? Methodological Reflections on Scalar Structuration." *Progress in Human Geography* 25, no. 4 (December): 591–614.

Brown, Wendy. 1995. *States of Injury: Power and Freedom in Late Modernity*. Princeton, NJ: Princeton University Press.

Brueck, Laura. 2012. "At the Intersection of Gender and Caste: Rescripting Rape in Dalit Feminist Narratives." In *South Asian Feminisms*, edited by Ania Loomba and Ritty Lukose, 224–43. Durham, NC: Duke University Press.

Campbell, Kristen. 2002. "Legal Memories: Sexual Assault, Memory, and International Humanitarian Law." *Signs: Journal of Women in Culture and Society* 28, no. 1: 149–78.

Caravan. 2020. "JNU Violence: Students Recount Attack by a Masked Mob, Said Delhi Police Watched." January 5. https://caravanmagazine.in/education/jnu-abvp-attack-5-january.

Chakravarti, Uma. 2018. *Gendering Caste: Through a Feminist Lens*. New Delhi: SAGE Publishing.

Chandran, Rita. 2019. "As Property Prices Rise, More Indian Women Claim Inheritance." *Reuters*, March 13. https://www.reuters.com/article/india-landrights-women/as-property-prices-rise-more-indian-women-claim-inheritance-idUSL8N20Z4XO.

Chowdhry, Prem. 2007. *Contentious Marriages, Eloping Couples: Gender, Caste, and Patriarchy in Northern India*. New Delhi: Oxford India Paperbacks.

Chowdhry, Prem. 2009a. "'First Our Jobs Then Our Girls': The Dominant Caste Perceptions on the 'Rising' Dalits." *Modern Asian Studies* 43, no. 2: 437–79.

Chowdhry, Prem, ed. 2009b. *Gender Discrimination in Land Ownership*. New Delhi: SAGE Publishing.

Chowdhry, Prem. 2011. *Political Economy of Production and Reproduction: Caste, Custom, and Community in North India*. New Delhi: Oxford University Press.

Ciotti, Manuela. 2014. "Dalit Women Between Social and Analytical Alterity: Rethinking the 'Quintessentially Marginal.'" In *Handbook of Gender in South Asia*, edited by Leela Fernandes, 305–17. London: Routledge.

Ciotti, Manuela. 2019. "For Another Difference: Agency, Representation and Dalit Women in Contemporary India." In *Dalit Women*, edited by S. Anandhi and Karin Kapadia, 75–94.

Clarke, Kamari Maxine. 2019. *Affective Justice: The International Criminal Court and the Pan-Africanist Pushback*. Durham, NC: Duke University Press.

Code, Lorraine. 2009. "A New Epistemology of Rape?" *Philosophical Papers* 38, no. 3: 327–45.

Coulthard, Glen Sean. 2014. *Red Skin, White Masks: Rejecting the Colonial Politics of Recognition*: Minneapolis: University of Minnesota Press.

Cox, Kevin R. 1998. "Spaces of Dependence, Spaces of Engagement and the Politics of Scale, or: Looking for Local Politics." *Political Geography* 17, no. 1: 1–23.

Criminal Law (Amendment) Act, 2013. 2013. *Gazette of India*, April 2. https://www.iitk.ac.in/wc/data/TheCriminalLaw.pdf.

Dangle, Arjun, ed. 2009. *Poisoned Bread: Translations from Modern Marathi Dalit Literature*. Hyderabad: Orient Blackswan.

Das, Veena. 1995. *Critical Events: An Anthropological Perspective on Contemporary India*. New Delhi: Oxford University Press.

Das, Veena. 1996. "Sexual Violence, Discursive Formations, and the State." *Economic and Political Weekly* 31, nos. 35/37: 2411–23.

Das, Veena. 2007. *Life and Words: Violence and the Descent into the Ordinary*: Berkeley: University of California Press.

Datta, Nonica. 1999. "Jats: Trading Caste Status for Empowerment." *Economic and Political Weekly* 34, no. 45: 3172.

Deere, Carmen Diana. 1995. "What Difference Does Gender Make? Rethinking Peasant Studies." *Feminist Economics* 1, no. 1: 53–72.

Deshpande, Swati, Swati Mathur, Kelly Kislaya, and Jaideep Mazumdar. 2013. "When Rape Becomes a Reason for Marriage." *Times of India*, August 29. https://timesofindia.indiatimes.com/india/when-rape-becomes-a-reason-for-marriage/articleshow/22131692.cms.

Dhanagare, D. N. 1987. "Green Revolution and Social Inequalities in Rural India." *Economic and Political Weekly* 22, no. 19/21: AN137–AN144.

Dhingra, Sanya. 2018. "Patriarchy, Popular Culture, Unemployment: Why Haryana Is India's Rape Capital." *Hindustan Times*, June 25. https://www.hindustantimes.com/india-news/patriarchy-popular-culture-unemployment-why-haryana-is-india-s-rape-capital/story-MGXBCioEeVZ9yNYEXmKsFJ.html.

Dogra, Chander Suta 2012. "Before the Roadblock Begins, Jat Quota Gets a Green Signal." *The Hindu*, December 14. https://www.thehindu.com/todays-paper/before-the-roadblock-begins-jat-quota-gets-green-signal/article4198118.ece.

Dutta, Ayona. 2016. "Another Rape? The Persistence of Public/Private Divides in Sexual Violence Debates in India." *Dialogues in Human Geography* 6, no. 2: 173–77.

Dutta, Debolina, and Oishik Sircar. 2013. "India's Winter of Discontent: Some Feminist Dilemmas in the Wake of a Rape." *Feminist Studies* 39, no. 1: 293–306.

Franco, Fernando, Jyotsna Macwan, and Suguna Ramanathan. 2000. *The Silken Swing: The Cultural Universe of Dalit Women*. Calcutta: Stree.

Fricker, Miranda. 2007. *Epistemic Injustice:Power and the Ethics of Knowing*. Oxford: Oxford University Press.

Fricker, Miranda. 2008. "Forum on Miranda Fricker's 'Epistemic Injustice: Power and the Ethics of Knowing': Précis." *Theoria: An International Journal for Theory, History and Foundations of Science* 23, no. 1(61): 69–71.

Gatade, Subhash. 2005. "Guilty of Gohana: In Search of the Real Perpetrators." *Countercurrents*, September 10. https://www.countercurrents.org/dalit-gatade100905.htm.

Geetha, V. 2016. *Undoing Impunity: Speech After Sexual Violence*. New Delhi: Zubaan.

Gettleman, Jeffrey, Hari Kumar, and Shalini Venugopal. 2020. "Men Convicted in Delhi Bus Rape Are Hanged in India." *New York Times*, March 19. https://www.nytimes.com/2020/03/19/world/asia/india-bus-rape-convicts-hanged.html.

Gilmore, Ruth Wilson. 2007. *Golden Gulag: Prisons, Surplus, Crisis, and Opposition in Globalizing California*. Berkeley: University of California Press.

Gopal, Meena. 2014. "Ruptures and Reproduction in Caste/Gender/Labour." In *The Problem of Caste*, edited by Satish Deshpande, 162–72. Bangalore: Orient Blackswan.

Gorringe, Hugo. 2017. "Questions of Honour: Dalit Women Activists and the Rumour Mill in Tamil Nadu." *Contemporary South Asia* 25, no. 3: 255–69.

Gupta, Akhil. 2012. *Red Tape: Bureaucracy, Structural Violence, and Poverty in India*. Durham, NC: Duke University Press.

Gupta, Charu. 2016. "Dalit Women as Victims: Iconographies of Suffering, Sympathy, and Subservience." *South Asian History and Culture* 7, no. 1: 55–72.

Gupta, Charu, K. Satyanarayana, and S. Shankar. 2020. "The History of Caste has Lessons on the Dangers of Social Distancing." *The Wire*, May1. https://thewire.in/caste/social-distancing-dangers-india.

Guru, Gopal. 1995. "Dalit Women Talk Differently." *Economic and Political Weekly* 30, nos. 41/42: 2548–50.

Halder, Debarati, and K. Jaishankar. 2008. "Property Rights of Hindu Women: A Feminist Review of Succession Laws of Ancient, Medieval, and Modern India." *Journal of Law and Religion* 24, no. 2: 663–87.

Halley, Janet. 2008. "Rape at Rome: Feminist Interventions in the Criminalization of Sex-Related Violence in Positive International Criminal Law." *Michigan Journal of International Law* 30, no. 1: 1–123.

Hartman, Saidiya V. 1997. *Scenes of Subjection: Terror, Slavery, and Self-Making in Nineteenth-Century America*. New York: Oxford University Press.

Hennefeld, Maggie, and Nicholas Sammond, eds. 2020. *Abjection Incorporated: Mediating the Politics of Pleasure and Violence*. Durham, NC: Duke University Press.

The Hindu. 2011. "15 Convicted, 82 Acquitted in Mirchpur Dalit Murder Case." September 24. https://www.thehindu.com/news/national//article61758191.ece.

Hindu Net Desk. 2017. "Jat Quots Protests: What Is It All About?" September 23. https://www.thehindu.com/specials/jat-quota-protests-what-is-it-all-about/article61470409.ece.

Hindustan Times. 2018a. "21-Year-Old Woman Gang Raped for Four Days in Panchkula." July 21. https://www.hindustantimes.com/punjab/22-year-old-alleges-rape-by-40-men-for-four-consecutive-days-in-haryana-s-panchkula/story-fLY6lOWhhQUvCNazQIDdtN.html#:~:text=Sunny%2C%20owner%20of%20hotel%20Lovely,complaint%20to%20the%20Chandigarh%20Police.

Hindustan Times. 2018b. "Crime Against Women on Rise in Haryana, Rape Cases Up By 47 Percent." September 15. https://www.hindustantimes.com/india-news/crime-against-women-on-rise-in-haryana-rape-cases-up-by-47/story-7PmHvhkGH27LbAGciOFHbN.html.

Hindustan Times. 2018c. "Haryana Witnesses 10 Rapes in Past 10 Days." January 23. https://www.hindustantimes.com/india-news/haryana-witnesses-10-rapes-in-past-10-days/story-87vLw3wMHZ3e7yFLooiZcM.html.

Howitt, Richard. 1998. "Scale as Relation: Musical Metaphors of Geographical Scale." *Area* 30, no. 1: 49–58.

Human Rights Law Network. 2011. "Mirchpur Carnage: Caste Violence in Haryana." Compiled and edited by Sarita Bhoi. New Delhi: Human Rights Law Network.

Human Rights Watch. 2017. "'Everyone Blames Me': Barriers to Justice and Support Services for Sexual Assault Survivors in India." Accessed April 15, 2022. https://www.hrw.org/report/2017/11/08/everyone-blames-me/barriers-justice-and-support-services-sexual-assault-survivors#.

Hussain, Mohammed Hamid. 2017. "Significance of the Institutions of Lambardars, Tehsildars, and Patwaris in the Operation of the Mahalwari System." *International Journal of Advanced Education and Research* 2, no. 3: 179–84.

Indian Express. 2014. "SC Issues Notice to Haryana Govt on Rising Rape Cases." February 18. https://indianexpress.com/article/india/punjab-and-haryana/sc-issues-notice-to-haryana-govt-on-rising-rape-cases/.

India Today Web Desk. 2020. "December 2012 Gangrape Case: Death Warrant Issued for Nirbhaya Rapists, to Be Hanged on January 22 at 7 am." *India Today*, January 7. https://www.indiatoday.in/india/story/nirbhaya-rapists-to-be-hanged-on-january-22-at-7am-16347182-0200-10-7.

Irving, Toni. 2007. "Borders of the Body: Black Women, Sexual Assault, and Citizenship." *Women's Studies Quarterly* 35, no. 1/2 (Spring–Summer): 67–92.

Jaffrelot, Christophe. 2000. "The Rise of the Other Backward Classes in the Hindi Belt." *Journal of Asian Studies* 59, no. 1: 86–108.

Jaffrelot, Christophe. 2003. *India's Silent Revolution: The Rise of Low Caste in North Indian Politics*. Delhi: Permanent Black.

Jaleel, Rana M. 2021. *The Work of Rape*. Durham, NC: Duke University Press.

Jamil, Ghazala. 2017. *Accumulation by Segregation: Muslim Localities in Delhi*. Delhi: Oxford University Press.

Jeffrey, Craig, Patricia Jeffrey, and Roger Jeffrey. 2002. "Dalit Revolution? New Politics in Utter Pradesh, India." *Journal of Asian Studies* 67, no. 4: 1365–96.

Jodhka, Surinder S. 1994. "Agrarian Changes and Attached Labour: Emerging Patterns in Haryana Agriculture." *Economic and Political Weekly* 29, no. 39: A102–A106.

Jodhka, Surinder S. 1999. "Community and Identities: Interrogating Contemporary Discourses on India." *Economic and Political Weekly* 34, no. 41: 2957–63.

Jodhka, Surinder S. 2006. "Beyond 'Crises.'" *Economic and Political Weekly* 41, no. 16: 1530–37.

Jodhka, Surinder S. 2012. "Agrarian Changes in the Times of (Neo-Liberal) 'Crises': Revisiting Attached Labour in Haryana." *Economic and Political Weekly* 48, nos. 26/27: 5–13.

Jodhka, Surinder S., and Murli Dhar. 2003. "Cow, Caste and Communal Politics: Dalit Killings in Jhajjar." *Economic and Political Weekly* 38, no. 3: 174–76.

John, Mary E. 2018. "The Political and Social Economy of Sex Selection: Exploring Family Development Linkages." New Delhi: Center for Women's Development Studies with assistance from United Nations Population Fund (UNFPA) and UN Women.

Kaba, Mariame. 2021. *We Do This 'Til We Free Us.* Chicago: Haymarket Books.

Kannabiran, Vasanth, and Kalpana Kannabiran. 2003. "Caste and Gender: Understanding the Dynamics of Power and Violence." In *Gender and Caste*, edited by Anupama Rao, 249–60. London: Zed.

Kapur, Ratna. 2005. *Erotic Justice: Law and the New Politics of Postcolonialism.* London: Cavendish Publishing.

Katz, Cindi. 2001. "Vagabond Capitalism and the Necessity of Social Reproduction." *Antipode* 33, no. 44: 709–28.

Khera, Reetika, ed. 2011. *The Battle for Employment Guarantee.* New Delhi: Oxford University Press.

Khoja-Moolji, Shenila S. 2017. "The Making of Humans and Their Others in and through Transnational Human Rights Advocacy: Exploring the Cases of Mukhtar Mai and Malala Yousafzai." *Signs: Journal of Women in Culture and Society* 42, no. 2: 377–402.

Kolsky, Elizabeth. 2010. "'The Body Evidencing the Crime': Rape on Trial in Colonial India, 1860–1947." *Gender and History* 22, no. 1: 109–30.

Kristeva, Julia. 1982 [1941]. *Powers of Horror: An Essay in Abjection.* Translated by Leon S. Roudiez. New York: Columbia University Press.

Kumar, Arjun. 2014. "Access to Basic Amenities: Aspects of Caste, Ethnicity, and Poverty in Rural and Urban India—1993 to 2008–2009." *Journal of Land and Rural Studies* 2, no. 1: 127–48.

Kumar, Radhika. 2016. "Stooping to Conquer: Jats and Reservations in Haryana." *Economic and Political Weekly* 51, no. 16: 15–18.

Kumari, Ved, and Ravinder Barn. 2017. "Sentencing in Rape Cases: A Critical Appraisal of Judicial Decisions in India." *Journal of Indian Law Institute* 59, no. 1: 1–25.

Lodhia, Sharmila. 2015. "From 'Living Corpse' to India's Daughter: Exploring the Social, Political and Legal Landscape of the 2012 Delhi Gang Rape." *Women's Studies International Forum* 50, no. 3: 89–101.

Lokaneeta, Jinee. 2020. *The Truth Machines: Policing, Violence, and Scientific Interrogations in India*. Ann Arbor: University of Michigan Press.

Mallapur, Chaitanya. 2017. "Crimes Against Women Up 83 Percent, But Conviction Rate Hits 10-Year Low; Delhi Reports Highest Crime Rate in India." *First Post*, December 12. https://www.firstpost.com/india/crimes-against-women-up-83-but-conviction-rate-hits-10-year-low-delhi-reports-highest-crime-rate-in-india-4254313.html.

Mamdani, Mahmood. 2010. "Responsibility to Protect or Right to Punish?" *Journal of Intervention and State Building*, 4, no 1: 53–67.

Manoj, C. G. 2015. "Haryana Dalit Attacks: 7-Fold Jump in 3 Govts." *Indian Express*, October 22. https://indianexpress.com/article/india/india-news-india/haryana-dalit-attacks-7-fold-jump-in-3-govts/.

Manorama, Ruth. 2008. "Dalit Women: The Downtrodden Among the Downtrodden." In *Women's Studies in India: A Reader*, edited by Mary E. John, 445–52. New Delhi: Penguin.

Marcus, Sharon. 1992. "Fighting Bodies, Fighting Words: A Theory and Politics of Rape." In *Feminists Theorize the Political*, edited by Judith Butler and Joan W. Scott, 385–403. New York: Routledge.

Marston, Sallie A. 2000. "The Social Construction of Scale." *Progress in Human Geography* 24, no. 2: 219–42.

Marston, Sallie A., John Paul Jones III, and Keith Woodward. 2005. "Human Geography Without Scale." *Transactions of the Institute of British Geographers* 30, no. 4: 416–32.

McGranahan, Carol. 2016a. "Refusal and the Gift of Citizenship." *Cultural Anthropology* 31, no. 3: 334–41.

McGranahan, Carol. 2016b. "Theorizing Refusal: An Introduction." *Cultural Anthropology* 31, no. 3: 319–25.

Menon, Nivedita. 2004. *Recovering Subversion: Feminist Politics Beyond the Law*. New Delhi: Permanent Black.

Mishra, Archana. 2015. "Devolution of Property of the Hindu Female: Autonomy, Relationality, and the Law." *International Journal of Law, Policy and the Family* 29, no. 2: 149–66.

Misri, Deepti. 2011. "'Are You a Man?': Performing Naked Protest in India." *Signs* 36, no. 3: 603–25.

Mitra, Dubra. 2020. *Indian Sex Life: Sexuality and the Colonial Origins of Modern Social Thought*. Princeton, NJ: Princeton University Press.

Mountz, Alison, and Jennifer Hyndman. 2006. "Feminist Approaches to the Global Intimate." *Women's Studies Quarterly* 34, no. 1/2 (Spring–Summer): 446–63.

Narayanamoorthy, A. 2006. "State of India's Farmers." *Economic and Political Weekly* 41, no. 6: 471–73.

National Crime Records Bureau. 2018. "Crime in India." New Delhi: Ministry of Home Affairs.

Nayar, Pramod K. 2006. "Bama's Karukku: Dalit Autobiography as Testimonio." *Journal of Commonwealth Literature* 41, no. 2: 83–100.

NDTV. 2015. "My Daughter's name is Jyoti Singh: Mother of Delhi Braveheart." *YouTube*, December 16. https://www.youtube.com/watch?v=ekk8P62uTTM.

Ok, Anand Raj, and Helen Roberts. 2013. "Delhi Bus Rape Victim's Mum Speaks Out." *Friday Magazine*, November 22. https://fridaymagazine.ae/life-culture/delhi-bus-rape-victim-s-mum-speaks-out-1.1258017.

Oza, Rupal. 2019. "Wrestling Women: Caste and Neoliberalism in Rural Haryana." *Gender, Place and Culture* 26, no. 4: 468–88.

Oza, Rupal. 2020."Sexual Subjectivity in Rape Narratives: Consent, Credibility and Coercion in Rural Haryana." *Signs: Journal of Women in Culture and Society* 46, no. 1 (September): 103–25.

Pahwa, Nitish. 2020. "India Just Had the Biggest Protest in World History: Will It Make a Difference?" *Slate*, December 9. https://slate.com/news-and-politics/2020/12/india-farmer-protests-modi.html.

Phadke, Shilpa. 2013. "Unfriendly Bodies, Hostile Cities: Reflections on Loitering and Gendered Public Space." *Economic & Political Weekly* 48, no. 39: 50–59.

Paik, Shailaja. 2014. "Building Bridges: Articulating Dalit and African American Women's Solidarity." *Women's Studies Quarterly* 42, no. 3/4 (Fall–Winter): 77–96.

Paik, Shailaja. 2018. "The Rise of *New* Dalit Women in Indian Historiography." *History Compass* 16, no. 10: 1–14

Pawar, Urmila, and Meenakshi Moon. 2008. *We Also Made History: Women in the Ambedkarite Movement*. New Delhi: Zubaan.

Pedot, Richard. 2013. "'He Was a Shit, to Boot': Abjection, Subjection, and Feminism in 'Black Venus.'" *Journal of the Short Story in English* 60 (Spring): 113–27.

People's Union for Democratic Rights (PUDR) and Association for Democratic Rights (AFDR). 2012. "This Village Is Mine Too: Dalit Assertion, Land Rights and Social Boycott in Bhagana." Joint report. New Delhi PUDR and AFDR.

Press Trust of India. 2015. "No Liberal Approach, Mediation or Compromise in Rape Cases: SC." *The Tribune*, July 1. https://www.business-standard.com/article/pti-stories/no-liberal-approach-mediation-or-compromise-in-rape-cases-sc-115070100732_1.html.

Press Trust of India. 2019. "Hry Govt to Double Monthly Honorarium of Lambardars to Rs 3,000." *Outlook*, February 4. https://www.business-standard.com/article/pti-stories/hry-govt-to-double-monthly-honorarium-of-lambardars-to-rs-30-001-19020401337_1.html.

Priya, Sasi. 2015. "Rape Cases in India: Has Anything Changed after the Nirbhaya Incident? Part I." *Factly*, March 10. https://factly.in/rape-cases-in-india-statistics-has-anything-changed-after-the-nirbhaya-incident-part-1/.

Rajalakshmi, T. K. 2010. "Upping the Ante." *Frontline*, October 9–22. https://frontline.thehindu.com/other/article30182168.ece.

Rao, Anupama. 2009. *The Caste Question: Dalits and the Politics of Modern India*. Berkeley: University of California Press.

Rao, Anupama. 2011. "Violence and Humanity: Or, Vulnerability as Political Subjectivity." *Social Research* 78, no. 2: 607–32.

Rao, Shakuntala. 2014. "Covering Rape in Shame Culture: Studying Journalism Ethics in India's New Television News Media." *Journal of Mass Media Ethics* 29, no. 3: 153–67.

Razavi, Shahra. 2009. "Engendering the Political Economy of Agrarian Change." *Journal of Peasant Studies* 36, no. 1: 197–226.

Rege, Sharmila. 1996. "Caste and Gender: The Violence Against Women in India." In *Dalit Women Issues and Perspectives*, edited by P. G. Jogdand, 18–36. Delhi: Gyan Publishing House.

Rege, Sharmila. 1998. "A Dalit Feminist Standpoint." *Seminar* 471: 47–52.

Ramesh and Others v. the State of Haryana. 2016. Criminal Appeal no. 2426. Available at https://indiankanoon.org/doc/191444115/.

Ritchie, Andrea J. 2017. *Invisible No More: Police Violence Against Black Women and Women of Color.* Boston: Beacon Press.

Roychowdhury, Poulami. 2013. "'The Delhi Gang Rape': The Making of International Causes." *Feminist Studies* 39, no. 1: 282–92.

Sarangi, Jaydeep. 2018. "Metaphors of Conquest: Towards the Aesthetics of Dalit Feminism Through Select Texts and Contexts." *Contemporary Voice of Dalit* 10, no. 1: 1–7.

Sarkar, Tanika. 2000. "A Prehistory of Rights: The Age of Consent Debate in Colonial Bengal." *Feminist Studies* 26, no. 3: 601–22.

Sarkar, Tanika. 2002. "Semiotics of Terror: Muslim Children and Women in Hindu Rashtra." *Economic and Political Weekly* 37, no. 28: 2872–76.

Satish, Mrinal. 2011. "Compromise Formula in Rape Sentencing." *Law and Other Things*, March 11. https://lawandotherthings.com/2011/03/compromise-formula-in-rape-sentencing/.

Satish, Mrinal. 2017. *Discretion, Discrimination and the Rule of Law: Reforming Rape Sentencing in India.* Cambridge: Cambridge University Press.

Scroll.in. 2018. "Haryana: Body of Dalit Girl with 19 Injuries Found in Jind, Medical Exam Reveals Gang-Rape." January 15. https://scroll.in/latest/865080/haryana-body-of-dalit-girl-with-19-injuries-found-in-jind-medical-exam-reveals-gang-rape.

Scroll.in. 2021. "Modi Announces Repeal of Farm Laws, Protest to Continue Till They Are Revoked in Parliament." November 19. https://scroll.in/latest/1010920/pm-modi-says-centre-will-repeal-three-new-farm-laws.

Sen, Paroma. 2015. "Customary Laws Over Land & Land Rights of Women in Haryana." *Journal of Humanities and Social Science* 20, no. 12: 10–24.

Sen, Rukmini. 2010. "Law Commission Reports on Rape." *Economic & Political Weekly* 45, no. 44: 81–87.

Shalhoub-Kevorkian, Nadera. 2011. "'It Is Up to Her': Rape and the Re-victimization of Palestinian Women in Multiple Legal Systems." *Social Difference* 1: 30–45.

Sharma, Bhushan, and Anurag Kumar. 2019. "Learning from the Outsider Within: The Sociological Significance of Dalit Women's Life Narratives." *Journal of International Women's Studies* 21, no. 6: 22–34.

Sharp, Jenny. 1991. "The Unspeakable Limits of Rape: Colonial Violence and Counterinsurgency." *Genders* 10 (Spring): 25–46.

Shepherd, Kancha Ilaiah. 2021. "Fielding Fire: The Farm Laws Are an Assault on Shudra Power." *Caravan*, February 28. https://caravanmagazine.in/politics/farmer-protests-caste-modi-shudra-obc.

Siddiqi, Dina M. 2015. "Scandals of Seduction and the Seductions of Scandal." *Comparative Studies of South Asia, Africa and the Middle East* 35, no. 3: 508–24.

Simpson, Audra. 2014. *Mohawk Interruptus: Political Life Across the Borders of Settles States*. Durham, NC: Duke University Press.

Simpson, Audra. 2016. "Consent's Revenge." *Cultural Anthropology* 31, no. 3: 326–33.

Singh, Soibam Rocky. 2018. "Mirchpur Killings: HC Dismisses Appeal of Convicts." *The Hindu*, August 24. https://www.thehindu.com/news/national/mirchpur-killings-hc-dismisses-appeal-of-convicts/article24768737.ece.

Smith, Neil. 1984. *Uneven Development: Nature, Capital, and the Production of Space*. Oxford: Basil Blackwell.

Srinivasan, Rama. 2020. *Courting Desire: Litigating for Love in North India*. New Brunswick, NJ: Rutgers University Press.

State of Gujarat v. Natwar Harchandji Thakor. 2005. CriL 2957, 1 GLR, 709. Accessed April 15, 2022. https://indiankanoon.org/doc/1439610/.

Sterngold, James. 1993. "Japan Admits Army Forced Women into War Brothels." *New York Times*, August 5. https://www.nytimes.com/1993/08/05/world/japan-admits-army-forced-women-into-war-brothels.html#:~:text=Confronted%20with%20overwhelming%20evidence%2C%20Japan,was%20no%20evidence%20of%20coercion.

Still, Clarinda. 2017. "Dalit Women, Rape and the Revitalisation of Patriarchy?" In *Dalit Women*, edited by S. Anandhi and Karin Kapadia, 189–217. London: Routledge.

Sunder Rajan, Rajeswari. 1993. *Real and Imagined Women: Gender, Culture, and Postcolonialism*. Abingdon: Routledge.

Tamalapakula, Sowjanya. n.d. "Understanding Dalit Feminism." Accessed June 14, 2021. https://www.academia.edu/10225419/Understanding_Dalit_Feminism.

Taylor, Charles. 1994. "The Politics of Recognition." In *Multiculturalism: Examining the Politics of Recognition*, edited by Amy Gutmann, 25–73. Princeton, NJ: Princeton University Press.

Teltumbde, Anand. 2013. "Delhi Gang Rape Case: Some Uncomfortable Questions." *Economic and Political Weekly* 48, no. 6: 10–11.

Teltumbde, Anand. 2019. "Foreword: Dalits, Dalit Women, and the Indian State." In *Dalit Women*, edited by S. Anandhi and Karin Kapadia, 53–74. London: Routledge.

Thebault, Reis, Andrew Ba Tran, and Vanessa Williams. 2020. "The Coronavirus Is Infecting and Killing Black Americans at an Alarmingly High Rate." *Washington Post*, April 7. https://www.washingtonpost.com/nation/2020/04/07/coronavirus-is-infecting-killing-black-americans-an-alarmingly-high-rate-post-analysis-shows/.

Thomas, Deborah A. 2019. *Political Life in the Wake of the Plantation: Sovereignty, Witness, Repair*. Durham, NC: Duke University Press.

Times of India. 2011. "Lambardars an Integral Part of the System: HC." October 17. https://timesofindia.indiatimes.com/city/chandigarh/lambardars-an-integral-part-of-the-system-hc/articleshow/10395414.cms.

Times of India. 2013a. "Foot in Mouth Statements." January 8. https://timesofindia.indiatimes.com/Foot-in-mouth-statements/articleshowpics/msid-17937075.cms.

Times of India. 2013b. "Rape Is Not the End of Life, I Want to Join Soon." August 25. https://timesofindia.indiatimes.com/city/mumbai/Rape-is-not-the-end-of-life-I-want-to-join-soon/articleshow_new/22040265.cms?from=mdr.

Tiwary, Deeptiman. 2020. "Explained: In Crimes against Women, Rise in Cases of Rape with Murder." *Indian Express*, January 10. https://indianexpress.com/article/explained/in-crimes-against-women-rise-in-cases-of-rape-with-murder-6208863/.

Tomar, Ruchi. 2013. "Dalit Feminism: A Transformation of Rejection into Resistance." *The Criterion* 4, no. 12: 1–8.

Tur, Jatinder Kaur. 2020. "Farm Bills: Farmer Unions in Punjab Ask Political Parties to Stay Away from Their Protests." *Caravan*, September 25. https://caravanmagazine.in/agriculture/farm-bills-unions-ask-political-parties-to-stay-away.

Tyler, Imogen. 2013. *Revolting Subjects: Social Abjection and Resistance in Neoliberal Britain*. London: Zed Books.

United Nations. 2012. "UN Human Rights Chief Calls for Profound Change in India in Wake of Gang-Rape Tragedy." Accessed April 15, 2022. https://news.un.org/en/story/2012/12/429242-un-human-rights-chief-calls-profound-change-india-wake-gang-rape-tragedy.

Vijayan, Prem Kumar. 2018. "The Absent Narrative of the Victim." *The Equator Line* 6, no. 1: 118–30.

Women Against Sexual Violence and State Repression. 2014. "Speak! The Truth Is Still Alive: Land, Caste and Sexual Violence against Dalit Girls & Women in Haryana." Dehli, Progressive Printers. http://www.dalits.nl/pdf/Speak.pdf.

Yadav, Anumeha. 2016. "Jat Violence: What Exactly Happened in Haryana (and Why)." *Scroll.in*, March 1. https://scroll.in/article/804313/jat-violence-what-exactly-happened-in-haryana-and-why.

Yadav, Yogendra. 1996. "Reconfiguration in Indian Politics: State Assembly Elections, 1993–95." *Economic and Political Weekly* 31, no. 2/3: 95–104.

Yengde, Suraj. 2013. "For a Rape 'Caste' (Does) Matter in India." *Sanhati*, January 26. http://sanhati.com/excerpted/6054/.

INDEX